A
WORLD
APART

A
WORLD
APART

by

Gustav Herling

TRANSLATED FROM THE POLISH BY
Andrzej Ciozkosz (Joseph Marek)

"Here there is a world apart, unlike everything else,
with laws of its own, its own manners and customs,
and here is the house of the living dead—life as
nowhere else and a people apart. It is this corner
apart that I am going to describe."
—DOSTOEVSKY—*The House of the Dead*

ARBOR HOUSE
NEW YORK

Manufactured in the United States of America

First published 1951
This edition published 1986

Library of Congress Cataloging in Publication Data

Herling-Grudziński, Gustaw, 1919-
  A world apart.

  Translation of: Inny świat.
  1. Concentration camps—Soviet Union. 2. Political
prisoners—Soviet Union—Biography. 3. Political
prisoners—Poland—Biography. I. Title.
HV8964.S65H47   1986   940.54′72′47   86-8066
ISBN: 0-87795-821-1

FOR

KRISTINA

CONTENTS

PREFACE TO THE FIRST EDITION

by

BERTRAND RUSSELL, O.M.

OF the many books that I have read relating the experiences of
victims in Soviet prisons and labour camps, Mr. Gustav Herling's
A World Apart is the most impressive and the best written. He
possesses in a very rare degree the power of simple and vivid
description, and it is quite impossible to question his sincerity at
any point.

In the years 1940–42 he was first in prison and then in a forced
labour camp near Archangel. The bulk of the book relates what
he saw and suffered in the camp. The book ends with letters from
eminent Communists saying that no such camps exist. Those who
write these letters and those fellow-travellers who allow themselves
to believe them share responsibility for the almost unbelievable
horrors which are being inflicted upon millions of wretched men
and women, slowly done to death by hard labour and starvation in
the Arctic cold. Fellow-travellers who refuse to believe the
evidence of books such as Mr. Herling's are necessarily people
devoid of humanity, for if they had any humanity they would not
merely dismiss the evidence, but would take some trouble to look
into it.

Communists and Nazis alike have tragically demonstrated that
in a large proportion of mankind the impulse to inflict torture
exists, and requires only opportunity to display itself in all its
naked horror. But I do not think that these evils can be cured by
blind hatred of their perpetrators. This will only lead us to become
like them. Although the effort is not easy, one should attempt, in
reading such a book as this one, to understand the circumstances
that turn men into fiends, and to realise that it is not by blind rage
that such evils will be prevented. I do not say that to understand
is to pardon; there are things which for my part I find I cannot
pardon. But I do say that to understand is absolutely necessary
if the spread of similar evils over the whole world is to be prevented.

I hope that Mr. Herling's book will be very widely read, and that

ix

it will rouse in its readers not useless vindictiveness, but a vast compassion for the petty criminals, almost as much as for their victims, and a determination to understand and eliminate the springs of cruelty in human nature that has become distorted by bad social systems. And apart from these general reflections, the reader will find the book absorbingly interesting and of the most profound psychological interest.

1951

A
WORLD
APART

PART I

CHAPTER 1

VITEBSK—LENINGRAD—VOLOGDA

THE summer of 1940 was nearly over when I was in Vitebsk. In the afternoons the sun still shone for a while on the paving-stones of the prison courtyard, and later set behind the red wall of the neighbouring block. Inside the cell familiar sounds reached us from the courtyard: the heavy tread of prisoners making their way to the bath-house, mingled with Russian words of command and the jingling of keys. The warder in the corridor sang quietly to himself; every now and then he put down his newspaper and, without undue hurry, came up to the little round window in the cell door. As if at a given signal two hundred pairs of eyes abandoned their indifferent scrutiny of the ceiling and transferred their gaze to the small pane of the judas. An enormous eye peered into the cell, looked round at all of us, and disappeared again; the small tin shield which covered the glass on the other side fell back into place. . . . Three kicks on the door meant: "Get ready for supper".

Half-naked, we would get up from the cement floor—the supper signal had put an end to our afternoon nap. While waiting with clay bowls in our hands for the liquid mess which was to be our supper, we took the opportunity to relieve ourselves of the liquid mess which had been our lunch. Six or eight streams of urine crossed in the air like the jets of a fountain, and met in a miniature whirlpool at the bottom of a high pail before us, raising the level of foam along its sides. Before buttoning up our trousers, some of us would look curiously at our shaved flesh: it was like seeing a tree, bent by the wind, standing solitary on the barren slopes of a field.

If I were asked what else we did in Soviet prisons, I should find it difficult to add anything to the above account. We were woken in the morning by a knock on the door, and soon our breakfast—a pail of cabbage-water—was brought into the cell, together with a basket containing our daily ration of bread. We munched the bread until lunch and our conversational capacity reached its peak. The Catholics would then gather round an ascetic priest, the Jews round an army rabbi with fish-like eyes and folds of skin, which had once been his belly, hanging loosely from his body; simple people

I

told each other their dreams and talked nostalgically about the past, while the intellectuals searched the cell for cigarette-ends which could be made into one common cigarette. Two kicks on the door put an end to the chatter, and the groups of prisoners, headed by their spiritual leaders, trooped out into the corridor and crowded round the pail of soup. But one day a dark Jew from Grodno joined us in the cell, and weeping bitterly announced that Paris had fallen. From that moment the patriotic whisperings and the political discussions on the palliasses came to an end.

Toward evening the air became cooler, woolly clouds sailed across the sky, and the first stars gleamed faintly. The rust-coloured wall opposite our window would burst briefly into a reddish flame, which was then suddenly extinguished by the sunset. Night came, and with it cool air for the lungs, rest for the eyes, and moisture for parched lips.

Just before evening roll-call the electric light came on in the cell, and its sudden brilliance accentuated the darkness of the sky outside. But only a moment later the night was pierced by the criss-crossing beams of searchlights, patrolling the darkness from the corner towers of the prison. Before the fall of Paris, a tail woman, her head and shoulders wrapped in a shawl, would pass at just about this hour through the small section of the street visible from our cell window. She would stop by the lamp-post opposite the prison wall to light a cigarette, and several times it happened that she lifted the burning match into the air like a torch and held it for a moment in that incomprehensible pose. We decided that this was a sign of Hope. After Paris fell, we did not see her for two months. It was not until an evening late in August that the sound of her hurried footsteps, echoing in the silence of the small street, woke us from our dreams; as before, she stood under the street-light and after she had lit her cigarette, she put out the match with a zig-zagging movement of the hand, like the motion of connecting-rods on railway-engine wheels. We all agreed that this could only mean a transfer, perhaps that very night. But they were in no hurry and we all remained in Vitebsk for another two months.

*   *   *   *   *

The investigations and hearings of my case had been completed some months ago, in the prison at Grodno. I did not behave heroically during those hearings, and I still admire those of my prison friends who had the courage to engage their interrogators in subtle verbal duels and dialectic colloquies. My answers were short and direct, and it was not until I was outside in the corridor, being led back to my cell, that glorious-sounding phrases from the catechism of Polish political martyrdom suggested themselves to my fevered imagination.

All that I desired during those hearings was sleep. Physically I cannot endure two things, an empty stomach and a full bladder. Both were torturing me when, woken in the middle of the night, I took my place on a hard stool before the officer in charge of my examination, with an incredibly strong light shining straight in my eyes.

The first accusation in my indictment was based on two points of evidence. First, the high leather boots which I wore supposedly proved that I was a Major of the Polish Army. (These boots had been given to me by my younger sister when I decided to try and make my way abroad after Poland had been defeated and partitioned between Germany and Russia in September 1939. I was then twenty, and the war had interrupted my university studies.) Secondly, my name, when transcribed into Russian, became Gerling* and this supposedly made me the relative of a well-known Field-Marshal of the German Air Force. The accusation therefore read: "Polish officer in the pay of the enemy". But fortunately it did not take me long to convince the interrogator that these accusations were quite without foundation, and we were able to dispense with them entirely. There remained the one undisputed fact—when arrested, I had been trying to cross the frontier between the Soviet Union and Lithuania. Then: "May I ask why you were trying to do that?"

"I wanted to fight the Germans."

"Yes. And are you aware that the Soviet Union has signed a pact of friendship with Germany?"

"Yes, but I am also aware that the Soviet Union has not declared war on France and England."

"That has not the slightest significance."

"Then how, finally, does the indictment stand?"

"Attempting to cross the Soviet-Lithuanian frontier in order to fight against the Soviet Union."

"Could you not substitute the words 'against Germany' for

* The Russian alphabet has no hard "H" and substitutes for it the letter "G'

'against the Soviet Union'?" A blow in the face brought me back to my senses. "It comes to the same thing, anyway," the judge consoled me as I signed the confession of guilt which had been placed in front of me.

It was not until the end of October, when I had already spent five months inside the Vitebsk prison, that, together with fifty of the two hundred prisoners in my cell, I was called out to hear my sentence. I walked to the office calmly, without a trace of excitement. After a sentence of five years' imprisonment had been read out to me, I was taken to a different cell, in the side-wing of the Vitebsk prison, to wait for my transport. There for the first time I came into contact with Russian prisoners. When I came in, several boys, aged between fourteen and sixteen, were lying on wooden bunks, and by the window, through which I could see a scrap of dark, lead-coloured sky, sat a small man with red eyes and a hooked nose, munching in silence a piece of stale brown bread. It had been raining for several days. The autumn sky hung over Vitebsk like a swollen fish-bladder; streams of dirty water poured down through the gutter and trickled over the netting which covered the lower half of the bars on our window.

Juvenile delinquents, like the boys in the cell, are the plague of the Soviet prisons, though they are almost never found in labour camps. Unnaturally excited, always ferreting in other men's bunks and inside their own trousers, they give themselves up passionately to the only two occupations of their lives, theft and self-abuse. Almost all of them either have no parents or else know nothing of their whereabouts. Throughout the vast expanse of the Russian Police State they manage to lead with astounding ease the typical life of "bzeprizornye" ("the homeless"), jumping goods-trains, constantly on the move from town to town, from settlement to settlement. They make a living by stealing and selling goods from government stores, and frequently they steal back what they have just sold, blackmailing unsuspecting purchasers with the threat of laying information against them. They sleep in railway stations, in municipal parks, in tram terminuses; often all their belongings can be wrapped in a small bundle tied with a leather strap. Only later I discovered that the bezprizornye constitute a most dangerous semi-legal mafia, organised on the pattern of masonic lodges, and surpassed only by the more powerful organisation of "urkas", or criminal prisoners. If in Russia anything like a black market exists, it is only thanks to the efforts of these urchins, always weaving in and out of crowds, besieging the "spectorgs" (special shops supplying exclusively the *élite* of the Soviet bureaucracy), creeping at dusk towards stores of corn and coal. The Soviet authorities wink at all this activity; they regard the bezprizornye as the only true proletariat free of the original sin of counter-revolution, as a plastic mass of raw material which can be moulded into any shape they choose. These young boys have come to look on prison as something like a holiday-camp, and they take advantage of a prison sentence to rest after the exertions of their life outside. Occasionally, a vospitatel (education officer), with an angelic face, flaxen hair and blue eyes, would come into our cell, and, in a voice which sounded like the gentle whisper of the confessional, call the handful of bezprizornye out for a "lesson": "Come, children, let us go and learn a little." When the "children" came back from their instruction, our ears burned at the obscenities which they mixed freely with the stock phrases of Soviet political propaganda. Accusations of "Trotskyism", "nationalism", and "counter-revolution" were constantly flung out at us from their corner, then assurances that "Comrade Stalin did well to lock you up," or that "the power of the Soviets will soon conquer the whole world"—all this repeated again and again with the cruel, sadistic persistence typical of homeless youth. Later in the labour camp I met an eighteen-year-old boy who had been appointed chief of the local "Kulturno-Vospitatelnaya Tchast" (cultural and educational section) only because once, as a bezprizorny, he had gone through such a course of instruction in prison.

My neighbour under the window looked at me with suspicion throughout the first day, incessantly chewing dry crusts of bread which he kept in a large sack; this sack lay on his bunk and served him as a pillow. He was the only man in the cell to whom I felt any desire to speak. Frequently in Soviet prisons one comes across people with the stamp of tragedy on their faces. This Jew's narrow mouth and hooked nose, the eyes which were always watering as if inflamed by dust, the broken sighs and the claw-like hands darting to the sack—these could mean all, or nothing. I remember him best as he walked to the latrine on our daily visit there, tripping along with little steps; when his turn came, he stood awkwardly over the hole and let down his trousers, then carefully lifted the long tail of his shirt, and, half-standing, puffed and reddened with the effort.

He was always the last to be chased out of the latrine, and he buttoned up his trousers in the corridor as he walked, hopping aside like a bird to avoid the warder's pushes. Back in the cell, he immediately lay down on his bunk, breathing heavily, his old face looking like a dried fig.

"Polish?" he finally asked one evening. I nodded.

"I'd like to know if my son could have been an army captain in Poland?" he screeched angrily.

"I wouldn't know," I answered. "Why are you here?"

"That isn't important. I can rot away in prison, but my son is a captain in the Air Force."

After the evening roll-call he told me his story, as we lay side by side and talked in whispers, careful not to wake our bezprizornye. The old Jew had for many years been a shoe-maker in Vitebsk; he remembered the Revolution of 1917 and sadly recalled all that had happened to him since the day of its outbreak. He had been sentenced to five years because, in the local shoe-makers' guild, he had opposed the use of leather scraps for soling new shoes. "That in itself is nothing," he kept repeating, "you understand, men are jealous everywhere. I gave my son a good education, I made him a captain in the Air Force—how could they be expected to like it that an old Jew like me should have a son in the Air Force? But he will petition the authorities and they will let me out before my time is up. Anyway, whoever heard of using such rubbish for new soles?" He raised himself on the bunk, and having made certain that the bezprizornye were asleep, ripped open the lining of his jacket sleeve, and drew out of the wadding a crumpled photograph of a young man with an intelligent face and a hooked nose, in the uniform of the Red Air Force.

Several minutes later, one of the bezprizornye rolled off his bunk, relieved himself into the bucket by the door, and knocked on the little window. From the corridor we heard the jingling of keys, a prolonged yawn, and the sound of studded boots on the stone floor. A sleepy eye appeared at the window. "What do you want?"

"Give me a fag, citizen warder."

"Back to your titty-bottle, little shit!" the warder growled, and the eye disappeared again.

The boy grabbed the door with both hands, and, standing on his toes, yelled into the closed window: "I've got something to tell you!"

At this, the key turned twice in the lock and the cell door opened slightly. Just inside stood a young warder, his cap twisted to one side of his head. "Well?"

"Not here—in the corridor."

The door, with a loud squeak, opened wider, and the boy ducked under the warder's hand which was resting on the lock; after a while he returned to the cell puffing at a cigarette. Inhaling the smoke in greedy gasps, he looked apprehensively in our direction and cowered in his corner like a young puppy trying to avoid a kick. A quarter of an hour later the door opened wide again, the warder entered the cell smartly and sharply called: "Up! Block sergeant! Search!"

The block sergeant began the search with the bezprizornye while the warder kept his eyes on the two rows of prisoners who stood to attention facing each other with their backs to the bunks. Practised hands quickly went through the palliasses of the boys, passed over my bunk, and finally plunged inside the old Jew's sack. I heard the rustling of paper, and then:

"What's this? Dollars?"

"No, that's a photograph of my son, Natan Abramovich Zygfeld, Captain of the Red Air Force."

"Why are you here?"

"Industrial sabotage."

"A saboteur of Soviet industry has no right to keep the photograph of a Red Army officer in his cell."

"But that is my son . . ."

"Silence. There are no sons in prison."

When, a few days later, I left the cell to join a transport, the old shoe-maker was still rocking on his bunk like a stunned parrot on its perch, chewing his crusts and mumbling a few monotonously repeated words.

It was late when we walked to the station, and the town was almost empty. The streets, washed down by rain, gleamed in the dark light of the evening, like long narrow sheets of mica. The air was close and muggy and it was difficult to breathe. The Dzvina river, dangerously swollen, rumbled threateningly under the sagging planks of the wooden bridge. In the small back streets I had a feeling which I cannot explain, that through cracks in the wooden shutters people were looking at us from every house. In the main street there was more traffic, but groups of people passed us in silence, without turning their heads in our direction, looking straight in front of them or down at the ground. Five months ago I had crossed the same streets of Vitebsk on my way to the prison, on a stifling June day, separated from the pavement by a thin steel line of bayonets. Then the Dzvina was slowly crawling along its dried-up bed; tired men and women walked along the pavements, talking little and careful not to stop in the street even for a moment, officials in caps with the peaks turned up, workers in overalls smeared with machine-oil, schoolboys with satchels on their backs, soldiers in high boots smelling of grease, women in drab cotton dresses. I would have given much that day to see a group of people standing idly and gaily talking together. We passed houses with open windows, but there were no gay coloured quilts hanging out to air; surreptitiously we looked over fences into gardens and court-yards, but there was no washing drying in the sun; we saw a closed church with the inscription "anti-religious museum" in front of it; we read the patriotic slogans on the streamers displayed across the street; we gazed at the enormous red star over the Town Hall. It was not so much a town of sadness—it was rather a town which had never known joy.

* * * * *

It was November when, after a week's journey, I arrived in Leningrad with a convoy of prisoners. On the station platform we were divided into groups of ten, which were taken, at short intervals, in black prison vans to the "Peresylka" (the Leningrad transit prison, a stopping-place for prisoners bound for the labour camps). Squeezed in among other prisoners, stifling in the wooden box without windows or ventilator, I had no opportunity of seeing the town. But when the car turned corners its motion threw me off the seat, and through a crack in the partition between the driver's cab and the rear of the van I could catch a glimpse of buildings, squares and trees. The day was cold but sunny. Snow had already fallen, and people in the streets were wearing high winter boots and fur caps with ear-flaps. The ear-flaps, like blinkers, allowed them to look straight in front without having to pay attention to what was happening around them: our transport passed through the town unnoticed.

Veteran prisoners told me afterwards that Leningrad prisons housed forty thousand people at that time. These calculations—

and I am sure that they were quite trustworthy—were based chiefly on judicious observation and comparison of various facts. In the famous Kresty prison, which was composed of one thousand single-person cells, the average number in each cell was thirty; we learnt this from prisoners from the Kresty, who usually spent the night before their transport to the labour camps in the Peresylka. We reckoned the numbers in our prison at ten thousand; in cell No. 37, to which I was taken, and which was intended, in normal conditions, to hold twenty prisoners, there were seventy of us. One of the most astonishing and admirable features of the starved intellectual life of inmates in these "houses of the dead" is the extent to which every experienced prisoner has developed his powers of observation. Every cell possesses at least one statistician, a scientific investigator of prison life, engrossed day and night in assembling a complicated jig-saw puzzle of stories, scraps of conversation overheard in corridors, old newspapers found in the latrine, administrative orders, movements of vehicles in the court-yards, and even the sound of advancing and receding footsteps in front of the gate; from these disjointed observations he manages to construct a composite picture of the surrounding reality. In Leningrad I first heard hypotheses as to the total number of prisoners, deportees and white slaves in the Soviet Union. In the prison discussions the amount guessed at was always between eighteen and twenty-five million.

After entering the prison, as we were walking along a corridor, the party was suddenly met by a group of prisoners marching in the opposite direction, towards the main doors. We stopped dead, held back by an impulse of fear. The group which had been advancing towards us also stopped and retreated a few steps. We stood face to face, our heads bowed—two worlds, joined by the same fate, yet divided by a barrier of fear and uncertainty. The warders held a hurried consultation, and decided that my transport would have to give way. A side-door was struck with an iron knocker, a face appeared behind the window, another short talk followed, and we were led into a wide, bright corridor, part of a block whose appearance seemed to contradict everything that I had so far seen in the course of my prison wanderings.

This luxurious building with large windows and shining corridors, such a fantastic change from the monastic decay characteristic of most Russian prisons, is the best wing of the Peresylka. Large grilles, sliding on rails, take the place of cell doors along the wall, giving an illusion of complete internal freedom and of that particular self-discipline which men isolated from the world evolve in order to forget their loneliness. The cells were empty and gave the impression of living-rooms whose tenants had gone out just before our arrival. Through the bars I could see beds with sheets on them, bed-side tables with family photographs in frames of coloured and silver paper, clothes-hangers, large tables strewn with books, newspapers, and chessmen, white shells of wash-basins in the corners, wireless-sets and portraits of Stalin; at the end of the corridor was a common dining-room, with a raised platform probably intended for the performances of musically talented prisoners. To appreciate the mental start of astonishment which I felt at the sight of Stalin's portrait in a prison cell, it must be understood that prisoners in Russia suffer a kind of excommunication from political life and are allowed to take no part in its liturgies and sacred rites. The period of repentance must be passed without their God, though also without the advantages of enforced political atheism. Thus they may not praise Stalin, but neither are they free to deny him.

This was the "Intourist" prison, I think most probably the one visited by Lenka von Koerber, the author of an enthusiastic book about the Soviet prison system. During the few minutes which I spent there I managed to exchange a few words with one of the prisoners, who was tidying the cells while the others were at work. Tinkering with a wireless-set and not looking in my direction, he told me that the prisoners here were full citizens of the Soviet Union, serving sentences not exceeding eighteen months for such crimes as "mielkaya krazha" (petty theft), "progul" (unpunctuality for work), "khuliganstvo" (hooliganism), and other offences against factory discipline. They spend their days in workshops within the prison boundaries, receive satisfactory wages for their work, eat well, and their families are allowed to visit them twice a week. If the Soviet authorities created similiar conditions of life for the twenty million prisoners and exiles on Russian soil, Stalin could probably keep the Army, the N.K.V.D. and the Party in check by the creation of a "fourth force". My prisoner did not in any way complain about his lack of freedom—he was quite comfortable there. I asked him if he knew of the fate of prisoners now in other blocks of the Peresylka, and in the thousands of camps and prisons spread like a wide net over the Soviet Union. Yes, he knew all about that, but then those were "politicals". "Those"—he nodded his head towards the small barred windows of the Peresylka's other block—"those are the living dead. Here one can breathe more freely than at liberty." "Our Winter Palace", he called it affectionately. Stalin knows well, from his own experience, that only the "bytoviks", the short-term criminal prisoners, can be forced into repentance and humiliation by the provision of humane conditions of life in prison, never the politicals. Moreover, the better his material conditions in prison, the more persistently does a political long for freedom, the more violently will he rebel against the authority which has imprisoned him. The prisoners and Siberian exiles of Tsarist times were allowed to lead an unbelievably comfortable and cultured life, yet these same men later overthrew the Tsars.

The bytovik, like the prisoner to whom I talked, must be distinguished from the urka, who is a hardened criminal. Although in the labour camps it is possible to come across bytoviks whose sentences exceed two years, yet in the hierarchy of the camp these occupy an exceptional position, nearer to the privileges of the administrative staff than to the status of the average prisoner. A bytovik becomes an urka only after he has served several terms. An urka seldom leaves the camp at all, but merely enjoys a few weeks' occasional freedom, time enough to see to his most urgent affairs and commit his next offence. The measure of his importance in the labour camp is not only the amount of years which he has spent wandering from one camp to another, and the seriousness of his offence, but also the size of the fortune which he has collected from the black market, theft, and frequently even the murder of "byelorutchki", as political prisoners are called (the word means "white hands"), the number of cooks and camp officials who are friendly to him, his professional qualifications to supervise the labour-gangs, or "brigades", of prisoners, and the number of women who wait for him, like fresh post-horses for a stage-coach, at various points in his journeys through the camps. The urka is an institution in the labour camp, the most important person after the commander of the guard; he judges the working capacity and the political orthodoxy of the prisoners in his brigade, and is often entrusted with the most responsible functions, assisted if necessary by a technical expert without the urka's camp experience. All newly-arrived young girls pass through his hands before landing up in the beds of the camp chiefs. Urkas dominate even the "cultural and educational section" of the camp. To these men the thought of freedom is as repugnant as the idea of the labour camp is to a normal person.

It was by accident that I joined cell 37 of the Leningrad Peresylka. When prisoners of the transport were being sorted out in the corridor and sent to their particular cells, it was found that my name was not on the list. The warder scratched his head helplessly, carefully went through the letter G, once more asked me my name and Christian name, and finally shrugged his shoulders. "What cell were you directed to?" he asked. From behind the doors on each side of the corridor came a restless murmur of voices above which I could hear occasional loud conversation and raucous singing. Only inside a cell situated a little farther along the corridor a pleasant silence seemed to reign, broken every few moments by the odd phrase of an exotic song sung in a hoarse, asthmatic voice and followed immediately by a sharp chord on the strings of an instrument. I made up my mind. "To cell 37," I answered calmly.

The cell was almost empty. Two rows of wooden bunks, packed closely together and each covered with a palliasse, gave some feeling of comfort and stability; but when I saw the improvised beds of jerkins and overcoats on the floor against the walls, and the bundles of clothing piled under the table (in overcrowded cells these are untied and laid out only at night, when every available scrap of floor-space, benches and even tables are occupied by sleeping prisoners), I guessed that there were too many people here already. On the ground by the door, next to the bucket, an enormous bearded man, with a magnificent head which might have been carved out of stone, was lying on a palliasse and calmly smoking a pipe. He was staring at the ceiling; one hand was under his head, with the other he smoothed and tugged at the jacket of an army uniform stripped of its insignia. With every pull at the pipe, a cloud of smoke emerged from the bristly beard. In another corner of the cell, a man of forty-odd with an intelligent, clean-shaven face, dressed in breeches, high boots, and a green wind-jammer, was lying on his back, a book propped against his knees. Opposite the bearded giant sat a fat Jew in an army uniform open across the chest to show bunches of black hair, his naked legs hanging down over the bunk. He wore a small beret on his head, and the woollen scarf round his neck accentuated the thick lips and the eyes which peered from his flabby face like currants pressed into dough, separated by a nose like a large gherkin. He was singing, with much choking and puffing, a song which I then thought was Italian, beating time with one hand on his knee. Next to him, leaning against the wall, stood a well-built athletic man, wearing a sailor's cap and a striped vest, who plucked idly at the strings of a guitar as he stared through the window at the misty outlines of Leningrad. The whole scene was reminiscent of a sailor's hostel in a French port.

Just before lunch the studded door opened wide and about seventy prisoners, with their hands still behind their backs, entered the room in pairs to the sound of the warder's monotonous counting —the cell was returning from its walk. Most of the newcomers were ageing men in military uniforms and coats which had been stripped of insignia; several of them went straight to their bunks, supporting themselves on sticks or on the shoulders of their companions. A few young sailors and civilians came in last, and elbowed their way through to the table. Three kicks on the door, here as in Vitebsk, meant—lunch.

During the meal I noticed a tall, handsome man, who looked at me with interest, eating slowly and meditatively, and with a certain elegance of gesture, his portion of boiled barley. His large, thoughtful eyes were set deep in a bony and wrinkled face: after every bite he moved his jaws slowly, as if savouring a rare delicacy. He spoke to me first, and told me his story in a stilted and archaically ceremonious Polish, a language which he had evidently not spoken for many years. He was the descendant of a Polish exile who had been sent to Siberia when the Polish Insurrection of 1863 against Russia was suppressed; his name was Shklovski and before his arrest he had been in command of an artillery regiment in Pushkino (formerly Tsarskoye Selo), near Leningrad. Russia he called "my country", of Poland he spoke as "the land of our fathers". He was in prison because as a colonel, and a Pole by origin, he had not been sufficiently interested in the political education of his soldiers. "You understand," he smiled gently, "when I was young they taught us that the army was there to think little and defend its country." I asked what had brought the others here. "These generals?" He shrugged his shoulders. "They are here because they took too much interest in politics."

Shklovski's neighbour at the table was the man in the green

wind-jammer, who had been reading a book when I first saw him. This was Colonel Lavrenti Ivanovich (unfortunately, I can no longer remember his surname). He and Shklovski were the most junior officers in the cell. When he found that I was a Pole and that I had been in Poland during the September campaign of 1939, he became interested and began to ask me questions. He told me that before he was arrested he had been in Army Intelligence on the Soviet-Polish frontier; he knew the whole region like the back of his hand, and four years of prison had not impaired the wonderful dossier of information which he carried in his head. He could remember the dispositions of garrisons, regiments and divisions of the Polish frontier guard, as well as the names and the personal idiosyncracies of their commanding officers; thus, this one was always short of money for cards, that one was mad about horses, a third lived in Lida but had a mistress in Baranoviche, while yet another was a model officer. He asked me excitedly what part each had taken in the September campaign, as a ruined horse-owner might enquire about the performances of his horses on foreign race-tracks. I knew little and was unwilling to tell him even that, for I was still under the impact of the bitter defeat which Poland had suffered in the first stages of the war.

The talks with Lavrenti Ivanovich soon made us close friends, and one day our conversation turned to the subject of our cell-mates. I remember that evening as if it were yesterday. We were sitting on his bunk: next to us dozed a young medical student from Leningrad, with a girlish face, who once, in the latrine, asked me in a whisper if I had read Gide's *Retour de l'U.R.S.S.*, for judging by the articles in the Soviet Press it must be a very interesting book. The lights had already come on in the cell, the sailors sat round the table playing cards, while the Soviet generals, frozen in attitudes of deep reflection, lay on their bunks like two rows of effigies. Lavrenti Ivanovich indicated each with a glance, moving only the muscles of his face, and throwing out quick explanations by the way, like a guide in a museum collection of Egyptian mummies. Of the fat Jew, who was as usual humming quietly and swinging his legs, he said: "Division political commissar in Spain. He had a hard time at the hearing." The large man with the beard he described as an engineer, a general of the Air Force, who had recently gone on a hunger-strike, demanding a revision of his trial "in view of the needs of the Soviet air industry". All the generals had been accused of espionage in 1937, and, in the opinion of Lavrenti Ivanovich, the whole affair was a German plot organised on a vast scale. German Intelligence had submitted to Soviet Intelligence, through a neutral intermediary,* faked proofs of espionage, heavily implicating many members of the Soviet General Staff, who at various periods during their service had spent some time in Germany. The Germans hoped to paralyse the Soviet high command, and Soviet Intelligence was still in a state of exaggerated suspicion after the Tukhachevsky plot. If the Russo-German war had broken out in 1938, the Staff reserves of the Red Army would have been extremely meagre. The opening of the Second World War had saved the prisoners of cell 37 from death sentences, and had suddenly stopped the wheel of investigation and torture on which they were being slowly broken. Their hopes lay with the outbreak of a Russo-German war, when they expected to be freed, reinstated in their posts and commands, and given full pay for the four years which they had spent in prison.† The sentences of ten years which had been read out to them after three and a half years imprisonment, a month before my arrival, they considered to be no more than a formality designed to save the face of the N.K.V.D. For to the occupants of cell 37 the opening of a Russo-German war was an unquestionable certainty even in November 1940; they believed in its victorious conclusion, but the idea that any fighting would take place inside Russian territory never even occurred to them. After the evening roll-call, when the perambulating shop which sold cigarettes, newspapers and sausages was wheeled into the cell,‡ Lavrenti Ivanovich—the most junior in age and rank—would climb on to the table and read aloud from *Pravda* and *Izvestia* identical news bulletins from the Western Front.

It was the only moment during the whole day when the generals

---

* I have since heard the theory that this neutral intermediary, acting at the time with the best of intentions, was actually Dr. Benes.

† It seems that their expectations were realised. Isaac Deutscher's biography of Stalin contains the following passage (p. 486): "Survivors of the crushed oppositions, who could be useful in the war effort, were brought out of concentration camps and assigned to important national work. Tukhachevsky's disciples who had been cashiered and deported were rushed back to military headquarters. Among them, according to one reliable report, was Rokossovsky, the victor of Stalingrad, a former Polish communist, who had served as liaison officer between Tukhachevsky's staff and the Comintern." I expect that among those freed were also the generals of cell 37, for their indictments were partly based on the Tukhachevsky plot.

‡ I never saw a similar shop in any other Russian prison, and I believe that this amenity was a privilege granted specially to the generals of cell 37.

roused themselves from their lethargy and discussed with animation the chances of both sides. It struck me that when the conversation turned on Russia's potential military strength, there was no trace of bitterness, rebellion or even complaint in their pronouncements, only the sadness of men who have been torn away from their life's work. I once asked Lavrenti Ivanovich about this. He said: "In a normal state, men are free to be contented, fairly contented, or discontented. In a state in which all are supposed to be contented, the suspicion arises that all are discontented. Either way, we form a solid whole."

General Artamian, the bearded Armenian from the Air Force, got up for a few minutes every evening, and took his massive body for a walk round the bunks "in order to stretch the bones a bit". After every such walk he lay down again in his old place, and puffing heavily, breathed in and out several times. He did all this with enormous gravity and an astonishing punctuality: his evening exercise told us that supper would soon be there.

My first day in cell 37 was also the third day of his hunger-strike; after I had been there ten days it was still on. Artamian grew pale, his walks and his breath became shorter every day, and he coughed violently after every first deep puff of a fresh pipe. He demanded to be freed and reinstated in his work, drawing attention to his revolutionary past and his services to the State. The N.K.V.D. offered to let him work under a guard in a Leningrad aeroplane factory, with a separate cell in the "Winter Palace". Every three days the warder brought him a magnificent food parcel "from his wife", though he heard and knew nothing of her, as she was most probably living in forced exile in some remote part of Russia. Artamian would get up from his bunk, offer the food all round, and when the offer was met by silence, would call the warder in from the corridor, and in his presence throw the whole lot into the bucket.

Though I slept on the floor near the bucket, and therefore next to his bunk, he never spoke to me. However, on my last night in the Leningrad prison, when unusual movements in the corridor seemed to warn us that a transfer was imminent, neither of us slept. I lay on my back, with my hands folded under my head, and listened to the noise of footsteps increasing on the other side of the door like the roar of a river gathering force behind a dam. The puffs of smoke from Artamian's pipe dimmed the light of the bulb, and the cell was in half-darkness. Suddenly his hand left the bunk and groped for mine. When I gave it to him, he raised himself slightly on the bedding, guided it under the blanket and pressed it to his chest. Through the ragged shirt I could feel uneven swellings and depressions on his ribs. He guided it farther down, below the knee—the same thing there. I had been told by Lavrenti Ivanovich that most of the generals had been beaten during their hearings, but I had not supposed that it was to the extent of broken bones. I wanted to speak to Artamian but he seemed to be deep in thought, and his immovable bearded face showed only exhaustion.

After midnight the movements in the corridor grew even louder; I could hear the opening and closing of cell doors, and monotonous voices chanting lists of names. After every "present" the stream of human bodies grew, their muffled whispers echoing in the corridor. At last the door of cell 37 opened—Shklovski and myself for the transport. While I knelt and rapidly tied up my ragged bundle, Artamian once more gripped my hand and squeezed it warmly. He did not say a word and did not look at me. We came out into the corridor and joined the crowd of sweat-drenched, steaming, sleepy bodies, crouched fearfully against the walls, like the rags of human misery in a city sewer.

Shklovski and I travelled together in the same compartment of a "Stolypin carriage".* He spread his greatcoat on the bench and remained in the corner of the compartment during the whole journey, sitting with straight back, silent and severe, his uniform buttoned up to the neck, hands folded across his knees. Besides us, there were three urkas, criminal prisoners, who immediately began to play cards on the upper, folding bench. One of them, a gorilla with a flat Mongolian face, told us before the train had even left the station that in Leningrad he had at last got a fifteen-year sentence for killing with an axe the cook at the Pechora camp, who had refused to give him an additional helping of barley. He said this with a certain pride in his voice, without interrupting the game. Shklovski sat unmoved with his eyes half-closed, while I forced myself to laugh.

It must have been much later, for the train had left the forest, and the grey light of dawn was showing over the snow-covered slopes, when the gorilla suddenly threw down his cards, jumped down from the bench and came up to Shklovski.

* These were railway carriages with barred windows for transporting prisoners, so called after the Tsarist minister who first introduced them in Russia

"Give me that coat," he yelled, "I've lost it at cards."

Shklovski opened his eyes and, without moving from his seat, shrugged his shoulders.

"Give it to me," the gorilla roared, enraged, "give it, or—glaza vykolu—I'll poke your eyes out!" The colonel slowly got up and handed over the coat.

Only later, in the labour camp, I understood the meaning of this fantastic scene. To stake the possessions of other prisoners in their games of cards is one of the urkas' most popular distractions, and its chief attraction lies in the fact that the loser is obliged to force from the victim the object previously agreed upon. In 1937, during the pioneer period of labour camps, they played for human lives, for there was then no more precious possession; a political prisoner, sitting at one end of a barrack, did not guess that the greasy cards, falling with a smack on the small plank spread across the knees of the players, were deciding his fate. "Glaza vykolu" was the greatest threat which the urkas wielded: two fingers of the right hand, outstretched in the shape of the letter V, made straight for the victim's eyes. The only defence against this movement was to bring the edge of the hand up rapidly and put it against the nose and forehead. The menacing fingers of the attacker split against it like waves against the prow of a ship. Later I noticed that Shklovski's gorilla had not much chance of carrying out his threat, for the index finger of his right hand was missing. This kind of self-mutilation was very common in the early years of the labour camps, when a leg or an arm, slashed with an axe on a pine block, was known, especially among the forest brigades, as the surest way of gaining access to a hospital when at the end of one's strength. The inhuman thoughtlessness of Soviet labour camp legislation has created a situation in which a prisoner who drops dead at his work from exhaustion is just a nameless unit of energy, which with one stroke of the pencil is eliminated from the plan of production, while a prisoner wounded at work is a damaged machine, which is sent off for repairs as soon as possible.

When the train reached Vologda I was the only one to be taken from the compartment. "Good-bye," I said to Shklovski. "Good-bye," he replied as we shook hands, "and may you return to the land of our fathers."

I passed a day and a night in the prison of Vologda, whose little corner towers and red wall surrounding a large courtyard gave it the appearance of a small medieval castle. In the cellars, in a small cell which had no window but only a hole the size of a man's head in the wall, I slept on the bare earth. Around me lay peasants from the neighbouring countryside, who could not tell day from night, did not remember the time of the year or the name of the month, had no idea why they were in prison, how long they had been there, or how long they would remain there. Lying on their fur greatcoats, fully dressed, in their shoes, and unwashed, they talked feverishly through their half-sleep of their families, homes and cattle.

The next night I travelled with another transport and arrived at dawn at the station of Yercevo, near Archangel, where an escort was waiting for us. We dispersed from the carriages on to the crackling snow amid the howling of bloodhounds and the orders of the guards. The sky was pale from the frost and the last stars still flickered. It seemed to me that they would go out any minute and then the dark, thick night would emerge from the still forest and swallow up the shimmering sky and the pale dawn concealed in the cold flames of the fires. But, round the first bend of the road, I could see on the horizon the silhouettes of four crow's-nests placed high on wooden stilts and surrounded by barbed wire. Lights gleamed in barrack windows and well-chains could be heard slipping on their frozen capstans.

CHAPTER 2

HUNTING BY NIGHT

THE word "proizvol" is now probably unknown to most Soviet prisoners. Roughly translated, it means the regime enforced by the urkas within the wired-off camp zone between late evening and dawn. The reign of the proizvol in the majority of Russian labour camps began in 1937 and was suppressed towards the end of 1940.

The "pioneer" period of Soviet labour camps is itself generally dated from 1937 until 1940, though it varied according to differences in local conditions. In the minds of old Russian prisoners, who were fortunate enough to survive the years of the Great Purge and of the "socialist construction in one country" based on mass use of forced labour, "'thirty-seven" is a date similar to the date of the birth of Christ in the mind of a Christian, or that of the destruction of Jerusalem in the mind of an Orthodox Jew. "It was in 'thirty-seven"—constantly I heard these words spoken at the camp in a whisper full of terror and unhealed suffering, as if that year had been one of famine, plague and civil war. In the revolutionary calendar there is a whole number of such fundamental historical occurrences, which, however, in the custom of the New Era, are seldom defined by dates. For very old people the turning-point is the October Revolution, and that date could more justifiably be accepted as the beginning of the New Era, for everything which has ever occurred in the annals of mankind is classified by the words "before" and "after". Thus, according to the political attitude of the speaker, "before" and "after" mean either poverty and contentment, or contentment and poverty; but in both cases anything which happened in Russia before the storming of the Winter Palace in St. Petersburg merges into the dusk of pre-history. Younger people (I am of course still speaking of the labour camps) reckon the Era differently. For them the Tsar means unquestionably "poverty, slavery, and oppression", and Lenin "white bread, sugar, and lard". These milestones are fixed in their primitive historical consciousness by the stories of their fathers, but the real turning-point for them is the year 1937, the year of the "second revolution".

The first two friends that I made in the camp both belonged to the remains of the "Old Guard" of 1937. The first, Polenko, an agricultural engineer, had been found guilty of sabotaging collectivisation, and the other, Karbonski, a telephone engineer from Kiev, was imprisoned for maintaining contact with his relatives in Poland. From what they told me I learnt that the Kargopol camp, which in 1940, at the time of my arrival, consisted of several "camp-sections" (the largest were Mostovitza, Ostrovnoye, Krouglitza, Nyandoma, the two Alexeyevkas, and my own Yercevo), each a camp in itself, distributed within a radius of about thirty-five miles, and containing altogether something like thirty thousand prisoners, had been founded four years before by six hundred prisoners, who one night were simply put out of a transport train near Yercevo station, in the middle of the virgin northern forest. Conditions were hard: the temperature was not infrequently as low as forty degrees below zero centigrade; their food did not exceed 300 grammes of black bread and a plate of hot soup every twenty-four hours; they slept in shacks of fir branches which they built round a constantly burning fire, while their guards lived in small huts fixed on sledge runners. The prisoners began their work by making a clearing in the forest and putting up a small hospital barrack in the middle of it. Then came the discovery that self-mutilation at work gave a prisoner the privilege of spending several weeks under a real roof which did not constantly send down a shower of melting snow, and near a small iron stove which was always red-hot; but the number of accidents at work became so great that the wounded were usually packed off on a sledge to the nearest hospital, at Nyandoma, about twenty-five miles from Yercevo. At the same time the death-rate among prisoners rose in an alarming way. The first to die were Polish and German communists who had fled to Russia from their own countries to avoid prison. According to my two friends, it was far more horrible to watch the death of Poles than to listen to the endless feverish delirium of Germans. Polish communists, mostly Jews, died suddenly, like birds falling off a branch in hard frost, or like those fishes of the ocean depths which burst from inner pressure when they are brought up to the surface from the deep. One short cough, one hardly audible gasp, a tiny, white cloud óf breath which hung for a moment in the air, and the head fell heavily on the breast while the hands, with a last movement, scraped the snow on

the ground. And that was all—not a cry, not even a complaint.
. . . After the Poles and the Germans it was the turn of the
Ukrainians and the natives of Central Asia, the Kazaks, Uzbeks,
Turcomen and Kirghiz who are all known as "nacmeny". Russians,
Balts and Finns (who are expert foresters) held out best, and their
daily rations were therefore increased by a hundred grammes of
bread and an additional ladleful of soup a day. During the first few
months, when the high mortality rate and the primitive conditions
of the camp made it difficult for the guards to keep a careful check
on prisoners, frozen bodies were sometimes concealed in the shacks
while their rations of bread and soup were collected by other
prisoners. Soon barracks sprang up in the clearing, which was
already surrounded by barbed wire, and every day the brigades of
"lesoruby" or foresters, swollen by fresh contingents from the
prisons, cut their way farther into the forest, leaving behind them
their dead and a wooden track for sledges and cars.

By 1940 Yercevo was already an important centre of the Kargopol
timber industry with a saw-mill, two branch lines from the railway,
its own food supply centre, and a separate village beyond the camp
zone for the free administrative staff. All this had been built by the
prisoners.

From these early pioneer days the tradition of the proizvol has
been handed down.* When there were as yet no sheds which could
be locked for the night, in which the prisoners were able to deposit
sharp tools such as saws, axes, and billhooks after work, and when
the control of the guards over prisoners did not go beyond the end
of a bayonet or the beam of a searchlight, some of the tools found
their way into the barracks in the evenings. The first contingents
of urkas, which came to the camp in 1938, took advantage of this
state of affairs to proclaim within the camp zone, from dusk till
dawn, a miniature "prisoners' republic", holding their own trials
and meting out justice to the politicals at night. No guard
would have dared to show himself inside the barracks after dark,
even when the horrible moans and cries of political prisoners who
were being slowly murdered could be heard all over the camp; he
could never be certain that a billhook would not appear from
behind one of the barrack corners and split his head open. As

---

* A certain Bessarabian communist told me that in 1938, in a camp in the
Solovetsky Islands, he witnessed the brutal beating-up of Karol Radek, one
of the victims of the "proizvol" there.

complaints to the authorities in the daytime produced little result, the political prisoners organised their own defence groups, and this civil war between a demoralised proletariat and a revolutionary intelligentsia lasted, though gradually weakening in tension, until the beginning of 1939. In that year new technical arrangements and strengthened garrisons in the camp allowed the N.K.V.D. to take the initiative into their own hands. In 1940 the remains of the prisoners' republic existed only in order to facilitate the night hunts for newly-arrived women which the urkas organised in the camp zone. A year and a half before my arrival there, the first women's barrack had been built in the camp. In justice to the N.K.V.D. it should be said that they tolerated these night hunts only within the open camp zone—the door of the women's barrack itself was within the distance of a rifle-shot from the guard-house. New women arrivals were usually warned by experienced women prisoners of the danger which threatened them, but it sometimes happened that they did not believe these warnings. If they complained in the guard-house the morning after the "accident", they were met with derision; and besides, what woman would have been willing to risk bringing on herself the merciless revenge of the urkas? From the moment of her arrival, she learnt the rules of the struggle for survival in the camp and instinctively obeyed them, either keeping to the barrack after dark, or else finding a protector among the urkas. In the beginning of 1941 these night hunts were also suppressed by the N.K.V.D. Life became for some more bearable, for others "just dull".

Arriving in the camp while the prisoners were at work, I spent the day in an empty barrack and toward evening, when I felt that I had a chill and a high temperature, I took the advice of the priest Dimka and crawled to the medical hut. Dimka, an old man with a wooden leg who was a kind of barrack orderly, advised me to pester the doctor until he agreed to send me to the hospital. "After a stretch in prison," he said, "you need a rest before you can take up honest work again." We both smiled at the word "honest". Then the priest picked up a wooden yoke, put it across his shoulders, and lifted two buckets from the ground with iron hooks which hung from the yoke. This was the most important hour of his idle day. He had already scrubbed the floor, thrown wood into the stove, and was now off to get boiled drinking water and "hvoya", a dark-green infusion of pine-needles, which was supposed to counteract vitamin deficiency. The few fortunate victims of scurvy in the camp could obtain from the doctor a certificate entitling them to receive "cyngotnoye pytanye"—a daily spoonful of chopped-up raw vegetables, usually onions, carrots, turnips and beetroots. Almost invariably requests for cyngotnoye were made in the hope of getting an extra spoonful of food, not medicine.

The sky over the camp zone was already grey, but the weather was almost mild. The first wisps of smoke were appearing above the barracks and sweeping the gables with their wide plumes, while the frosty window-panes shone with a dim light. All round the horizon stretched the dark wall of the forest. The paths through the camp zone were made of two planks, laid side by side; they were swept every day by the priests, who cleared away the snow with large wooden shovels, and piled it in heaps, which sometimes reached to the waist, on either side. The whole camp looked like an enormous clay-pit, covered with a network of small channels for railway trucks. The doors of the guard-house were already open to admit the first brigades returning from work. On a high platform outside the kitchen stood a queue of ragged shadows, in fur caps with flaps over their ears, their feet and legs wrapped in rags and tied about with string, who were reminding the cook of their existence with an impatient tinkling of billy-cans.

The medical hut was situated near the women's barrack. The doctor and his orderly received patients behind a plywood partition; in the corner by the door sat a ragged, shaggy old man with steel spectacles, who welcomed all who came in with a gentle look from his little eyes, and with undisguised joy entered their names on the list of patients. He seemed to be quite at home there; not only did he inscribe, in a beautiful handwriting, the names of patients on his list, and constantly throw small logs into the stove, but he also asked each newcomer, with a comical gravity, about his troubles and symptoms, and every now and then would shout—poking his shaggy head round the partition—"Tatiana Pavlovna, it seems to me that this is a very serious case," and, returning to his stool with satisfaction, would stir the remains of some soup warming in a small billy-can on the edge of the stove. A pleasant female voice would invariably answer: "Be good enough to wait a moment, Matvei Kirylovich," which caused the old man to spread his hands in the gesture of a busy official. These vestiges of an unusual, exaggerated courtesy could be found in camps only among older people.

The majority of those waiting in the hut were nacmeny, the Mongolian inhabitants of Central Asia. Even in the waiting-room they clasped their stomachs in pain, and the moment they entered behind the partition burst into a sorrowful whining, in which moans were mixed indistinguishably with their curious broken Russian. There was no remedy for their disease, and they were usually regarded as incurable simulants. They were dying simply of homesickness, of longing for their native country, of hunger, cold and of the monotonous whiteness of snow. Their slanting eyes, unused to the northern landscape, were always watering and their eyelashes were stuck together by a thin yellow crust. On the rare days on which we were free from work, the Uzbeks, Turcomen and Kirghiz gathered in a corner of the barrack, dressed in their holiday clothes, long coloured silk robes and embroidered skull-caps. It was impossible to guess of what they talked with such great animation and excitement, gesticulating, shouting each other down and nodding their heads sadly, but I was certain that it was not of the camp. Often, late in the evening, after the old men among them had wandered off to their own barracks for the night, the young men stayed in pairs on their bunks and for hours at a time stroked each other's necks, faces and backs. As their movements became slower, their bodies stiffened with tension, and their eyes were glazed and misted. I have no idea how these caresses ended, and I never saw any actual sodomy among the nacmeny, but during the whole year and a half which I spent in the camp, only once did a Turcoman woman pass through Yercevo. The group of Mongolians received her as an honoured guest in their corner, and she was escorted back to the women's barrack before nightfall; the next day she left with a transport.

Tatiana Pavlovna, the doctor, turned out to be a polite, elderly woman, who directed me to the hospital without making any difficulties when she found that I really had a high temperature. "The card I've given you won't take care of everything," she said as I left, "sometimes one has to wait a very long time for a free bed." As I returned to the barrack to collect my belongings, the camp zone was already quite dark. I could see, stumbling down the paths, several victims of the night blindness which is a common result of malnutrition, carefully groping along the slippery, ice-covered barrack walls, and warding off with fluttering fingers the black curtain before their eyes. Occasionally one of them fell into a snow-

drift, and dug himself out again with awkward despairing movements of the body, softly calling for help. Healthy prisoners passed
them by unheeding and walked quickly on, their eyes fixed on the
welcoming lights of barrack windows.

In the hospital I had to spend only one night on the floor in the
passage, and then two weeks in a clean bed in the ward. That
period I remember as one of the happiest of my life. My skin,
which had not known the touch of sheets for a whole year, seemed
to open all its pores with relief, and a deep sleep brought me
feverish recollections—I slept for twenty-four hours. In the bed
next to mine lay a large man suffering from "pylagra", a mysterious
disease of which I know only that its symptoms are loss of hair and
teeth, attacks of prolonged melancholia, and also, I believe,
rupture. Every day, after waking up, my neighbour threw off his
bedclothes and for several minutes ponderously weighed his
testicles in the palm of his hand. His cure consisted exclusively of
lumps of margarine like small boxes, which he received for breakfast with a portion of white bread. Those who had once contracted
pylagra never returned to normal health. After leaving the
hospital they were moved straight to the barrack where those no
longer fit for work could spend the whole day lying on their bunks
without stirring, and were fed on smaller rations; this barrack was
known in the camp as the bone-shop or the mortuary. During my
stay in hospital I made friends with the nurse, an unusually devoted
and helpful Russian woman from Vyatka, who had been sentenced
to ten years for her father's counter-revolutionary activities; the
father, if he was still alive, had spent the years since 1937 in closed,
isolated camps, and as he was not allowed to write or receive letters,
his daughter knew neither where nor in what conditions he was
living. Sister Tamara gave me Griboyedov's *Collected Works*, and,
apart from Dostoevsky's *The House of the Dead*, this was the only
book which I ever tried to read during my stay in the camp.

When I returned to the barrack, I was allowed three days' further
rest, so that I had plenty of time in which to consider my position.
In theory, there were three possibilities before me: I would be
assigned to one of the brigades of foresters, or I would be sent to
another section of the Kargopol camp, or, if I wished to avoid
either alternative, I would have to start looking after my own
interests. Work in the forest from dawn to dusk, standing up to the
waist in snow, was not above the capacities of a healthy man, but I

dreaded the walk of three miles to and from work, through a forest full of snowdrifts and large treacherous pits which were dug to catch wolves; my legs had swollen so much in prison that I could hardly stand in the food-line. From the accounts of other prisoners I gathered that Yercevo was the best section of the Kargopol camp, while the others, especially the penal camp of the second Alexeyevka, were for the most part full of Poles who had been sent there to die by inches. Following the advice of Dimka, who became my best friend, I sold my high officer's boots for 900 grammes of bread to an urka from the railway porters' brigade. The same evening he gave me his answer: the camp command had agreed that I should join brigade 42, and recommended me to report at the camp store to draw out a "bushlat" (a long-sleeved jerkin lined with wadding), a cap with ear-flaps, wadded trousers, waterproof gloves made of sailcloth, and "valonki" (shoes made of sheepskin, cowhide and horsehide) of best quality, i.e. new or worn only a little—a full set of clothing such as is usually issued only to the best "stakhanovite" brigades of prisoners. I knew from Dimka what to expect from the work of a porter at the food supply centre. The work itself was heavy, for an average twelve-hour working day meant carrying twenty-five tons of flour in sacks, or eighteen tons of rye without sacks, over a distance of thirty yards from the truck to the store: as the number of trucks on the siding was greater than usual, we had to work sometimes for twenty hours at a stretch. On the other hand, the supply centre was beyond the camp zone, and it was possible to steal food there. "You'll have to work a bit," Dimka told me, "but you'll also eat well. In the forest, you can warm yourself at the fire and die of hunger. You can't eat bark. But here I shall have your hvoya waiting for you." For the moment, then, I was saved. Lying on an upper bunk by the window, I looked round the 42nd "international brigade". The eight best places out of about two hundred in the barrack were taken up by a gang of urkas, led by Koval, the pock-marked Ukrainian bandit to whom I had sold my boots. The rest were a mixture of communists from all over Europe, and one Chinaman.

That same evening, shortly before midnight—Dimka usually got up at that hour, to rummage in the refuse buckets for herring-heads which would make the soup for his next day's lunch—Koval, who was lying on his stomach by the window, his face pressed to the glass, suddenly jumped off the bunk and with a few quick nudges woke up his companions. After a while they all gathered round a small space in the window where the frost had melted, looked out at the camp zone, whispered among themselves and walked out. All this took no more than a minute, during which I lay with my eyes closed, breathing heavily as if asleep. There was complete silence in the barrack after they left; along the two rows of bunks men were sleeping in their clothes, open mouths greedily gasping at the hot air. After the last urka had disappeared through the door, I quickly turned over on my stomach and breathed on the window over my bunk until I had cleared a small round judas in the frost. A hundred yards beyond our barrack the ground sloped to form a large hollow which continued on the other side of the barbed wire. The neighbouring barracks were placed at the edge of the hollow, so that it was out of sight of the guard-house and the upper part of the camp zone. The bottom of the hollow could be seen well only from the top of the highest watch-tower, but if the guard was sitting with his face turned towards the camp and his back against the wall of his crow's-nest he could see only the further, outlying part of the slope. From the direction of the hospital a young well-built girl was crossing the deserted zone on her way to the women's barrack, and in order to make a short cut and avoid walking round by the barbed wire, she would have to pass along the inner edge of the hollow, just in front of our barrack. Eight shadows rapidly dispersed among the barracks on the left side of the hollow, so that each outlet of the path was guarded. The girl was walking straight into the trap. In the snow-muffled silence of the camp the night hunt was on.

The girl was now walking along the path on a level with our barrack, half-hidden by a large snowdrift. From the distance I could see only that she had broad shoulders and a wide face, tied round with a head scarf whose ends fluttered behind her in the wind like the tail of a kite. Before she reached the bend of the path, the first shadow stepped out from behind a barrack and stood in her way. The girl started and gave a short cry, which was stifled as the shadow jumped at her throat, caught the back of her neck with one hand and put the other over her mouth. The girl bent back like a bow, and raising her left leg from the ground, pushed the knee into the attacker's stomach, and at the same time grasped his beard with both hands, pushing the great fur-capped head away with all her strength. The shadow made a half-circle with his left foot, and with

a sharp kick knocked her right leg from under her. They both fell
into the snowdrift together at the very moment when the other
seven ran up from all directions.

They dragged her, holding her by the hands and legs, while her
hair tumbled loosely behind, to the bottom of the hollow, and threw
her down on a snow-covered bench, about twenty-five yards from
the barrack. She met the first with a furious kicking of her legs,
freed for a moment from his grasp, but soon she was quiet again,
choked by the skirt which was thrown over her head, and Koval's
great paw, which he placed over her face, forcing her head down on
the bench. The first pinned her right leg to the back of the bench
with one knee, and with his other leg pressed on the inside of the
thigh which was hanging in mid-air and moving convulsively.
While two others held her wrists, the first, half-kneeling, was tearing
off her underclothes and calmly unbuttoning his trousers. After a
moment her body began to rock convulsively and Koval had to
loosen the grip of his fingers with each uneven jerk of her head.
The second and third had an easier task, and, encouraged by the
sudden calm of her body, impatiently dug for her breasts in the
rumpled bundle of her skirt and blouses. But, when it was the turn
of the fourth, she managed for a moment to free her head from
Koval's relaxed fingers, and in the frosty silence she let out a short,
throaty cry, full of tears and muffled by her skirt. A sleepy voice
called from the nearest watch-tower: "Come, come, boys, what are
you doing? Have you no shame?"

They pulled her off the bench, and, like a limp rag doll, dragged
her behind the barrack, to the latrine. The space before my window
was empty; only round the bench and on both sides of the path there
were dark rifts where the high banks of snow had been trampled.
After about an hour seven of them returned to the barrack. Then
I saw Koval taking the girl back to the women's barrack. She
walked slowly, stumbling and tripping on the path, head drooping
to one side, with arms folded across her breasts, supported round
the waist by the strong arm of her companion.

The next evening Marusia came to our barrack. There were still
traces of congealed blood on her cheeks, and her eyes were bruised,
but she looked pretty in a coloured skirt and a white, embroidered
linen blouse, in which two large breasts swung loosely like round
loaves of bread. She sat, as if nothing had happened, on Koval's
bunk, with her back to the other urkas, and gently pressing close to

him she kept whispering in his ear, kissing his pock-marked cheek with tears in her eyes. Koval at first sat grumpily by her side and from under his low forehead threw embarrassed glances at his companions, but in the end he let her persuade him. She stayed, and throughout that night we were constantly woken from our feverish sleep by her tender exclamations of love, cries of pain, and Koval's rhythmical breathing. She stole out of the barrack before dawn, followed by the careful, wavering tread of her exhausted lover. After that she came every evening and often sang before nightfall, in a strong voice which trailed off into a mournful squeal at the end of each phrase, Ukrainian songs about "the boy who used to come to my house" and "the fine life a man can have with a milkmaid". She became a water-carrier in the camp, and we all liked her broad, swarthy face, her fair hair loose and flying in the wind as she sat on the sled and spurred her horse with loud cracks of the whip or nervous tugs at the reins. Beyond the zone, where, as a criminal prisoner, she was allowed to go for water without a guard, she sometimes begged a few gay pictures or coloured paper cut-outs, and in the evenings they would be pinned on the dirty wall above her lover's bunk.

But the brigade was not working well since the memorable night of the hunt. Koval went to work half-conscious; his legs bowed under the weight of heavy sacks, he often missed his turn at the trucks, and several times even fell off the loading-stage on to the rails. Once, while we were enjoying a short break from work inside a small watchman's hut, Wang the Chinaman observed that "One of the horses in the team ought to be changed," and was immediately silenced by a look from the other urkas. We noticed, however, that they too stopped talking and smiled contemptuously whenever Koval came near them for a cigarette. He took to going about by himself, ate from his own separate bowl, and after supper would put on my officer's boots and an embroidered Ukrainian shirt, then lie down on his bunk with a cigarette and listen for the sound of splashing water as the last barrel of the day was driven to the kitchen.

One evening, when Marusia, who never spoke to anyone in our barrack, was sitting as usual next to Koval, her arms entwined round his waist, one of the urkas tapped her lightly on the shoulder and spoke a few words to her. The girl slowly unwound her arms, turned her head and looked at the man with loathing; suddenly she raised her whole body and, with the gleam of a mortally wounded animal in her eyes, spat straight in his face. The blinded urka took a step back, wiped his face with his sleeve, and spreading out the two fingers of his right hand, drew back for the dreaded blow. At that moment Koval sprang up from the bunk and threw himself at the other. They struggled for a moment, and when they were separated, Koval found himself facing seven pairs of hostile eyes. He turned to the girl, who was cowering in the corner, pulled his torn shirt round him and through clenched teeth said in a voice which chilled my blood: "Lie down, you bitch, and off with your clothes, or I'll choke the life out of you." Then to his friends: "She's yours, brothers."

First came the urka at whom she had spat. Marusia now took them without any resistance, gently opening her thighs, cupping her hands round the swinging buttocks above her, and not complaining even when their impatient hands crushed her breasts. Her head hung down over the end of the bunk, and her wide eyes looked persistently at Koval, who was sitting by the table, while her pale lips whispered softly: "Forgive me, Timosha, forgive me." Koval did not get up from his seat even when, as she was leaving the barrack, she looked back at him once more with eyes full of an unbounded, down-trodden love. Long after she left, the air was full of a sharp smell of sweat, sperm and hvoya.

After three days, at her own request, Marusia left Yercevo for Ostrovnoye. The eight urkas in the barrack returned to their former brotherhood, which until the end of my stay in the camp was never again disturbed by the slightest symptoms of human feeling.

CHAPTER 3

WORK

1. DAY AFTER DAY.

AT half-past five in the morning the barrack doors opened with a clatter, and the silence, disturbed only by the last sighs of sleep, was broken by a loud shout of "Padyom—let's go." A moment later the "razvodchyk", a prisoner responsible for the march-out of the brigades to work, walked briskly along the rows of bunks, tugging the sleepers by their legs. The prisoners moved heavily on their bunks, threw aside the coats covering their heads, and slowly, as if their bodies were held down by invisible bonds, sat up, only to fall back on to the bunks with moans of pain a moment later. Then the "dnevalny", the barrack orderly, walked slowly up and down, repeating "To work, children, to work" in a monotonous whisper; he had to see that all the occupants of the barrack were up and on their feet before the kitchens opened. He performed his work gently and politely, not like the razvodchyk, but more as befits a man who, himself free from work, is forced to send others to it, and whose low status of a slaves' servant does not allow him to speak with the harshness used by free men and their camp servants when they address the prisoners.

Those few minutes after reveille, while the inhabitants of each barrack lay on their bunks without moving, were devoted to our peculiar form of prayer. It began invariably with swearing and curses, and ended almost as invariably with the sacramental formula: "Oh, what a bloody life. . . !" That expression, which I heard repeated every day on all sides, was a hideous complaint which contained everything that a prisoner knew and could say about his living death. In other lands and other conditions, in normal prisons, the place of this short cry of despair is taken by a real prayer or by the remission of one day of the total sentence, for it is only too understandable that a man robbed of everything but hope should begin his day by turning his thoughts to hope. Soviet prisoners have been deprived even of hope, for not one of them can ever know with any certainty when his sentence will come to an end. He can remember literally hundreds of cases where sentences have been prolonged by another ten years with one stroke of a pen at the Special Council of the N.K.V.D. in Moscow. Only someone who has been in prison can appreciate the whole implication of cruelty in the fact that during my year and a half in the camp only a few times did I hear prisoners counting aloud the number of years, months, days and hours which still remained of their sentences. This silence seemed to be a tacit agreement not to tempt providence. The less we talked about our sentences, the less hope we cherished of ever regaining freedom, the more likely it seemed that "just this once" everything would be well. Hope contains the terrible danger of disappointment. In our silence, rather like the taboo which forbids the men of certain primitive tribes to pronounce the names of vengeful deities, humility was combined with a quiet resignation and anticipation of the worst. Disappointment was a fatal blow to a prisoner who lacked this armour against fate. I remember an old railwayman from Kiev, called Ponomarenko, who had spent ten years in various Soviet camps, and who alone among us all talked of his approaching release with a confidence that dispelled fear, excluding all uncertainty. In July 1941, two weeks after the outbreak of the Russo-German war, he was summoned to the N.K.V.D. office beyond the zone on the last day of his sentence to hear that it had been prolonged "indefinitely". When we came back from work that evening, he was already dead. Dimka told us later that he had come back from the Second Section* looking pale, and had seemed suddenly aged by the ten years which he had spent in the camp. He lay down on his bunk without a word, and to all questions would answer only: "My life is finished, it's all over"; and he, an old bolshevik, alternately prayed soundlessly or beat his grey head against the planks of the bunk. He died between four and five in the afternoon, when Dimka as usual went out for hvoya and hot water. I can only guess what was happening in his heart, but one thing is certain—that besides despair, pain, and helpless anger, he felt also regret for his thoughtless faith in hope. In his last moments, looking back on his wasted life, he must have reproached himself bitterly for provoking fate by his light-hearted confidence. In the

* The Second Section of the N.K.V.D. was concerned with the quotas of prisoners and their distribution among the camps. Like all other camp authorities, it was under the ultimate control of the Third Section, which, by the extensive use of informers, watched over the political behaviour of the prisoners and the loyalty of the free camp officials, and decided all questions with even the slightest political aspect.

barrack I heard more condemnation than sympathy for him. He had suffered, yes: but had he not brought it upon himself? Was it not playing with fire to talk freely about his release? Did he not invoke freedom, instead of putting his faith humbly in the sentences of destiny? He was no inexperienced novice, for he himself, in 1936, had seen men who were due for release at four o'clock in the afternoon cut the veins of their wrists when, at twelve o'clock, an order had come from Moscow abolishing the system of remission of two days for every day of stakhanovite work. He had told us this himself, laughing and pleased because his own good sense had always told him to work only so much that a day should be counted as a day. And now he had been cheated of 3,650 days of unfailing, honest work. It was considered that he had been deservedly punished for breaking the prisoners' code.

Everything went on as before: Ponomarenko's bunk was taken by another prisoner, the place of his faith in justice by the old taboo, and the place of his daily sentence-litany by the only words which we used to express hopelessness without provoking hope.

By a quarter to six only those prisoners who had obtained a medical dispensation from work on the previous day were still lying on their bunks, while the rest were beginning to dress. Prisoners bent over their bare legs, attempting to construct from rags, pieces of string or lengths of wire, torn felt boots and scraps of car tyres a warm and enduring foot-covering which would last for an eleven-hour day of work. Only the specially picked brigades, mine among them, engaged in work directly concerned with the camp's production plan, were issued with new clothing and allowed to exchange it when it was worn out. But about three-quarters of all prisoners walked out to work in rags which exposed parts of their legs, arms and chests. It was not surprising, then, that many of them did not undress at night for fear that their clothing, put together with difficulty, would simply disintegrate. For them the morning reveille was like a signal in the waiting-room of a railway station. They shook the sleep out of themselves, dragged themselves off the bunks, moistened their eyes and mouths in the corner of the barrack, and walked out to the kitchen. They left the zone for work with a surreptitious hope that this time the frostbite on the exposed parts of their bodies would be bad enough to merit at least a few days' dispensation from work.

The zone was still quite dark. Only just before the morning

roll-call the sky became pink on the edge of the horizon, melting after a while in the steel-blue glare of the snow. It was difficult to distinguish faces even at the distance of an extended hand. We all walked in the direction of the kitchen, bumping into each other and clanging our mess-cans. By the well and round the small hut where the hot drinking water was boiled could be heard the jangling of buckets, the crunching of frozen snow and the quiet whispers of the imprisoned priests, who, like Dimka, usually did the work of barrack orderlies, calmly conducting their morning exchange of courtesies. The sombre ceiling of the sky closed upon us from above, and the still invisible barbed wire separated us from the outer world which was beginning to go about its business by the light of electric lamps.

On the raised platform in front of the kitchen formed three queues, epitomising the social divisions of the camp proletariat. Before the serving-hatch with the inscription "third cauldron" stood the best-dressed and fittest prisoners—stakhanovites, whose daily production capacity reached or surpassed 125 per cent of the prescribed norm; their morning meal consisted of a large spoonful of thick boiled barley and a scrap of salted "treska" (a large northern fish similar in flavour to the cod) or herring. The second cauldron was for prisoners with a daily production capacity of 100 per cent of the norm—a spoonful of barley without the piece of fish. At the front of this queue stood old men and women from those brigades where it was impossible to reckon the work in terms of percentages, who were therefore automatically issued with the second cauldron. But the most terrible sight was the first cauldron queue, a long row of beggars in torn rags, shoes tied with string and worn caps with ear-flaps, waiting for their spoonful of the thinnest barley. Their faces were shrivelled with pain and dried like parchment, their eyes suppurating and distended by hunger, their hands convulsively gripping the billy-cans as if their stiff fingers had frozen to the tin handles. Dazed with exhaustion and swooning on their thin legs, they pushed their way through to the hatch, whined plaintively, begging for an extra dribble, and peered greedily into the cans of second- and third-cauldron prisoners as they left the hatches. In this queue arguments were most frequent, here the humble whining changed most frequently into the shrill falsetto of anger, envy and hatred. The queue for the first cauldron was always the longest in the camp. Apart from the most numerous class of prisoners, those who with the best will in the world could not attain 100 per cent of the norm because their physical condition was too poor, there were many who purposely spared themselves at work, convinced that it was better to work little and eat little than to work hard and eat almost as little. All the barrack orderlies, and a few prisoners from the staff and administration of the camp, also belonged to the first cauldron.

Prisoners who left the zone without an escort, by special passes, had their breakfast before six. Besides water-carriers and servants employed in the houses of free administrative staff, this group also included the technical experts and engineers who had to be at their places before the arrival of the brigades. The meal of their special "iteerovski" (I.T.R.—engineering and technical work) cauldron surpassed in quantity and to some extent in quality the rations even of stakhanovites on general work. At half-past six all the serving-hatches were closed, though they opened again, after the brigades had left for work, to feed prisoners with medical dispensations from work, the inhabitants of the mortuary, and those working inside the zone itself on the second cauldron.

Very few prisoners had enough strength of will to carry their meals from the kitchen all the way back to the barracks. For the most part they ate standing up at the bottom of the platform, swallowing in two or three hasty gulps all that the cook's ladle had poured into the dirty can. Small groups of prisoners began to join the black crowd gathering by the guard-house immediately after breakfast. The zone was already light, and from the dispersing darkness could be made out first the frost-rimed wires, then the enormous sheet of snow, extending to the hardly visible line of the forest on the horizon. In the village and in the barracks the lights were going out and the chimneys were sending dirty yellow clouds of smoke into the air. The moon was fading gently, frozen in the icy sky like a slice of lemon in a jelly, and the last stars still twinkled. The morning "razvod"—the brigades' march out to work—was starting.

At a given signal the prisoners drew themselves up into brigades, standing in twos. In normal brigades the old were at the front and the young at the back, but in brigades whose output did not come up to the prescribed norm the order was reversed. This practice must be explained more fully. There were very few prisoners who believed that it was better to work less and eat less, and in the overwhelming majority of cases the cauldron system was successful in obtaining the maximum physical effort from the prisoners for an insignificant increase in their rations. A hungry man does not stop to think, but is ready to do anything for an extra spoonful of soup. The fascination of the norm was not the exclusive privilege of the free men who imposed it, but also the dominating instinct of the slaves who worked to it. In those brigades where the work was done by teams of men working together, the most conscientious and fervent foremen were the prisoners themselves, for there the norms were reckoned collectively by dividing the total output by the number of workers. Any feeling of mutual friendliness was completely abolished in favour of a demented race for percentages. An unqualified prisoner who found himself assigned to a co-ordinated team of experienced workers could not expect to have any consideration shown to him; after a short struggle he was forced to give up and transfer to a team in which he in his turn frequently had to watch over weaker comrades. There was in all this something inhuman, mercilessly breaking the only natural bond between prisoners—their solidarity in face of their persecutors. The formation of brigades in the morning brought this system to monstrous cruelty. In brigades which failed to come up to the norm the pace of the march was set by the youngest prisoners to save time, while the older and feebler ones were dragged behind. This natural selection resulted in rapid rejuvenation of the brigades in question, for the old ones who could not keep up gradually disappeared for good.

The first to leave the zone were the brigades of foresters, who had to walk between five and seven kilometres to their work; leaving the camp at half-past six, they would arrive at their sector of the forest at half-past seven, and finish work at five. The razvodchyk, who acted as the master of ceremonies at the morning roll-call, standing with a board and a pencil exactly on the border-line between the zone and free territory, called each brigade in turn to the gates and reported its presence to the officer of the guard. Beyond the gate waited with mounted bayonets a detachment of the "Vohra" (the labour camp garrisons) in long greatcoats and fur caps. The chief officer of the guard formally handed the brigade over to its permanent escorting soldier, who stepped out of his rank, called out his name and the number of his brigade, checked the number of prisoners and repeated it aloud to the officer, acknowledging the receipt of so many men for such and such work. From that moment he was responsible for them with his own life, so that a moment before marching off he repeated to the prisoners the sacred, invariable formula: "Brigade such and such, I am warning you: one single step to the right or the left, and you get a bullet through the head." Then he gave the signal to move off, and lowering his rifle as if for attack, with his finger on the trigger, sent the brigadier to the front and himself brought up the rear. After the forest brigades went those for the saw-mill, the brigades of joiners going to the town, then the digging, the food-centre, the road-building, the water-works and the electricity-plant brigades. From the gates of the camp black crocodiles of men—stooping, shivering with cold and dragging their legs—dispersed in all directions and disappeared on the horizon after a few minutes like scattered lines of letters, gathered with one pull of the hand from a white sheet of paper.

The journey to work was exhausting, but contained some variety compared with the work itself. Even prisoners whose brigades worked at a distance of less than a mile from the zone found great pleasure in passing familiar places, trees, frozen streams, dilapidated sheds and wolf-traps, perhaps asserting their own existence by observation of the unchanging laws of nature. In some brigades, too, the degree of friendliness between the prisoners and their guard was so close that, as soon as they were out of sight of the guard-house, the "strelok" put his rifle on his shoulder and began to chat pleasantly with the last few pairs. This insignificant expression of human feelings gave us not so much the pleasure of raising ourselves from humiliation and contempt, but rather excitement at an infringement of prison rules. Occasionally the guard treated his brigade with politeness, and even showed signs of a rudimentary guilty conscience towards them. Therefore the days when the guard of a particular brigade was changed were among the most memorable for the prisoners, and were eagerly discussed in the barracks. Some time had always to pass before a fresh understanding could develop between the slaves and their new overseer. It was quite a different case if the escorting guard looked upon the prisoners as his natural enemies and treated them accordingly; that brigade did not miss the slightest opportunity of annoying him and making his work difficult.

The first hours of the day were always the most difficult to bear. Our bodies, stiffened rather than rested by sleep on hard bunks, had to struggle against great pain in order to recapture the rhythm of work. Besides, there was really nothing to wait for in the morning. Only the stakhanovites received a midday meal—a spoonful of boiled soya-beans and a hundred grammes of bread; this "extra" was brought by one of the water-carriers, under the supervision of a cook, in a large bucket fixed to sledge runners. Other workers spent the midday break sitting round the fire in a position where they could not see the stakhanovites' "extra", smoking one common cigarette which was passed from Land to hand.

It was rarely that a prisoner had saved a slice of bread from the previous evening's meal. Bread rations were issued daily according to the cauldrons: third—700 grammes, second—500 grammes, and first—400 grammes.* Bread—apart from the spoonful of boiled barley in the mornings and the portion of weak soup in the evenings —was the camp's basic food. To restrain oneself from gulping all of it down immediately after receiving it required a superhuman effort of will. Only those prisoners who walked out again to the kitchen after their evening meal, and bought additional portions of soup from the cooks with the rapidly vanishing items of their pre-camp clothing, could bring themselves to put a little bread by for the morning.

Two hours before their return to the zone the prisoners came to life again. The prospect of rest and of momentary satisfaction of tormenting hunger had such an effect on us that not only the return, but even the anticipation of it was the day's most important event. As in every idealised picture, there was more illusion than reality in the expectation. The agony of prison life did not end for us when we returned to the barracks, but on the contrary became the agony of waiting for death. Yet it contained a mysterious attraction in the intimacy of suffering. Lying alone on one's bunk, one was at last free—free from work, from the company of one's fellow-prisoners, free, finally, from time, which dragged so slowly for us. Only in prison is it easy to understand that life without any expectation of the future becomes meaningless and flooded with despair. We feared solitude while waiting for it. It was our only substitute for freedom, and in moments of complete relaxation it gave us the relief and the almost physical pain of tears.

The first, instinctive reaction of hopelessness is always the faith that in loneliness suffering will become hardened and sublimated as

* 1 lb. = approximately 450 grammes.

in a purgatory fire. Though many long for solitude as their last refuge, few are capable of bearing it. The idea of loneliness, as that of suicide, is most frequently the only protest which we can make when everything else has failed us, and before death has begun to hold more attraction than terror for us. It is never more than an idea, for despair enlightened by consciousness would be greater than the despair of torpidity. A prisoner walking back to the zone was like a drowning man who has survived a shipwreck and is swimming with a last effort of will towards a desert island. As long as he is struggling with the waves and catching gusts of air into lungs which are already bursting with pain, but always nearer and nearer to the land, his life is still worth living, for he still has hope. But there is no torture worse than the sudden realisation that this hope itself was only the delusion of unsteady senses. To find oneself on a desert island, without the slightest prospect of rescue and salvation, after the efforts to survive in the sea—that may indeed be called suffering. We lived through that every day; every day shortly before the return to the zone, the prisoners laughed and talked like free men; and every day they would lie down on their bunks after work like men choking with despair.

In the forest brigades, which in the north were the basis of the labour camps' production plan, the work was divided among several teams of four or five prisoners. The functions of each prisoner were constantly varied so that each would in turn perform the heavier and the lighter tasks; thus, one felled the pines with a thin curved saw, one cleared them of bark and boughs, one burnt the cleared branches and bark on the fire (this was a form of rest which was taken in turn), and the remaining two sawed the felled trunks into logs of a prescribed length, stacking them in piles a yard or two in height. Under this system of division of labour the most important person at the wood-cutting was the foreman, a prisoner who walked about without an escort or a free supervisor, who measured the cut wood, and stamped the counted logs with the camp seal. His reckonings became the basis on which the brigadier calculated the output of each team in his brigade. I can no longer remember what the prescribed norm was in the forest, but I do know that the Finns, who are deservedly reputed to be the world's best woodcutters, considered it to be excessively high even for free and well-fed workers. It was impossible for a forest brigade to surpass its norm except with the help of what was known as "toufta", a whole system of ingenious cheating. The authority of a brigadier among his workers was measured by his talents in this direction, which were also a source of income to him in the form of bribes from weaker prisoners. Various methods were used; the logs were stacked so that the piles would look full from outside and yet be loose inside, with spaces between logs—this could be successful only when the foreman was himself a prisoner, and for a bribe of bread would ignore the hollowness of the piles. If the foreman happened to be an incorruptible free official (though even these could occasionally be bribed, usually with a civilian suit), we would saw off thinly the stamped end of the log and insert this "new" log into an uncounted pile, while the shavings were quickly burnt in the fire. In any case it is a fact that without the toufta and its accompanying bribery, on all sectors of the camp's industry, no brigade could ever have reached even a hundred per cent output.

Forest work was considered to be one of the heaviest forms of labour in the camp. The distance from work to the camp was usually about three miles; the prisoners worked all day under the open sky, up to their waist in snow, drenched to the skin, hungry and exhausted. I never came across a prisoner who had worked in the forest for more than two years. As a rule they left after a year, with incurable disease of the heart, and were transferred to brigades engaged at lighter work; from these they soon "retired"— to the mortuary. Whenever a fresh transport of prisoners arrived in Yercevo, the youngest and strongest were always picked to be "put through the forest". This selection of slaves was sometimes similar even in the details of its decor to the illustrations of books about negro slavery, when the chief of the Yercevo camp section, Samsonov, honoured the medical examination with his presence, and with a smile of satisfaction felt the biceps, shoulders and backs of the new arrivals.

The length of a working day was basically eleven hours in all brigades, increased after the outbreak of the Russo-German war to twelve. But in the porters' brigade which worked at the food supply centre, and in which I spent most of my time in the camp, these limits were non-existent—the duration of work depended on the number of railway-wagons, and the wagons could not be delayed overtime, as the camp had to pay the railway executive for each additional hour beyond the prescribed time. In practice we worked sometimes as long as twenty hours a day, with only short

breaks for meals. If we returned to the zone after midnight, we
were not forced to rise with the others, but returned to the food
supply centre only about eleven in the morning, working again as
long as was necessary in order that the empty wagons could return
on time from our siding to Yercevo station. It was thus that by
overtime alone our output was usually between 150 and 200 per cent
of the norm. Even so toufta was applied very frequently in our
brigade as the majority of the porters desired to be maintained on
the "red list" of the stakhanovites, which gave them the privilege of
buying a piece of horse-sausage in the camp shop. The toufta at the
food supply centre consisted of adding, on paper, several yards to
the distance between the wagon and the warehouse with the
agreement of the foreman who signed the index figure of production
for the brigade. The norm of the porters' brigade was calculated on
the basis of two factors—the amount of unloaded goods, and the
distance between the wagon and the warehouse. The first could not
be altered, for each wagon carried a list of the amount and contents
of the freight, but the second left a margin of free numerical
calculation to the brigadier.

It is not easy to understand why, under these conditions, admission to the porters' brigade at the food supply centre was looked
upon in the camp as a certain social promotion. It must be remembered that overtime work was the rule rather than the exception at the supply centre, where twenty-five of us had to unload food for the 30,000 prisoners in all the camp sections of the
Kargopol camp, and for the co-operative store outside the camp.
And yet dozens of prisoners were waiting eagerly to take the place
of any one of us who would leave. There were two principal reasons
for this—one purely material, the other moral or rather psychological. Working at the centre, we had many opportunities of
stealing a piece of salted fish, a little flour, or a few potatoes. We
also had the right to negotiate with our foremen, and frequently
even with free officials, on an equal footing, for we were always
formally *asked* to work overtime. Our supervisors could, of course,
have appealed to the camp authorities in the event of our refusal,
thus substituting coercion for a procedure of good-will, but they
never had recourse to force before first exhausting every possibility
of obtaining their object by kindness and persuasion. We ourselves
took care not to be deprived even of these modest illusions of
freedom, for every prisoner feels the need to preserve the vestiges of

his own free will. Forgetting that the first law of camp life is physical self-preservation, we looked upon our freedom to sanctify the unlimited exploitation of our labour by a pretence of voluntary agreement as a precious privilege. It was like an echo of Dostoevsky's "The word convict means nothing else but a man with no will of his own, and in spending money he is showing a will of his own." We had no money, but we could bargain with the remnants of our strength, and we were as lavish with them as Tsarist exiles with their kopeks, when it was a question of maintaining the barest appearance of our humanity.

After the return from work every brigadier neatly filled in the form of output and carried it to the camp accountants' office; there the submitted figures were translated into percentages according to special tables and the calculations were sent to the camp administration office. This procedure employed, according to my approximate reckoning, about thirty officials for the two thousand prisoners of Yercevo alone. The percentage figures were then passed to the supply office, where the prisoners were assigned to cauldrons on their basis, and to the camp pay office, where the prisoners' individual cards were covered with long columns of figures, stating their earnings in roubles and kopeks according to the tariff of wages established for all labour camps. During my whole stay in Yercevo only once—on May 1st, 1941—did a camp pay officer come to our barrack with statements of our earnings. I signed an enormous form, from which I gathered that my earnings over the past six months were barely sufficient to cover the costs of my stay in the camp ("repairs" to barracks, clothing, food, administrative expenses), leaving me ten roubles—the equivalent of sixpence—in cash. I was glad to be paying my way in the camp, and justifying the expense of maintaining guards to escort me to work and N.K.V.D. officers to watch carefully whether my remarks in the camp could not be punished with an additional sentence. I knew many prisoners whose earnings were not as high even as mine, and who, on every first of May, were told that they had a deficit on their sheets. I have no idea whether this additional payment to the cost of our "corrective institution" was paid from their earnings in freedom after release, whether they remained after their sentences were finished to work off their debt in the camp, or finally whether their families were forced to pay in a certain sum as caution money.

Shortly before ending their work for the day the prisoners took their tools back to the shed and sat round the fire in a circle. A row of hands, covered with veins and patches of congealed blood, dirty and blackened by the work and at the same time whitened by frost-bite, was raised over the fire, the eyes gleamed with a diseased spark, the shadows of the flames played on faces numb from pain. This was the end, the end of yet another day. They felt the weight of their hands, the stitch in the lungs from frozen icicles of breath, the contraction of the throat, the pangs of an empty stomach under their ribs, the aching bones of legs and shoulders. At a signal from the escorting guard they left the fire and got up, some of them raising themselves with the help of sticks made at work. By six o'clock, from all sides of the empty, white plain, the brigades converged on the camp, like funeral processions of shadows carrying their own bodies across their shoulders. Walking along tortuous paths we looked like the legs of some enormous black caterpillar, whose head, pierced in the zone by the four blades of the searchlights, bared the teeth of gleaming barrack windows at the sky. In the deep silence of the evening we could hear only the tread of boots on the snow, broken by the whip-lashes of the escort's "Faster! faster!" But it was beyond us to walk faster; silently we walked, almost pressed against each other, as if, by growing together, we could more easily reach the lighted camp gates. Only the last few hundred yards, only one more final effort, and then the zone, a spoonful of soup, a morsel of bread, a bunk and solitude—a longed-for and yet how deceptive solitude.

And yet this was still not the end. The last three—two—one hundred yards to the gate required enormous effort: the brigades were searched at the guard-house as they arrived. Sometimes, at the gate itself, one of the crowd of prisoners would fall to the ground like a sack thrown off one's back; we would lift him up by his arms so as not to delay the search. If some forbidden object or a stolen scrap of food was found on a prisoner, the whole brigade was marched aside and in the frost, on the snow, stripped almost naked for the search. There were searches which were prolonged with sadistic slowness from seven till ten at night.

Only beyond the gate, in the zone, was it really the end. The prisoners stopped for a while before the alphabetical list of the daily post, dispersed slowly to their barracks for their mess-cans, and moved towards the kitchen. The zone was again dark as in the morning, the queues grew and the cans rattled on the lighted platform before the kitchen. We passed each other without a word, like the inhabitants of a plague infested town. And this silence would suddenly be broken by a despairing cry: somebody's canful of soup was being snatched away from him at the edge of the platform.

2. THROWN TO THE WOLVES.

What our work was, or rather what it could be in the hands of those who choose to use it as an instrument of torture, is best shown by this example of a man who, in the winter of 1941, was murdered with work in one of the forest brigades, by a method which was completely legal and only slightly infringed the code of the camp.

A month after my arrival a new transport, containing a hundred political prisoners and twenty bytoviks, came to Yercevo. The bytoviks remained in Yercevo, and the politicals were transported to the other camp sections, with the sole exception of a young, well-built prisoner with the blunt face of the fanatic, called Gorcev, who was detained in Yercevo and directed to the forest.

Various strange rumours were current in the camp about Gorcev, for he himself, disregarding the prisoners' time-honoured custom, never spoke a word about his own past. This fact alone was sufficient to arouse the prisoners' hostility, for those who guarded closely the secret of their sentence and imprisonment were considered either to be too proud to be admitted to the solidarity of the prisoners, or else as potential spies and informers. This was not his worst offence, for spying and denunciation were looked upon in the camp as the most natural thing; we were irritated particularly by Gorcev's behaviour. His attitude was that of a man who has accidentally slipped into the camp, while keeping a firm foothold on freedom. Only the technical experts of the I.T.R. cauldron were allowed to behave like that, never ordinary prisoners. It was whispered that Gorcev had been an N.K.V.D. officer before his arrest.

He himself—unconsciously, or else through simple stupidity—did everything to confirm this suspicion in our minds. Whenever he opened his mouth as the prisoners sat round the fire in the forest, it was to pronounce short, violent harangues against "the enemies of the people" imprisoned in the camps, defending the action of the Party and the Government in placing them out of harm's way. His dull face, with the cunning eyes of a knave and a large scar on the

right cheek, lit up with an instinctive smile of humility and sub-
servience whenever he pronounced the words of that magic formula
—"the Party and the Government". Once he unwarily revealed
that he found himself in the camp only "through error", and that he
would soon return to his former "position of responsibility". The
other prisoners began to treat him with open and undisguised
hatred.

I made several attempts to gain his confidence, not through
sympathy but simply from curiosity. I was fascinated by the
opportunity of talking to a man who, imprisoned in a labour camp,
observed it through the eyes of a free communist. But Gorcev
avoided me as he did the others, snubbed me whenever I asked a
question, and even provocative jeers produced no reaction from
him. Only once did I manage to engage him in conversation, and
we discussed capitalist encirclement. This discussion convinced me
of the error of the popular belief that the young generation of
Soviet communists is only a band of condottieri, who obey their
leader but are ready to abandon him at the first good opportunity.
For hundreds of thousands of Gorcevs bolshevism is the only
religion and the only possible attitude to the world, for it has been
thoroughly instilled into them during childhood and youth. Older
men like Zinoviev, Kamenev or Bukharin may have looked upon
their "ideological deviation" as a great personal defeat which
suddenly robbed their lives of meaning, they may have suffered and
considered themselves to have been betrayed, they may even have
broken down completely—but despite everything they must still
have retained enough of their critical faculty to enable them to
consider what was being done to them and around them with
historical detachment in their sober moments. But for the Gorcevs
the breakdown of their faith in communism, the only faith which
has directed their lives, would mean the loss of the five basic senses,
which recognise, define and appraise the surrounding reality. Even
imprisonment cannot goad them into breaking their priestly vows,
for they treat it as temporary isolation for a breach of monastic
discipline, and wait for the day of release with even greater
acquiescence and humility in their hearts. The fact that their
period of seclusion and meditation has to be spent in hell does
not prove anything for them, or rather it proves only that hell
really does exist, and woe to those who suffer expulsion from
paradise for sins against the doctrines of the Almighty.

One evening the veil concealing Gorcev's past was lifted slightly. He had quarrelled over some trifle with a group of Mongol nacmeny in the corner of the barrack, and fell into a rage such as we had never seen in him before. He seized one of the old Uzbeks by the collar of his robe and, shaking him furiously, hissed through clenched teeth: "I used to shoot you Asiatic bastards by the dozen—like sparrows off a branch!" The Uzbek, sitting on his folded legs on a lower bunk, rattled in his throat in his own language, and his face changed in a split second so as to become unrecognisable. His eyes darted steel at the attacker from under his lowered eyelids, his upper lip trembled nervously under the thin drooping moustache, revealing a row of white teeth. Suddenly, with a lightning thrust, he knocked Gorcev's hands into the air, and moving his body slightly forward, spat with all his force in the other's face. Gorcev tried to throw himself on the old man, but he was held still by the iron grip of two young Mongols who had jumped down from an upper bunk and caught his arms. We watched this scene in silence without moving from our places. So it seemed that he had been employed in suppressing the great native insurrection of Central Asia; and we knew that this task was entrusted only to those in the confidence of the authorities, the *élite* of the party and the N.K.V.D. Gorcev went to the Third Section with a complaint, but the old Uzbek was not even summoned for questioning beyond the zone. Perhaps because he had unintentionally confirmed the existence of the rebellion of which it was forbidden to speak throughout Russia, or perhaps because, despite appearances, he had no powerful protector beyond the zone, his old connections could not help him, and he was defenceless before the approaching blow. At any rate, his brigade took this failure as a good sign. All they wanted was that the Third Section should refrain from intervention in this matter, that it should throw at least one of its own people to the wolves, giving him up to the prisoners' revenge.

Some time about Christmas a transport from Krouglitza to the Pechora camps passed through Yercevo. The prisoners spent three days in the peresylny barrack, walking round our barracks in the evenings and looking for friends. It was one of these who stopped suddenly and went pale as he passed Gorcev's bunk.

"You—here?" he whispered.

Gorcev raised his head, blenched, and backed against the wall.

"Here?" repeated the new arrival, approaching him slowly. Then suddenly he jumped at Gorcev's throat, threw him down on his back across the bunk, and pressing his right shoulder into Gorcev's chest, started hammering his head furiously against the planks.

"So you fell too, did you?" he shouted, punctuating almost every word with a thud from Gorcev's head. "You fell at last, did you? You could break fingers in doors, push needles under finger-nails, beat our faces and kick us in the balls and the stomach . . . couldn't you . . . couldn't you? My fingers have grown again . . . they'll choke you yet . . . they'll choke you . . ."

Although younger and apparently stronger than his attacker, Gorcev behaved as if he was paralysed and did not attempt to defend himself. Only after a few moments did he seem to come to life, and he kicked the other man with his bent knee and fell with him to the floor. Supporting himself on the nearest bench, his face twisted with fear, he got up and started to run towards the barrack door. But there he found a barrier of Uzbeks who had left their corner to prevent his escape. He turned back—his brigade was waiting for him, looking at him with hostility. The attacker now walked towards him, holding an iron bar which someone on an upper bunk had thrust into his hand. The circle began to close round Gorcev. He opened his mouth to shout, but at that very instant one of the nacmeny hit his head with the wooden cover of a bucket, and he fell to the floor, dripping with blood. With the remnants of his strength he raised himself on his knees, looked at the slowly advancing prisoners and shrieked horribly: "They'll kill me! Guard! They'll kill me!"

In the deep silence, Dimka crawled off his bunk, limped over to the barrack door and bolted it. A jerkin, thrown from an upper bunk, fell on Gorcev ánd immediately the furious blows of the iron bar rained on his head. He threw the jerkin off and, stumbling like a drunkard, rushed towards his own brigade. There he was met by an extended fist, and he bounced off it like a rubber ball, vomiting blood, his legs giving way. He was passed from hand to hand, until he slid to the floor quite helpless, instinctively folding his hands round his head and protecting his stomach with drawn-up knees. He remained crouching like that, crumpled and dripping blood like a wet rag. Several prisoners came up to him and nudged him with their boots, but he made no movement.

"Is he still alive?" asked the one who had unmasked him. "Examining judge from the Kharkov prison, brothers. He used to beat good men so that their own mothers wouldn't know them. What a bastard, oh! what a bastard . . ." he lamented.

Dimka came up with a pailful of hvoya and threw it over Gorcev's head. He stirred, sighed deeply, and stiffened again.

"He's alive," said the forester-brigadier, "but he won't live long."

The next morning Gorcev washed the dry, congealed blood off his face and crawled to the medical hut, where he was given one day's dispensation from work. He went again beyond the zone, with another complaint to the Third Section, and returned empty-handed. It was now clear to us that the N.K.V.D. was giving up to the prisoners one of its own former men. A strange game, in which the persecutors entered upon a silent gentleman's agreement with their victims, was played out in the camp.

After the discovery of his past Gorcev was given the hardest work in the forest brigade: the sawing of pines with the "little bow". For a man unaccustomed to physical labour, and to forestry in particular, this work means certain death unless he is relieved at least once a day and given a rest at burning cleared branches. But Gorcev was never relieved, and he sawed eleven hours a day, frequently falling from exhaustion, catching at the air like a drowning man, spitting blood and rubbing his fever-ridden face with snow. Whenever he rebelled and threw the saw aside with a gesture of desperate bravado, the brigadier came up to him and said quietly: "Back to work, Gorcev, or we'll finish you off in the barrack," and back to work he would go. The prisoners watched his agonies with pleasure and satisfaction. They could indeed have finished him off in the course of one evening, now that they had their sanction from above, but they would have prolonged his death into infinity to make him suffer the agonies to which he had once condemned thousands.

Gorcev tried to fight back, although he must have known that it was as hopeless as the resistance of his victims had once been at the interrogations. He went to the doctor for a further dispensation, but old Matvei Kirylovich refused to put him on the sick list. Once he refused to march out to work, and was sent to solitary confinement on water alone for forty-eight hours, then driven out to work on the third day. The understanding was working well. Gorcev

crawled out every day at the end of the brigade, he walked about
dirty and half-conscious, he was feverish, moaned terribly, spat
blood and cried like a baby at night, and begged for mercy in the
daytime. He received the stakhanovite third cauldron, so that he
would not die immediately, for though his work did not entitle him
even to the first cauldron, yet the other prisoners did not stint their
own percentages to fatten up their victim. Finally, towards the end
of January, after a month had gone by, he lost consciousness at
work. The prisoners were worried that this time they could not
avoid sending him to the hospital. It was agreed that the water-
carrier who drove out to the forest every day with the stakhanovites'
extra portion, and who was friendly with the forest brigades, should
take him back on the sledge after the day's work. In the evening the
brigade marched slowly off towards home, and several hundred
yards behind crawled the sledge with Gorcev's unconscious body.
He never reached the zone again, for at the guard-house it was found
that the sledge was empty. The water-carrier explained that he had
sat in the front of the sledge the whole time, and probably had not
heard the fall of the body in the soft snow, piled up on either side of
the track. It was not until nine—after the guard had eaten his
supper—that an expedition with a lighted torch set out to find the
lost man. Before midnight, through the windows of our barrack,
we saw a wavering point of light on the road from the forest, but the
sledge, instead of coming straight to the zone, turned off in the
direction of the town. Gorcev had been found in a snowdrift two
yards deep which was covering one of the frozen streams—his legs
hanging out of the sledge, must of course have caught in the rail of
the wooden bridge. The body, frozen like an icicle, was taken
straight to Yercevo mortuary.

Long after his death, the prisoners still cherished their memories
of this revenge. One of my friends among the technical experts,
when I had in confidence told him the background of this accident
at the forest clearing, laughed bitterly and said: "Well, at last even
we can feel that the revolution has reversed the old order of things.
Once they used to throw slaves to the lions, now it is the lions who
are thrown to the slaves."

3. "STALIN'S MURDERER."

An additional hindrance at work was night-blindness, an illness
which sooner or later afflicts the majority of prisoners in the labour

camps of the north as a result of bad feeding, and lack of fats in particular.

A man with night-blindness stops seeing only at dusk, and must therefore accustom himself anew to his disablement every evening. This is probably responsible for his constant irritation and nervousness, his panicky fear of night and darkness. In the forest brigades, which worked only in the daytime, but at a distance of several miles from the camp, already at about three o'clock in the afternoon, when the dusk only just drew a faint veil over the pale-blue enamel of the sky, the night-blind began to moan at the escorting guard: "Back to the zone, to the zone, or we'll never get there." This was repeated every day with unfailing regularity, and always with the same result: the brigades left the forest at five and reached the camp after an hour's march through snowdrifts and hollows, at six, when it was already quite dark.

The sight of the night-blind, walking slowly through the zone in the early mornings and evenings, their hands fluttering in front of them, was as normal in the zone as that of the water-carriers who, bowed under the weight of their wooden yokes, were walking from all directions, crunching the snow blown on to the paths during the night, and converging on the well in a black, sharply silhouetted group. At those moments of the day the camp reminded me of a huge aquarium, filled to the brim with black water and trembling with the shadows of deep-sea fishes.

The night-blind were naturally never assigned to work which sometimes lasted far into the night. They were never found in the porters' brigade, even though only in that brigade, with a possibility of stealing a rare piece of pork fat, could they have any chance of being cured—it was in its way a perfect vicious circle: with us they could have been cured of night-blindness, but they never came to us because they suffered from night-blindness.

I remember, though, that once a new worker walked out to work with my brigade, a small, silent man with a severe face and red-rimmed eyes. He was serving a ten-year sentence for a ludicrous misdemeanour. Once, as a high official in one of the people's commissariats, he had had a few drinks with a friend in his office, and made a wager that with one revolver shot he could hit Stalin, whose picture was as usual hanging on the wall, "right in the eye". He won the bet, but it cost him his life when, a few months later, after he had forgotten all about the incident, he happened to quarrel with the friend. The next day he found two officers of the N.K.V.D. waiting for him in the office, where they examined the portrait and immediately drew up an indictment. He was sentenced by the N.K.V.D. Special Council. He had already served seven years, and always providing that his sentence was not prolonged, he still had the worst three years before him. He was assigned to our brigade after much pleading, in order to "improve his health a little", as he told us, making a wide circle in the air with his hand.

Divided into teams of seven, we were that day unloading three enormous railway trucks of flour. We were working like men possessed, for we had been told that we would return to the zone as soon as the work was finished. The new prisoner worked well enough to begin with, but as soon as it began to get dark, he slackened speed, began to miss his turns with the sacks, dropped them inside the wagon on purpose and spent a long time sewing them up again, and kept on going aside more and more frequently. Fortunately, our team contained only one urka, and the politicals assumed complete indifference. "The old one can't keep it up," the Finn Rusto Karinen said to me with his strange accent.

When it was almost dark, the new man reported an urgent need to the guard, and with a slow, wavering step, putting his legs carefully before him like an acrobat on a tight rope, he went to the latrine. He stayed there for a long time, so long that the urka Ivan, with the muttered approval of the two Germans, appealed to the whole team, reminding us that we were working together, and that the percentages were calculated on average output. Then the new one's face, pale as paper, loomed up beside me by the wagon, and I noticed that he was trembling all over.

"What's the matter with you?" I asked, stopping for a moment.

"Nothing," he replied, and I noticed that his hand was groping in the air before him looking for me, even though against the surrounding whiteness of the snow everything could be clearly seen within a radius of five yards. "Nothing," he repeated, "I feel a bit weak, that's all."

"Go and take a sack, or they'll drive you out of here!" I shouted at him, and ran back to the wagon. And a moment later I saw him climbing up on the loading plank which stretched between the train and the warehouse. He walked slowly, but surely enough, like a pedigree horse with bound fetlocks. He stayed in the wagon a long time, and again we became impatient and irritated. The two prisoners who were inside the wagon handing the sacks out later told us that he had asked them to place the sack on his shoulder, with a short, trembling "for pity's sake". Finally he appeared in the door of the wagon and a moment searched for the gangway with his outstretched foot. When his leg found it, he walked halfway across in a few long steps and suddenly stopped. Then he raised his right leg into the air and waved it several times in mid-air like a ballerina, but every time it landed again in empty space—the plank was very narrow—and he put it down again and froze in expectation. It was all obscurely funny and did not arouse our sympathy. Only later we understood that we had been watching a grotesque dance of death. But at the time Karinen only laughed shortly, and Ivan shouted angrily: "Hey, you, Stalin's murderer, what sort of a circus do you think this is?"

Then we heard a strange sound, something between a sigh and a sob, and Stalin's murderer turned slowly round on his heels in the direction of the wagon—he had evidently decided to go back.

"Have you gone mad?" I shouted at him. "Wait, I'll help you!" But it was already too late, for he suddenly straightened himself, jerked his body, tried for a moment to regain his balance on the plank, and then fell with the sack on the snow-covered rails.

We all ran from the platform and surrounded him in a closed circle. He brushed the flour off his jerkin and wiped his bleeding forehead. "Night-blindness," he explained briefly, and added: "I thought I'd got over it."

Later I watched him running about with sacks under the plank, bending over the snow as he carefully scraped the flour out of it and gathered it together with both hands; he looked as if he had been exiled from heaven into the depths of hell. I believe that he was crying quietly. Perhaps he was only gathering up a handful of flour for himself, and hiding it in his clothes, as if he was willing to risk everything now. I have no idea how he had succeeded in concealing his night-blindness and how he imagined that he would "get over it". Our brigadier led him back to the zone after work. When they searched us at the guard-house, his pockets were empty and there was nothing in his handkerchief. The next morning he went to the forest with a penal brigade. . . . For a man who had survived seven years in a labour camp, the forest was a slow, lingering death.

He died of exhaustion a few months later. When I met him, a few days before his death, he had stopped washing a long time before, his face had the appearance of a wrinkled lemon, but underneath his pus-encrusted eyelashes the fever-consumed eyes, which hunger was beginning to cover with a film of madness, still gleamed defiantly at the world. It did not need an experienced prisoner to tell that only a few days separated him from complete madness, and now the last remnants of his human dignity were burning out within him. He stood, with an empty can in his hand, leaning against the balustrade on the kitchen platform, and I bumped into him just at the moment when the cook was pushing my canful of soup through his serving-hatch. He smelt so abominably that I instinctively moved away; he had probably lost all control over the simplest mechanisms of his body, and slept without undressing, weak and feverish, surrounded by the shell of his dried excrement. He did not recognise me, but looking in front of him only whined: "Give me some soup." And then, as if justifying this audacious request, he added: "Even the dregs."

I poured all I had into his can and watched him, holding my breath. With trembling hands he brought the can to his mouth, and burning his lips gulped down the hot fluid, while a rattling noise came from his throat. Two thin streams of soup trickled from the corners of his mouth and froze almost instantly. When he had finished he went up to the kitchen window, as if I was not there at all, and flattened his stubbly face against the window. On the other side of the window, leaning against a steaming cauldron of soup, stood the Leningrad thief Fyedka (political prisoners were usually not allowed to work in the kitchens) laughing at him. "There aren't any extras for counter-revolutionists!" he shouted.

I stayed a moment looking at those two faces divided by the filmy glass. "Stalin's murderer" was looking at the cauldron of soup with a stare which contained all the mortal, exhausted powers of his mind and body. His face expressed an inhuman effort to remember something, to understand. His emaciated, angular features attempted in vain to pierce the glass barrier. His weakening, broken breath steamed on the tile of ice, like an enormous winking eye. Suddenly he drew back his right hand, as if for a blow: I caught it in mid-air.

"Come," I said, "this won't get you anywhere. I'll take you back to your barrack."

He did not attempt to escape me, but walked obediently, stooping and crumpled. Again, as on the loading plank, he half-sobbed, half-sighed.

"Robbers," he finally brought out, "robbers, robbers . . ."

"Who?" I asked thoughtlessly.

"You, you, all of you here," he cried in a heart-rending voice, and freeing himself from my grasp, started to run. He looked like a huge sewer rat covered with slime, caught suddenly in a beam of light. He turned round several times on one spot as if there was no escape from it, then suddenly stopped, facing me.

"I killed Stalin!" His voice changed into the throaty whine of the madman. "I shot him like a dog . . . like a dog . . ." He laughed with bitter triumph.

He was too weak to understand everything. But he was unfortunately still strong enough to understand that slow, choking death was approaching. Before he died, like a last sacrament he wanted to take upon himself the crime that he had not committed. Defending himself against an unknown future, struggling in the bonds of the present, he acknowledged the past which had been thrust upon him. And perhaps, a few moments before his death, he had saved his belief in the reality and value of his own extinguished existence.

CHAPTER 4

DREI KAMERADEN

ALL fresh transports of prisoners arrived first at Yercevo, which was the starting-point of the route to all other sections of the Kargopol camp. Prisoners who were not fortunate enough to be allowed to stay in Yercevo always spent several nights waiting for their moves to other sections in a small transit barrack, where they did not receive water or hvoya, situated near the guard-house, and known as the peresylny. In the evenings, if I was quite certain that my brigade would not be called out to the food supply centre in the middle of the night, I would often visit the peresylny. Of the prisoners there the greatest number was always destined for the small penal camp of the Second Alexeyevka, which seemed literally to swallow up endless numbers of prisoners who never returned. Only once, after the general amnesty of Poles which followed the Russo-Polish pact of 1941, I met in the transit barrack a prisoner who was returning to freedom from the Second Alexeyevka through Yercevo. This was Andrzej K., a friendly Trotskyist worker from Warsaw, whom I had already met in the Grodno prison where I was first taken after my arrest. From what he very unwillingly told me, I gathered that prisoners in the Second Alexeyevka are used only for forest work, and that the conditions there are extremely bad compared with those of Yercevo. The Alexeyevka, K. told me, was a camp isolated in the heart of the Archangel forest, far from any human settlements and about twenty miles from the railway line, though connected with Yercevo by the internal branch line which kept up its food supply. It was under the absolute control of the degenerate camp commander, an N.K.V.D. officer, and his confidential staff. The prisoners in this penal camp lived in ramshackle barracks with leaking roofs, received only the second cauldron, were issued with worn-out and torn clothing, worked in the forest thirteen instead of twelve hours a day, often waited as long as two or three months for the ceremonious proclamation of a free day in the camp and, since there was no proper hospital accommodation, were moved straight into the mortuary at any sign of illness. Only in July and August, when the endless

56

northern winter gives place to a short but hot summer, the marshy forest clearings offered to the wretched scurvy-ridden prisoners a rich crop of berries, small mushrooms, and the bitter, red fruit of the sorb tree. Then a spark of life gleamed through the sticky yellow matter which surrounded their inflamed eyes, and the grimy, dirt-encrusted faces were raised up towards the sun with gratitude and fresh hope. The official name of "penal camp" which was given to the Alexeyevka was apparently no more than a courtesy title; in reality the camp was like a wide net which swallows up an entire school of sprats—in this case foreign prisoners, who could hardly have had time to commit an offence against discipline which would merit removal to the penal camp during the few days they spent in the transit barrack at Yercevo before they were sent to the Alexeyevka. Among them was the "lumpenproletariat" of the Warsaw "ghetto", who had made their escape from the hell of Nazi occupation, across the River Bug, to the paradise of the Soviet Union. These Jewish journeymen, tailors and carters died like flies in the Alexeyevka. K. told me that he frequently saw them rooting in the rubbish heaps for rotten cabbage leaves and potato peelings. In this penal camp mutinies were constantly breaking out among the prisoners. They were suppressed without bloodshed—the camp command merely stopped the issue of rations for several days, and some time later thin skeletons, barely covered with skin yellow as the parchment of old holy books, their skulls unblemished by the bullets of the victorious revolution, were removed beyond the camp zone. After a taste of life at Yercevo, K., who despite his Trotskyism retained an instinctive habit of looking on "the bright side" of everything in Soviet Russia, decided that the farther away from Moscow, the worse the conditions become—in other words, that the intention is good, but badly carried out.

The wooden path which led to the transit barrack ended in several steps down to the door, which were cut in the snow. The hut itself was dark, dirty, its roof lower than other barracks, so that on the upper bunks one could only talk lying down, or sitting bent double, with one's back curved against the ceiling. Large vertical beams supported the roof, and framed the closely-packed shelves of bunks round the walls. Nails had been knocked into the beams, and water dripped on to the floor from the wet boots which were hung there. The curved stove-pipe was covered with steaming, sweaty rags which the prisoners wrapped round their feet. It was so dark that one could see nothing as one came in, and only when the eyes had become accustomed to the dim light of one small bulb on the opposite wall could one make out two rows of bare feet protruding from the grey, shapeless bundles of rags huddled on the bunks, and three or four shadows bent over the stove, their fingers spread out above the hot metal. The first visitor to the transit barrack, arriving before evening, would break its habitual silence with a nudge at the nearest pair of bare feet and the four customary questions: Who are you? Where do you come from? Where are you going? Why are you here? Occasionally, after such an attempt at conversation, a feverish face with demented eyes emerged from its pile of rags, threw out a furious "pashol von—get away", and burrowed down again into its stinking litter. But usually several attempts were enough to rouse the grey figures on the bunks, who raised themselves up, ready for conversation and barter. By evening the transit barrack was full of people. Local prisoners leaned against the beams and exchanged stories, observations and overheard news, and bartered bread for tobacco, with the transit prisoners, who, anxious for the safety of their few belongings, seldom left the bunks. The atmosphere of the peresylny barrack pleased me; by a stretch of the imagination it could be made to appear as a cross between a hostel for tramps, setting out on a quest for the golden fleece, and a normal pre-war European café. Here it was possible to make new friends, receive news from other camps and prisons, buy a little tobacco, complain of one's hard fate, and even, since in this temporary stopping-place there was little danger of denunciation, grumble a little about Stalin and his prætorian guard. Only after the war I learnt with sorrow, but also with a secret satisfaction, that even in this respect the cafés of Europe had become for millions of people exactly what the transit barrack in Yercevo became for me. Crowds of refugees on the move took the place of a handful of *habitués*, until the cafés came to resemble the small wooden boxes which in my native countryside we nailed to trees to rest and house the flocks of chattering birds on their flight to a warmer country, rather than the Kaffenhausen of Vienna or the "cafés-chantants" of Paris.

The transit barrack also fulfilled the function of an Institute for Research into Political Tendencies, which, basing its investigations on the character of each fresh wave of prisoners, made it possible to deduce from it current indications of the price of slave labour, and the extent of ideological deviations in politics. Thus—I learnt from the stories of my companions in the camp—in 1939 the barrack housed the remnants of those caught in the Great Purges, now imprisoned chaotically and without any apparent reason. 1940 saw the arrival of regular contingents of Poles, Western Ukrainians, White Russians and Jews from Eastern Poland, as well as Balts from the north and inhabitants of Sub-Carpathian Ukraine. In 1941 came the first convoys of Finns and detachments of Red Army soldiers who had been captured on the Finnish front; these soldiers had marched under a decorated triumphal arch in Leningrad, welcomed by streamers with the legend "The Fatherland greets its heroes", and to the strains of the Budyenny March had been led straight to a railway siding beyond the town where sealed cattle trucks were waiting to take them to the camps. In the first months after the outbreak of the Russo-German war in 1941 the transit barrack was full of completely russified Germans from the German settlements on the Volga, and bewildered groups of Ukrainians and White Russians, fleeing into Russia from their native villages as the front rapidly moved forward. I remember the nicknames which were given to some of these victims of the war in the "technical" barrack. The Poles were called "anti-Nazi fascists", the Red Army men "heroes of the Finnish front", and the Ukrainians and White Russians who were flying before the Germans became known as "partisans of the war for the Fatherland".

In February 1941 I met in a transit barrack three Germans who stood out from the rest of its inmates by a certain instinctive haughtiness of gesture and fairly decent European clothing. Also between them they possessed something like a rudimentary tourist outfit. Otto, a short, stout, dark man with a broad face and small piercing eyes, always wore a black beret perched on the top of his head; Hans, tall, broad-shouldered and fair, kept a sports scarf perpetually tied round his neck; while Stefan, a thin young man with a long, intelligent face, would not be parted from his studded ski boots. At first sight they might have passed for three poor intellectuals in a hostel somewhere high in the mountains, and I was astonished when I learnt that only Stefan, the youngest, had been a student, at Hamburg, while the other two had both worked in factories at Düsseldorf. We started talking in Russian (all three spoke, with difficulty, a stiff and horribly unmusical Russian, mixed with a good deal of Ukrainian) but after a few minutes we changed to German, and I climbed up to their bunk, where we could talk undisturbed by the noise of the black-market deals which were flourishing below us in the barrack.

The three Germans had all belonged to the German Communist Party before the Nazi Putsch, but even though Hans and Otto had worked in the same town, none of them had known each other then. After the Reichstag Fire trial, when the Party, corroded by the activities of agents-provocateurs, was falling to pieces before the eyes of millions of its members, the three of them were sent abroad; the object of their escape could only be to reach the adopted country of Dimitrov, which was the adopted country of all communists. Hans travelled through Denmark, Sweden and Finland, Stefan and Otto through Paris, Italy and the Balkans. They marvelled at the efficiency of European communist organisations, which passed them without difficulty across frontiers from country to country, and during the long hours of the night, always at some new stopping place, they talked with other comrades they met during the journey of the fatherland of the world's proletariat, as they remembered it from illustrated party propaganda and from the stories of envoys who had returned from Russia. During the first year of terror in Germany, the "Sunday schools" which the party organised for its members were usually held in the countryside beyond the towns. Thus everything connected with Russia they associated in their minds with the ripe beauty of forests, fields and rivers, with the effortless abundance of orchards and the slow floating majesty of spring clouds, with that pleasant exhaustion which overcame the whole body as, dragging their feet, they returned to the town from their excursion to the edge of the distant horizon.

Otto and Hans met in 1936 in a Kharkov factory; Stefan after arriving in Russia attempted to study in Kiev. Their first impressions hardly corresponded with the ideal picture which they had formed at their Sunday gatherings, but many disappointments could then still be blamed on the difficulties of acclimatisation in a foreign country, and on the everlasting, mythical capitalist encirclement. Otto and Hans worked hard, earned well, and lived comfortably, and in the evenings, when they knew enough of the language, they delighted in listening to the well-informed lectures, full of political propaganda, which were held in the factory reading-room. But their first attempts to take part in the "free discussion" which followed each of these lectures cooled their ardour, and after a time Otto would often slip away for beer and billiards straight after work, while Hans began going out with a young Ukrainian woman who worked in the factory. Both were struck by the lies which were told during these discussions about the standard of living in the West. When Hans once tried to explain to the meeting that "capitalist slavery in the West is based on something quite different", he was silenced by the lecturer's sharp question: "Perhaps, comrade, you wish to return where you came from, or to think everything over again from the beginning?" Hans did not then know what it meant to "think everything over again from the beginning", though it sounded oddly like a threat, but he had no wish to "return where he came from". So from that evening he listened in silence, only looking across the room at the Ukrainian girl, who once, when saying good-bye to him, had stood on her toes and whispered in his ear: "You mustn't argue when members of the government are lecturing." Otto's usual place at the lectures remained empty. Towards the middle of 1936 Hans married the girl, left the room which he had shared with Otto, and went to live with his wife's family. At his friend's wedding, after several elderly guests had proposed the couple's health, Otto, already drunk, lifted his glass of vodka into the air, and spreading his short legs apart like a puffing bull, shouted loudly: "The Invincible Soviet Union is dreck—nothing but shit!" The Russian company evidently took "dreck" to be the German equivalent of "hurra", for clinking their glasses they nodded and murmured "right, right," but Hans pushed Otto out of the door and quickly took him home. Stefan at this time was still in Kiev, not studying as he had not yet mastered the language, but already an honorary member of the students' committee and a valuable speaker at their international meetings.

Then came the memorable year 1937. The Great Purge hung in the air like an approaching storm, but so far was only heralding its arrival by flashes of lightning and roars of thunder from beyond the seven mountains and the seven rivers. It was hard to believe the strange rumours, contradictory reports, and mysterious letters from Moscow and Leningrad. But the swollen wave of arrests and persecution finally broke through the Russian flood-gates and thundered into the Ukraine, sweeping away whomever it came upon, like a flood which carries with it roofs, beams, window-frames, furniture and hayricks. . . . Then people would come into offices, factories, schools and homes with the same question on all lips: "Whom will they take today?" But soon the flood was under control, and the swollen river flowed only through artificial channels. The foreigners were the first to go. Otto was arrested in his factory, Stefan at the University. Hans was taken from his home, without time to say good-bye to his terrified wife and child. He had heard nothing of them since, and received no answer to the letters which he wrote.

Their hearings were monotonous, turning during whole months on the accusation of espionage. Hans and Stefan were beaten only a few times and comparatively mildly, but Otto suffered for his drunken "dreck": his front teeth were knocked out, and his stomach and intestines never recovered from the repeated kickings. In the first months of 1939, five hundred and seventy German communists were placed together in a separate wing of one of the Moscow prisons (I can no longer remember whether Hans mentioned the Lubyanka or the Butyrki prison) and there, in a common cell, Hans and Otto found and befriended the terrified, wretched Stefan.

It must have been toward the middle of September, for every day the delighted warder brought them fresh news of the victorious march of the German Army across Poland, that one of the prisoners found in the latrine a scrap of newspaper containing the text of the Russo-German pact. The news spread in the prison and a decision was immediately made—from the morning of the next day all prisoners were to go on hunger-strike demanding that the German Ambassador, the representative of their now friendly country, should visit them in prison and arrange for their repatriation. The Russians ignored it for a week, but before the hunger-strike was over representatives of the prisoners, one from each cell, were called out to meet a German official sent there by Count Schulenburg, the German Ambassador. The prisoners made only one condition, that, after repatriation, they should not be punished for their communism or for their illegal escape from Germany. Otherwise they were quite indifferent to their fate, they were even willing to be taken into the Wehrmacht immediately after crossing the frontier. The hunger-strike was joined by German Jews, as well as a few pure Germans who would rather have stayed in a Russian prison than return to Germany, as an expression of their solidarity with the other prisoners. The Soviet authorities had not attempted to suppress the hunger-strike, and while their negotiations with the German Embassy dragged on for several months, the prisoners were given more and better food and taken out for daily exercise in the prison courtyard. Finally the same delegation of prisoners was summoned to hear the decision. The Russians agreed in principle to the repatriation of former German communists, though reserving the right to retain some of them in Russia "at their own discretion". The German official added that a second hunger-strike would produce no further result, as the Embassy had accepted the Russian terms. The prisoners thus had no choice and agreed. Hans, Otto and Stefan were among those who remained in the prison. In January 1940, in another cell, sentences of ten years each were read out to them, and in February they were transported to Yercevo. They knew nothing of the five hundred or so fortunate prisoners who had left for Germany.

When Hans finished telling me his story, I asked all three if they really believed that German concentration camps were better than Soviet labour camps like this one. Hans shrugged his shoulders and muttered something contemptuously, but Stefan seemed to understand my point of view. Then Otto, who had been silent up till then, raised his large head, and piercing Stefan with the gaze of his pig-like eyes said almost in these very words: "You have a dangerous tendency to philosophise, Stefan. The Fatherland is always the Fatherland, and Russia will always be—dreck." I, too, gave up this "philosophising". In the situation in which we found ourselves, to talk to them about the horrors of Nazi rule would mean as much as telling three rats caught in a trap that the nearest hole in the floor leads to a similar trap.

The next day, at dawn, they were taken to the Nyandoma camp section. Stefan noticed me as I stood at the camp gate in the crowd of prisoners forming ranks in brigades, waiting to be marched out beyond the zone, and lifting his hand, cried: "Auf Wiedersehen, mein Freund!" In April I received a letter from Hans, which I have kept to this day. "Stefan"—he wrote—"is working as best as he can at general work. I, Hans, have managed to get work as a mechanic, Otto is still at the saw-mill. We have no news of our dear ones in the U.S.S.R. The northern spring is so sad, especially in the conditions in which we live here."

   *   *   *   *   *

Until 1947 I was convinced that the most probable ending of the Moscow episode was that the Russian authorities, with the connivance of the German Embassy, divided the striking prisoners into several large newly-mixed groups, and retained each of these, "at their own discretion", in a different Soviet prison, so that not a single one ever reached Germany. But in London I was told by Alex Weissberg, once an outstanding Viennese communist who was the companion of Arthur Koestler's youth, the true ending of this story, and his testimony was confirmed a year later by Margaret Buber-Neumann's book *Under Two Dictators*. It took place in the winter of 1940, on the bridge which spans the River Bug at Brest. At night, the group of Germans crossed the river, which was then the frontier between the Russian and the German zones of demarcation in Poland, and, without an arch of triumph, made their way back to the Fatherland, where their fate was to stay all quiet on the Western front. My three comrades were not among them. The German Jews, who were attempting to resist, were forced by the N.K.V.D. across the river and straight into the hands of the Gestapo. Alex Weissberg was released beyond the Bug, and spent the whole war in hiding in Poland.

CHAPTER 5

THE ICE-BREAKER

"... and as life is impossible without hope he found a means of escape in a voluntary and almost artificial martyrdom."
—DOSTOEVSKY—*The House of the Dead.*

THE whole system of forced labour in Soviet Russia—in all its stages, the interrogations and hearings, the preliminary imprisonment, and the camp itself—is intended primarily not to punish the criminal, but rather to exploit him economically and transform him psychologically. Torture is applied at the hearings not on principle, but as an auxiliary instrument. The real object of a hearing is not the extortion from the accused of the prisoner's signature to a fictitious indictment, but the complete disintegration of his individual personality.

A man woken up in the middle of the night, unable to satisfy his most elementary physical needs during the hearing, sitting for hours at a time on a small hard stool, blinded by the light of a powerful bulb directed straight at his eyes, surprised by sudden, cunning questions and by an overwhelming crescendo of fictitious accusations, sadistically taunted with the sight of cigarettes and hot coffee on the other side of the table, and all this going on for months, sometimes even years—under these circumstances he is ready to sign anything. That, however, is not the essential point. A prisoner is considered to have been sufficiently prepared for the final achievement of the signature only when his personality has been thoroughly dismantled into its component parts. Gaps appear in the logical association of ideas; thoughts and emotions become loosened in their original positions and rattle against each other like the parts of a broken-down machine; the driving-belts connecting the past with the present slip off their wheels and fall sloppily to the bottom of the mind; all the weights and levers of mind and will-power become jammed and refuse to function; the indicators of the pressure gauges jump as if possessed from zero to maximum and back again. The machine still runs on larger revolutions, but it does not work as it did—all that had a moment before appeared absurd now becomes probable even though still not true, emotions lose their colour, will-power its capacity. The prisoner is now willing to admit that he had betrayed the interests of the proletariat by writing to his relatives abroad, that his slackness at work was sabotage of socialist industry. This is the crucial moment for the examining judge. One final blow at the rusty mechanism of resistance, and the machine will stop altogether. A man sleeping under an anæsthetic remains for a split-second suspended in a vacuum, when he feels, thinks and understands nothing. When the patient's heart stops beating for that fraction of a second, then is the time for immediate action. A trifling oversight, a slight delay, and the patient will regain consciousness on the operating table and then either rebel and shout out, or break down and retire into perpetual apathy. For the judge it is now or never. His eyes glance at the single piece of factual evidence, prepared for just this moment, his hands pick up the document like a scalpel. Only a few hours ago it could have been dismissed as insignificant, but as it is the only proof which has any foundation in fact, it grows now in the scorched imagination of the accused to gigantic proportions. The scalpel has found the right spot and the incision deepens. In feverish haste the surgeon cuts out the heart, his probing instruments transplant it to the body's right side, strip flakes of infected tissue from the brain, graft small patches of skin, change the direction of the blood flow, repair the torn network of the nervous system. The human mechanism, arrested at its lowest ebb and taken to pieces, is reconstructed and altered; those gaps between disjointed ideas are filled by new connections; thoughts and feelings settle in new bearings; the driving belts start to turn in the opposite direction, transmitting not the past to the present, but the present to the past; the efforts of mind and will are directed to different purposes; the arrows of the gauges will always point to maximum. The prisoner wakes from his trance, turns an exhausted but smiling face towards his benefactor, and with a deep sigh admits that now everything is clear to him, that he had erred all his life, but that now all will be well. The operation has been successful, the patient is reborn. Only once more, after his return to the cell, as he stands over the bucket and relieves his long-suffering bladder, when he feels drops of sweat on his forehead and the relaxation of tension in his whole body, he hesitates, and wonders whether he has dreamt or really lived through this re-incarnation. For the last time in his life he falls asleep with a sensation of tormenting uncertainty—the next morning he wakes feeling empty as a nut without a kernel and weak after the inhuman strain to which his whole organism has been subjected during the past few months, but dazzled by the thought that everything is already behind him. When a prisoner walks between the bunks without saying a word to anyone, it is easy for the others to guess that he is a convalescent with rapidly healing scars and a newly-assembled personality, taking his first uncertain steps in a new world.

In the period between the hearings and the sentence (which will be passed in his absence and probably send him on a quick journey to the camp), the prisoner becomes acclimatised in the cell to his new situation. Instinct warns him against talking to prisoners who have not yet undergone the Great Change, for the stitches on his scars are still too fresh to withstand the sharp pulls of ruthless tearing hands. He is afraid above all of the moment when the whole of his new reality will topple from one blow like a house of cards, when the old brain, ruining the patient work of months, shows enough determination to understand that the new heart beats differently and elsewhere than before, and some atavistic voice, echoing from the rubble of the past, sends him rushing at the cell door with clenched fists and a desperate cry: "I lied, I lied! I withdraw everything! I'm innocent, take me to the judge! I want to see the judge, I'm innocent!" If he is fortunate enough to be spared that crisis, the prisoner can lie for days on his bunk, calm and indifferent to everything, simply waiting for a transfer to his camp. In this somnambulistic state he notices the feeble light of his last hope seeping into his own prison through a narrow breach in its cold wall: he begins to long for the camp, timidly at first, then with growing impatience. An unknown voice—a precious relic of his old personality, an assurance that he had been and still could be different —deceives him with the illusion of a free life in the camp, among men of whom some must surely still remember the past. He now needs only two things: work and pity. It is not pity for himself that he requires, since he regards what he has just gone through as basically his own victory. He feels dimly that if he is to save the slight thread that still binds him to the buried past in which he was a different person, he must at all costs generate in himself a feeling of pity for his companions in misery, and of compassion for the suffering of others, which could prove to him that, despite his inner transformation, he has remained a human being. "Can one live without pity?" he asks himself at night, turning from side to side and mopping his forehead anxiously as he tries to remember whether once, in that obliterated past, his only reaction to human suffering had been the same painful indifference that he has felt since his rebirth. Can one live without pity?

In the camp he learns that it is only too easy. At first he shares his bread with hunger-demented prisoners, leads the night-blind on the way home from work, shouts for help when his neighbour at work in the forest has chopped off two fingers, and surreptitiously carries cans of soup and herring-heads to the mortuary. After several weeks he realises that his motives in all this are neither pure nor really disinterested, that he is following the egoistic injunctions of his brain and saving first of all himself. The camp, where prisoners live at the lowest level of humanity and follow their own brutal code of behaviour toward others, helps him to reach this conclusion. How could he have supposed, back in the prison, that a man can be so degraded as to arouse not compassion but only loathing and repugnance in his fellow-prisoners? How can he help the night-blind, when every day he sees them being jolted with rifle-butts because they are delaying the brigade's return to work, and then impatiently pushed off the paths by prisoners hurrying to the kitchen for their soup; how visit the mortuary and brave the constant darkness and the stench of excrement; how share his bread with a hungry madman who on the very next day will greet him in the barrack with a demanding, persistent stare? After two or three months of this struggle, the prisoner who has undergone the Great Change and is now making a desperate attempt to recover some of the past conceptions which were submerged at the hearing finally gives in. He listens without contradiction to the daily grumbling in his barrack: "Those bastards in the mortuary stuff themselves with our bread, and don't even work for it"; "Those night-blind lower our norms after dark and then sprawl all over the paths so that you can't even move"; "Those madmen ought to be locked up in the punishment cells, they'll be stealing our bread soon." He remembers and believes the words of his examining judge, who told him that the iron broom of Soviet justice sweeps only rubbish into its camps, and that men worthy of the name are able to prove that their imprisonment is due to a judicial error. The last thread has snapped, the prisoner's education is complete.

There remains only the exploitation of his cheap labour, and if he survives eight or ten years of the work, he will be fit to take the place of the examining judge behind a table, confronting the future prisoner who will be sitting where he had once sat.

There are, however, some who wake suddenly during this final trial, and stand at the crossroads of their lives to look back and realise clearly that they have been cheated, not convinced or converted, only destroyed as human beings, their feelings cauterised with a hot poker. They are still capable of one emotional effort. It is too late to jump at the door with raised fists and the cry "I want the judge, I am innocent!" but there is still time to blow the dying embers of his human feelings into a flame which will take the place of defeated compassion—the flame of voluntary and almost artificial martyrdom.

*　　　*　　　*　　　*　　　*

Without this introduction it is impossible to understand the story of Mikhail Alexeyevich Kostylev, a prisoner who was assigned to my brigade after his arrival from the camp section of Mostovitza. It is in no way typical of Russian prisoners, and differs particularly from that of the Poles.

As a general rule, the interrogation of Poles imprisoned after the annexation of Eastern Poland by Russia in 1939 had different aims and methods from that of Russians. Its object was not the re-education of future Soviet citizens, but simply the extortion of a signature to a fictitious confession, which provided the officers in charge of slave labour recruitment, and of the elimination of Polish influence from the newly-acquired territories, with a simple pretext for their work. The haste and muddle with which their examinations were conducted led me to the conclusion that the Russians looked upon their recruitment of slave labour in Eastern Poland as a precaution in the period of transition, and that, despite their self-confident declarations, they had considered the possibility of bargaining over the Poles at the post-war international conference. In the opinion of the Soviet Government, Eastern Poland had been permanently annexed to Russia by the Ribbentrop-Molotov partition treaty, but its Polish inhabitants were to serve as security until the end of the war, a kind of pledge which was to be exploited and circulated like the assets of a debtor, sequestered by his creditor. If the war had taken a different turn and if the Russians could have stood by and watched it without participating, waiting for the final victory of Germany, I have no doubt that this "pledge" would eventually have become the property of this strange "creditor", and one and a half million citizens of Eastern Poland would have begun the procedure of hearings and prison all over again, this time under the supervision of trained and experienced examiners who would go into their cases thoroughly.

When Kostylev awoke from the two-year trance which followed his hearing, it became clear to him that he had been cheated, and how he had been cheated. All that I have written above is not an artificial theory of the corrective function of Soviet labour camps which, wise after the event, I have myself constructed, nor a psychological interpretation of the life and death of M. A. Kostylev, but his own, frequently repeated story. Like a bloodhound who has once found the right scent, Kostylev carefully traced all the details of his imprisonment, his interrogation, and his life in the camp, and he had learnt to describe them calmly, convincingly and with knowledge, like a consumptive who, with feigned detachment, follows the progress of the disease in his own body. Neither did I invent the formula of voluntary martyrdom which follows a prisoner's failure to save himself by compassion; I heard it from Kostylev when I asked him what he hoped to gain by torturing himself physically every three or four days. The manner of his conversation might have given rise to the suspicion that Kostylev was suffering from a peculiar form of religious mania, inherited from generations of Russian mystics, or else from a gentle schizo-phrenia which, imperceptibly even to himself, had developed as a result of the shock of almost a year's hearings and of the first few months in the camp. He talked quietly, concisely and intelligently, with a persuasive conviction, so typical of the mentally deranged, which denies and abolishes all argument and, having gained the listener over to the premises and the logical connections of ideas, leads him into agreement with the conclusions. I do not exclude either of these possibilities, but this cannot prevent me from repeating here his whole story as I heard it from him. It is important because, in one way or another, my friendship with Kostylev has coloured the recollection of my Soviet experiences, and his death did not pass without an echo even among the other prisoners of Yercevo.

Kostylev was twenty-four when, at the request of the Party, he left his engineering studies at the Moscow Polytechnic and entered the naval school at Vladivostok. He came originally from Voronezh; his father died when he was very young, and from his earliest years he had to look after his mother, who after her husband's death transferred to her son all the unfulfilled love of a young widow. Love for his mother was the only point of stability in Kostylev's surrounding reality. He belonged to the Komsomol (the Communist Youth Organisation), and later to the Party, but his individuality was constantly escaping from the repressive framework of political training into the arms of his mother. His father, on his death-bed, had enjoined of him loyalty to his mother and to the "great achievement of the October Revolution". Kostylev had from childhood grown up in an atmosphere of communism and he did not even suppose that a third object of loyalty could exist in the world. He did not, therefore, hesitate when the Komsomol asked him to study engineering in Moscow, even though, as he asserted, he had always been attracted to literature; neither did he oppose the Party's decision to send him to a naval school in Vladivostok as a young student-engineer.

Here, before describing the further events of his life, it would be useful to consider the nature and the peculiar characteristics of Kostylev's communism. His mother, a simple and rather religious woman, understood little of what her husband said to her about politics, but reverence for his memory, and an instinctive anticipation of the family's safety, caused her to applaud and feed her son's revolutionary fervour. Her naïve faith satisfied him in his early youth, but after he had entered the Moscow Polytechnic his mature intelligence needed a rational foundation for the beliefs to which he had so far been faithful with his heart. He became acquainted with the classics of Marxism, studied Lenin and Stalin thoroughly, took an active part in Party meetings and discussions. He saw himself as a missionary, a communist engineer who was spreading the new technical civilisation in a Russia which was then "catching up and out-distancing the West." During the years of secluded life with his mother, when he would see her severe profile outlined against the window of the small cottage in Voronezh as he returned from school, and later, in the half-darkness inside, bend over her work-hardened hands with pain in his heart, he gradually felt the need to sacrifice himself, to suffer that others might be happy. Party propaganda told him that real suffering existed only in the capitalist West, and he became fired with the idea of a world revolution. An important element in the shaping of his personality was the fact that, undeterred by the wild, frenzied attacks on the capitalist world which emanated from the Soviet press and propaganda, Kostylev swore devotion to the cause of liberating enslaved Europeans in the name not of hatred, but of love for the unknown West.

It is not easy to understand how this young boy, who until he left home to study in Moscow had never known any world but his native Voronezh and the walls of the modest workers' flat, could have formed such an idealised picture of the West. The most likely explanation is that, naturally inclined to enthusiasm rather than to hatred, his imagination was caught by the figures of the Western "fighters for freedom" officially canonised by Party propaganda, figures who stood out clearly in all their glory when the economic, religious and social background of their activity was condemned by the vulgar catch-phrases of the same propaganda. Soviet educators have still not completely understood the functioning of the immature imagination; the sharply-contoured silhouettes of saints make a far deeper and more lasting impression on it than all the horrors of hell. It was comic and at the same time tragic to see Kostylev, in March 1941, trembling with admiration at the very mention of Thorez. He considered him to be the only true heir of the Great French Revolution, though he could not understand why the heir should be so blindly obedient to the man who had "betrayed the October Revolution".

Young Misha lost no time, and during four years in Moscow, besides his studies and his Party activities, he learnt enough French at evening classes to be able to read it freely. In Vladivostok he began to read in earnest, and by chance came upon Goncharov's diary of his journey round the world, *The Frigate Pallada*. This journal turned his youthful dreams into more realistic channels— he studied with redoubled energy and enthusiasm, possessed by a restless urge to travel. There is no doubt that the pattern of his life was becoming at least unusual; he was going through the imaginative experiences of a boy at a mature age, making up for a childhood which had been deformed by the responsibilities thrust upon it.

During his second year at the naval school, Kostylev found a small private lending library in Vladivostok, and in it several torn

French books: Balzac, Stendhal, Flaubert's *Education Sentimentale,* Musset's *Confession d'un Enfant de Siècle,* and the *Adolphe* of Benjamin Constant. He did not expect to read anything exceptional in them—his only intention was to practise his French—but the world which they opened up to him surpassed his wildest dreams, seemed indeed to be some unreal dream-world. From that time he lived in a state of continual excitement. He read through the nights, neglected his work, stopped attending Party meetings, became secretive and avoided his best friends. Many times he tried to explain to me the feelings which this discovery of French literature awoke in him.

"I was sick with longing for something indefinable," he told me, stroking his angular, shaved head with his good hand. "I breathed different air; I felt like a man who has been choking all his life without knowing it. You must understand that it isn't a question of facts, for, after all, men love, die, amuse themselves, plot and suffer all over the world in the same way. No, it was a question of atmosphere. All that I read about seemed to be taking place in a tropical climate, while I had lived from my birth in a desert of ice. . . . It's true that I had seen another life in Moscow, but there I couldn't share it, it was like a sectarian debauch which did not flow out into the streets through the doors of closed hotels. . . ."

"But, Misha," I would argue obstinately, "that is only literature. You've no idea how much misery and suffering exists in the West."

"I know, I know"—he would shake his head—"my examining judge said the same thing. But if I have ever known, even for a short time, what freedom is, then it was while I was reading those old French books. I was like an ice-bound ship, and it's no wonder that I tried to escape into warm waters."

Kostylev frequently made use of unfortunate literary comparisons in his conversation, but that one happened to be unusually apt. Large, powerful, with his head bowed like some iron battering-ram, and a fist the size of a blacksmith's hammer, he really did look like an ice-breaker.

Kostylev's story, not altogether clear to me when I first heard it and saw its epilogue, now becomes as understandable as a deciphered palimpsest. While reading the original text, it was essential not to accept Kostylev's own interpretation of it, not to see his tragedy as it impressed itself upon his primeval, subconscious memory. But alas! Kostylev fancied himself as a researcher, and before he would allow others to interpret the story of his life, he insisted on making a detailed and very one-sided analysis of it. He was convinced, for instance, that he owed his "resurrection" to several French romances; in my opinion, he merely read them too late, and unfortunately in French. As far as I know, all the books that Kostylev "discovered" had been translated into Russian, embellished with irritating Marxist commentaries which could be ignored, and made easily available in the cheap editions of the State Publishing House. It happened accidentally that Kostylev read them, in French, at an age when long repression had given to his belated, undischarged youthful rebelliousness a morbid and even maniacal character; he persuaded himself that he had been cheated, that the "whole truth" had been concealed from him. His attitude to the West was that of a converted neophyte, who blames a conspiracy of lies and the perfidy of rival priests for his erring in the old faith. He drew away from the Party, he did not even hesitate to lay part of the blame for his devotion to false gods on his mother and his upbringing. One day he forgot himself in a discussion with his friends and shouted:

"Liberate the West! From what? From a life of happiness such as we have never known?"

There was an immediate silence in the group, but the incident was temporarily forgotten.

The owner of the private lending library was a German from the Volga settlements called Berger; in 1937 he was arrested, and several weeks later he dragged Kostylev into prison after him. The first hearing showed that Kostylev's implication in Berger's case was merely accidental: when giving the police a list of the people who frequented his library, the old German had not failed to include "a tall, broad-shouldered student from the naval school". Even though Berger was arrested during the Great Purges, when suspicion could fall on anybody, there were several authentic aspects of his case which would have awoken the suspicions of any normal police. He was beyond doubt the intermediary in the exchange of gold for foreign currency and Japanese luxury goods, of which the Kolyma camp chiefs had been guilty.

Kostylev was repeatedly beaten unconscious in prison, then beaten again after a bucket of cold water had brought him round; he was hardly able to see through the chinks in the plaster of dried blood over his eyes, and his mouth was swollen with torn jaws and loose teeth. He would not admit his "guilt", and his determination grew in proportion to the increased intensity of his sufferings. The human organism is an unfathomable machine; it is true that it possesses a certain limit of endurance, but beyond that limit there is either complete submission, or else unexpected rebellion which is itself only a form of anæsthetic in extremis. The condition of lasting psychological apathy, caused by a break-down in the first line of physical resistance and the crushing of all the centres which send out together with waves of pain the command to stop and surrender, usually ends with total paralysis of the will and a dislocation of the backbone which beating has anyway made as useless as a cracked stick in a rag doll; but sometimes it also happens that the organism, though numbed by continual beating, mechanically repeats the remembered efforts of the submerging consciousness, like the instinctive conditioned reflexes of a body in its final agony. Kostylev remembered only that he had hissed with determination through clenched teeth: "I'm innocent, I've never been a spy". He fainted for a long while at the moment when, having cried "No!" for the last time, he felt the convulsive clashing of his jaws dislocating his front teeth and spat them out, choking, together with a stream of warm blood and vomit which broke through his closed gullet and gushed at the wall like oil from a pierced shaft. He felt relief, then all was darkness. His fainting saved him, for when he woke a few days later he was in the prison hospital, where he had been washed and bandaged.

At the next hearing the accusation of espionage was dropped and the interrogation took the form of casual conversations about Kostylev's general political opinions. It was clear that the N.K.V.D. had no intention of sending him back to the naval school in such a condition, and had decided to investigate in a different direction. It was too late to save the young engineer's massacred face, but it was still possible to save the face of that powerful institution which for twenty years had watched over the safety of the revolution. The theory of Soviet law is based on the principle that no one is innocent. An examining judge who receives a prisoner into his care can after many unsuccessful investigations abandon the original indictment, but this does not mean that he should not try his luck elsewhere. The prisoners have found an excellent expression to describe this curious proceeding—"What have they pinned on you?" they ask their companions who return from a hearing. As a result the sentence is always to a certain extent a compromise; the accused is made to realise that "he wasn't brought there for nothing", and the N.K.V.D., continues without hindrance to cultivate the myth of its infallibility.

There is no need to describe Kostylev's interrogation in detail, since the disintegration and transformation of a prisoner's personality has been reconstructed at the beginning of this chapter from his own accounts of his experiences. Kostylev's case was taken out of the general Berger dossier, and put into the hands of another judge. Misha breathed freely again. During the whole of this second interrogation, which, with only short interludes, continued during a whole year in the Vladivostok prison, he was not once beaten or even struck. At times the nightly hearings resembled eager discussions between young students; Kostylev defended his own position, attacked the other's, made long speeches, and after his return to the cell prepared for the next verbal encounter like a barrister marshalling his case for the court. All this time the examining judge listened politely, interposing only an occasional remark and making notes. For Kostylev, who already knew that the N.K.V.D. had other methods and arguments at its disposal, those first three months of gradual awakening were like fresh morning sleep after a night of bad dreams. He even came to like his taciturn but always smiling judge, who would offer him coffee and cigarettes, enquire solicitously about the wounds on his head and bend closer to catch every word whenever Kostylev lowered his voice. But the first phase of the hearing led nowhere. Kostylev had confessed everything about himself to the judge and admitted his sinful love for the West, and he now requested that the case should be taken out of the hands of the prison authorities and put before the plenum of the Party organisation at the naval school. The accusation of "succumbing to the influence of bourgeois liberalism" would have been more properly discussed by the students' central committee, which prolongs or cancels Party membership cards, instead of forming the only accusation in an N.K.V.D. prison. His inquisitor was of a different opinion, and now he opened the attack.

The decor of the hearings changed as if on a revolving stage. Kostylev was now woken in the night, taken back to the cell after a few hours, woken again at dawn, called out to hearings during meals and during the time reserved for the daily visit to the latrine; he was forbidden to wash, and deprived of his daily walk in the prison courtyard. There was no suggestion now of cigarettes and hot coffee. Kostylev walked about stunned and bewildered, his eyes were red from lack of sleep, his head burned from the still unhealed wounds, and the blood inside it roared like boiling water at the bottom of a pan. There were times when in full daylight, on his way to the hearing, he would stagger on his legs and lean against the wall of the corridor like a blind man; other times when he would faint on the stool before the judge's table. He now spent most of his hours in the small room where, day and night, dark blinds were drawn across the bars, shutting him off from time, which flowed beyond the windows, and making him easy prey for cunning questions in the fierce circle of electric light. At times he felt as if his head was an enormous pin-cushion, stuffed with horsehair and bristling with a thousand needles. He felt their painful, repeated stabs, and in an access of despair he would try to smother the pain by tearing at the bandages on his forehead, brow and cheeks, or by putting his hands to his ears, where the pricking of sharp needles was transformed into the crumbling sound of steel shavings falling to the bottom of an empty shell. He lost all consciousness of the passing of time, he was weakened by frequent emissions in his sleep, he would jerk up on the bunk at the sound of his name, suffocated and half-conscious, staring all round with burning, uncomprehending eyes.

He was now in principle ready and willing to admit some abstract guilt, and he even tried to suggest the idea to the judge. But the inquisitor, whose expression had changed as if a mask had dropped off his face, needed more facts. Who belonged to the secret organisation in the naval school? Where and when did its meetings take place? What were the organisation's practical aims? What contacts did it have outside? Who was its leader? Kostylev denied everything with a last effort of his will, but he knew that if the hearings continued much longer he would begin to invent names and circumstances, escaping from the menace of an empty reality by recourse to fiction. This stage of the hearing continued for three months, which approached in their tension and mental agony the short episode of physical torture when the Berger case was still at issue. But one night the hearing took an unexpected turn; he was told to sign a document which stated that his seditious agitation in the naval school was never based on any definite organisation.

In its third stage the interrogation again became easier. Kostylev was summoned on one evening a week, sometimes even one a fortnight, for informal discussions about "the actual conditions prevailing in Western Europe". Now it was the examining judge who talked—polite, smiling and forbearing as before—while Kostylev listened and asked questions; the lectures were interesting and intelligent, the arguments supported with books, figures and facts.

After what he had just gone through, the changed tone of the hearing was in itself sufficient to dispose Kostylev to make a moderate gesture of repentance. But he went even further and allowed himself to be really convinced, believing everything that his former persecutor told him. He listened attentively, quietly whispering "But that's terrible," he asked for details, drew the expected logical conclusions from the facts provided—in one word, he was now discovering the perfidy of the West with the same sincere exaltation with which he had once discovered its truth. It might have seemed that the infection under the skin had at last gathered into an overcharged abscess, ready for the incision. But the judge prolonged the interrogation artificially as if to make sure that the sinner's conversion was not merely the dissembling escape of a helpless victim. What else was there to discuss? The prisoner was willing to atone for all the moments of weakness and hesitation, for his faith had returned to him. He was ready to show by his work that he was glad to sacrifice his life for what he had learnt to love.

"Well, Kostylev," the examining judge said one evening, "we can finish the interrogation today. You must sign a confession, and then it will be over. It all boils down to this: you intended to abolish the present government of the Soviet Union with the aid of foreign powers."

Kostylev crouched and drew back as if to leap up suddenly. The blood rushed to his head, and in another moment he would have shouted "It's a lie!" But in his astonishment he only managed to repeat:

"Abolish the government of the Soviet Union—with the aid of foreign powers?"

Then, without taking his eyes off Kostylev, the examining judge drew out of his brief-case and threw on the table the signed testimony of three students from the naval school. One sentence had been underlined with a red pencil.

"Read it aloud!" the judge ordered sharply.

" 'Liberate the West! From what? From a life of happiness such as we have never known?' "

Kostylev let the paper fall on the table and lowered his head. He thought of his imaginary travels, his dreams of a journey to the West. After all, who knows. . . . Everything seemed logical—unreal, but terribly logical. Before him lay a column of checked and re-checked figures—it only remained to underline it and add the total. He asked for the confession and slowly put his name to it.

"May I write to my mother?" he asked quietly. "I haven't written to her for a year."

"You'll get paper and an envelope in your cell tomorrow."

After the completed hearing Kostylev returned to his solitary cell only to collect his possessions, and was then taken to a common cell. He lay on his bunk in silence, avoiding all conversation, and stared at the ceiling. The nightmare of sleepless nights and days of agonising tension had come to an end. He was glad to be leaving for a camp. After nearly a year's idleness, almost as tormenting as the hearings and beatings, he wanted to work and live among normal men. At night he thought of his future companions, and repeated to himself the question: "Can one live without pity? *Can* one live without pity?"

In January 1939 he was given a sentence of ten years and sent to the Kargopol camp, and after a few days in Yercevo, transferred under the "technical experts scheme" to Mostovitza. He acquired the reputation of a saint among the prisoners in that camp section. Long after his death, whenever a larger transport from Mostovitza passed through the peresylny barrack in Yercevo, the name of "the engineer Mikhail Alexeyevich Kostylev" was pronounced with awe and reverence. As an engineer from the "technical barrack", Kostylev lived in better conditions than the others and his work was comparatively light. He gave most of his own bread away, carried soup tickets to the mortuary, took advantage of the fact that he was allowed to go beyond the zone without an escort to bring back an occasional scrap of fat or vegetables for the sick. He reported the norms of all prisoners in the brigades which were under his command at the saw-mill as higher than their actual output, and this piece of toufta finished him. He was denounced by one of the brigadiers, and an administrative order from the chief of the whole Kargopol camp deprived him of the right to work as a technical expert for the whole duration of his sentence. He was assigned to a brigade of foresters, where he soon forgot pity and compassion; indeed, he needed it more than the others. Physical labour crushed and degraded him to such a degree that he would have stopped at nothing to get an additional scrap of bread. He hated his fellow-prisoners, and from that time looked upon them as his natural, greatest enemies. It is possible that he would have sunk even lower, to the greatest crime which a man worthy of the name can commit in the camp—the crime of spying and denunciation— if, by accident, he had not come across one of the books which he had read at liberty, in Vladivostok. He read it again in the camp, crying like a child who has found his mother's hand in the dark. And for the second time he realised that he had been cheated.

In March 1941 he came to Yercevo, with his right arm in a sling, and was formally included in the porters' brigade.

*   *   *   *   *

At dawn the barrack was already light, but over twenty porters were still asleep in their corner, undisturbed by Dimka's shouted announcement that breakfast was over. After working all night at the supply centre, we were allowed to sleep through the morning reveille, and to collect our breakfast during the lunch break, before marching out to work again.

At that time I had still not accustomed myself to heavy physical labour. I slept deeply, heavily, as if I had lost consciousness, but often only for two hours a night. Then I would wake and lie without stirring on my bunk among my sleeping neighbours, slowly accustoming myself to the thought of a fresh day's work.

It was because I seldom managed to sleep after the general awakening that I discovered the secret of Kostylev's bandaged right arm on the day after his arrival in the camp. Dimka, having made the formal declaration that the kitchen had finished issuing breakfast, had gone out as usual into the zone. The barrack was empty, except for the sleeping porters and a young man who sat by the fire, reading a book with evident emotion. The day before we had been told that a new prisoner from Mostovitza had joined us, and that he would go out to work with us as soon as his arm was healed and his dispensation from work withdrawn. He was tall, but his head was somehow too large and angular, as if chipped from living stone; two bushy eyebrows sprouted from the low, over-hanging forehead and almost hid the tiny, blazing eyes, sunk like two pieces of coal in his famine-swollen cheeks. Only the lower part of his face gave it an unforgettable expression of intelligence, combined with a fanatic, implacable obstinacy. The narrow lips, convulsively tightened, at once brought to mind the portraits of mediæval monks. I remember my instant delight in this mixture of sensitivity and almost brutal harshness. The hair which hung over his forehead emphasised his likeness to a statue. His left hand turned over the pages of the book with instinctive reverence, and the useless right arm held it in place on his knees. While he read, a charmingly naïve, childish smile played in the corners of his mouth.

Suddenly he looked round to make certain that no one was stirring in our corner, then laid the book aside and began to unwind with his good hand the bandage on his arm. It took him two or three minutes, and during that time he stopped once or twice to throw more wood on the fire. Before finally pulling the crusted layer of cloth and dried matter off his wound, he looked again in our direction and, turning his head away so as not to see the hand, gave a violent tug at the bandage. I thought that he was looking at me, but he did not see me, for his eyes closed suddenly as he drew in his cheeks, and his teeth bit into his lower lip from pain. Still without turning his head, he crawled nearer to the fire and blindly thrust the arm into the flames. Through his face passed a spasm of pain, his eyes seemed to be retreating into his head, his teeth released the bottom lip, his jaws met with a grating sound, and large drops of sweat stood out on his forehead. During those few seconds I saw not only the face, pierced with pain, but also the arm—a swollen block, wrapped in strips of burnt and peeling skin and dripping with blood and pus which fell in small drops on to the hot logs, hissing like burning oil. Finally he drew it out of the fire, then fell heavily on to the bench, and hiding his head between his knees, wiped the perspiration from his face with the sleeve of his left hand. He seemed to be relaxing and loosening after the hideous ordeal, like a street acrobat who tenses all the muscles of his body to escape from the chains which bind him, and then collapses on the pave-ment like a punctured balloon.

I climbed down from my bunk and sat down at the table, but he noticed my presence only when I picked up the dirty, saturated rag

to help him bandage the arm. He looked at me with surprise and
gratitude, but his tired eyes immediately gleamed with anxiety.

"Did you see?"

I nodded without a word.

"You won't tell?"

No, I would not tell. I did not disclose his secret to anyone for
many years, even though Kostylev died a month after our meeting.
And having once gained his secret, I soon gained his friendship.

This happened, as far as I can remember, almost exactly in the
middle of March 1941; on April 15th Kostylev's body was taken out
beyond the zone. Thus we knew each other only a month, not long
enough to return friendship, but enough to gain it. Kostylev became
attached to me like a dog and, if this expression can be applied to
the camp, we became inseparable. In reality, we were separated
during most of the day by my work. Kostylev still figured on the
list of dispensations, and every third evening he went to the
infirmary for an inspection of his arm; doubtless before every such
visit he found an opportunity to burn it in the barrack. Even
though he told me the story of his life in detail, and explained the
motives of his voluntary martyrdom, I believe that his self-torture
had as much to do with dispensation from work as with martyrdom.
Two facts seemed to support this view incontestably. First, the
circumstances in which the idea had first occurred to him. One day,
in the forest at Mostovitza, he was drying a piece of bread over the
fire, and carelessly let it fall into the flames; terrified by the prospect
of hunger, he plunged his hand in the fire without any hesitation.
That evening he was given seven days' dispensation, and then he
had formed his plan. And secondly, there was the way in which
Kostylev spent his free time in the barrack. It remained a mystery
to me throughout our friendship, a mystery which Kostylev was
unwilling to elucidate, where and how he managed to procure so
many books in the camp. He read through the whole day, he read
at night, perched on an upper bunk by the bulb, he read even in the
infirmary while waiting for his turn with the doctor.

Kostylev's dossier must have contained a note from the
examining judge recommending leniency and better treatment, for
despite the crime of toufta he was sent to Yercevo after his
accident in the forest, and with a direct assignment to the porters'
brigade. It is also possible that his transfer to Yercevo was
connected with a promised visit from his mother, the first since his

arrest in 1937. It had been arranged in Mostovitza that Mrs. Kostylev should travel from Voronezh to Yercevo to spend three days at the beginning of May in the "house of meetings" with her son. Misha lived in a state of such excitement at the prospect of this visit that he did not perceive the danger which threatened him. A healthy prisoner whose hand, for some mysterious reason, would not heal, was something quite exceptional and unforeseen in the Soviet system of forced labour, and could not be tolerated for long. I frequently advised him to give up the practice of burning his arm and to walk out to the supply centre with us a few times, at least until the time of the visit. After that he would be free to do as he pleased. But he only smiled at my warnings and repeated with childish obstinacy: "I shall never work for them again. Never, do you understand? Never!"

In the first days of April we suddenly heard that a transport for Kolyma was being prepared in our camp. Now that I have read something about German concentration camps, I realise that a transfer to Kolyma was in Soviet labour camps the equivalent of the German "selection for the gas-chamber". The analogy becomes even more accurate when it is seen that, as for the gas-chambers, the prisoners for Kolyma were taken from among those in the worst state of health, though in Russia they were being sent not to an immediate death but to hard labour which required exceptional physical strength and endurance. The secret of this nightmarish paradox is that every camp chief is responsible first of all for his own camp, and for the fulfilment of the production plan assigned to it; when he receives an order to supply so many of his prisoners for a convoy, he gets rid of the weakest and retains the strongest. Our camp froze in fear and expectation at the news: the conversations in the barracks died down, no one grumbled at work, the infirmary was empty of patients. The day of our last judgement was approaching, and we faced the countenance of our Lord with humble faces, following the lightning thrusts of his sword with a suppliant gaze.

Even then I could not persuade Kostylev to attempt some work, and he was in the infirmary every third day, the only patient there besides the nacmeny from the mortuary. On the evening of April 10th he was informed that his name had been included in the Kolyma list and told to report at the bath-house the next morning for what was known as a "sanitary preparation". He took this

blow calmly, but seemed to be stupefied, and only whispered:
"Now I shall never see my mother."

Even today I cannot say why, the same evening, I went to the
camp chief's office and offered to take Kostylev's place in the
transport, but I believe that my physical and psychological condition was responsible. I was at the lowest ebb of my endurance,
and the prospect of three months' idleness—this was the length of
the journey to Kolyma—was a temptation; I was still young enough
to be thrilled by some indefinable hope of exploration on this
journey to the edge of the world; finally, I was emotionally involved
with Kostylev so deeply that I could not draw back before this
trial of the permanence of our friendship. Enough to say that in the
camp chief's office I put my request to Samsonov's deputy. He
looked at me with astonishment but without a trace of anger.

"This is a labour camp," he said briefly, "not a sentimental
romance."

Kostylev was not surprised to hear that I had tried to save him.
He was really living in a "romance", though not perhaps such a
sentimental one as may have appeared to Samsonov's assistant, a
romance with a tragic ending, of which he was probably certain by
now, and to him it seemed perfectly consistent that his "good friend
from the West" should make an attempt to avert the catastrophe.
He pressed my hand warmly and went out without a word. I knew
that I might never see him again, for prisoners for distant destinations
were sometimes taken straight from the bath-house to the station.

But the next evening, as I came back from work, I found Dimka
waiting for me at the guard-house.

"Gustav Yosifovich," he whispered, catching my hand,
"Kostylev has poured a bucket of boiling water over himself in the
bath-house. He's in the hospital."

They would not allow me to see him in the hospital, and there was
nothing that I could have done there. Kostylev was dying in slow
agony, and until the end he did not regain consciousness. He had
obtained his final dispensation. And though he died not as he had
lived, when I knew him and in my way loved him, I see him still
today, the symbolic picture of a man who has repeatedly lost
everything in which he believed, with his face twisted by pain and his
arm plunged into the fire like the tempered blade of a sword.

They must have forgotten to inform Kostylev's mother of her

son's death, for in the first days of May, as we waited before the gate for the evening search, a soldier pointed her out to us at the guard-house. Through the frosted window-pane we saw her trembling hands, gathering a few mementoes of Misha into a small bundle, and her severe, wrinkled face, convulsed by tearless sobbing.

CHAPTER 6

THE HOUSE OF MEETINGS

"Dom svidanyi", literally "the house of meetings", was the name which we gave to a newly-built wing of the guard-house, where prisoners were allowed to spend between one and three days with their relatives, who had come from all parts of Russia to the Kargopol camp for this short visit. Its topographic situation in the camp zone was to some extent symbolic: our entrance to the barrack was through the guard-house, from the zone, and the way out was already on the other side of the barbed wire, at liberty. Thus it was easy to think that the house in which the prisoners saw their relatives for the first time after so many years was on the borderline between freedom and slavery; a prisoner, shaved, washed and neatly dressed, having shown his pass and the official permit for the visit, walked through the partition straight into arms extended to him from liberty.

Permission for such a visit was granted only after the most complicated and trying procedure had been undergone by the prisoner as well as by his family. As far as I can remember, every prisoner was in theory allowed to have one visitor a year, but the majority of prisoners had to wait three, sometimes even five, years for it. The prisoner's part was limited: when a year had passed from the moment of his arrest, he was free to present to the Third Section a written request for a visit, together with a letter from his family, which made it quite unmistakably clear that one of them wished to see him, and a certificate of his good behaviour, both at work and in the barrack, from the camp authorities. This meant that a prisoner who wanted to see his mother or his wife had to work at the level of at least the second cauldron, or full norm, for a year; the inhabitants of the mortuary were as a rule excluded from the privilege of a visit. The letter from the family was no mere formality. Where the connections between a prisoner and a free person were not those of blood, but of marriage, the greatest pressure was put on those outside to sever all relations with the "enemy of the people", and many wives broke down under it. I read many letters in which wives wrote to their husbands in the camp: "I can't go on living like this," asking to be freed from their marriage vows. Occasionally, when the prisoner had every hope that permission for the visit would be granted, the procedure suddenly stopped dead, and only a year or two later did he learn that his relatives at liberty had thought better of it and withdrawn the original request. At other times, a prisoner who went to the house of meetings was welcomed not by extended arms, trembling with desire and longing, but by a look of weariness and words begging for mercy and release. Such visits confined themselves to the few hours necessary to settle the fate of the children, while the unfortunate prisoner's heart withered like a dried nut, beating helplessly within its hard shell.

The initiative in the efforts to obtain permission naturally belongs to the family at liberty. From letters which I was shown by other prisoners I gathered that the procedure is prolonged, intricate, and even dangerous. The decision does not rest with GULAG (the Central Office of Camp Administration), which is concerned only with the administration of the camps and has nothing to do with the sentences or the indictments which produced them, but nominally with the Chief Prosecutor of the U.S.S.R., and actually with the local N.K.V.D. office in the petitioner's place of domicile. A free person who is sufficiently obstinate to persist in his audaciousness, undeterred by the initial obstacles, finds himself the victim of a vicious circle from which he can seldom escape. Only a person with an absolutely blameless political past, one who can prove that he is immune from the germ of counter-revolution, can obtain the precious permission. Now in Russia no one would dare enter a hearing of interrogation even with a totally clear conscience; in this case, too, the certificate of political health is demanded by officials who are the only ones with the authority to give it. Apart from this evident contradiction, we find another, even more fantastic. The presence in one's family of an enemy of the people is in itself sufficient proof of contamination, for someone who has lived with him during many years cannot be free from the plague of counter-revolution.

The N.K.V.D. treat political offences as a contagious disease. Thus when a petitioner arrives at the N.K.V.D. office for a certificate of health, that in itself is evidence of his probable infection. But let us suppose that the political blood tests have not shown the presence of infection in the organism, and the petitioner has been vaccinated and remains in quarantine for an indefinite time. If all goes well, he then receives permission for a direct, three-day contact with the sick man, whose very existence seemed at the interrogation to be dangerous even at a distance of several thousand miles. The cruel, discouraging paradox of this situation is that during the hearings at the N.K.V.D. the petitioner must do everything to convince the interrogator that he has broken all relations with the prisoner and eradicated all emotional ties with him. And back comes the obvious question: in that case, why should he be willing to undertake a distant and expensive journey in order to see the prisoner? There is no way out of this conundrum. No obstacle is put in the way of wives who ask for a visit to the camp in order to end their marriages, thus freeing themselves from the nightmare of a life in half-slavery, in an atmosphere of constant suspicion, and with the brand of shared responsibility for the crimes of others. Others either give it up or else take the final, desperate step—a journey to Moscow to obtain the permission through special influence there. Even if they do somehow succeed by this method, they will have to face the vengefulness of the local N.K.V.D. whom they have slighted to achieve their object, when they return from the camp to their native town. It is easy to guess how many are brave enough to risk asking for permission under these circumstances.

It is natural to ask why these monstrous difficulties and obstacles are put in the way of a visit, since the contingent of workers has already been supplied to the camps, and the costs of the journey there are covered by the visitor himself. I can only suggest three possible conjectures, of which one at least is accurate. Either the N.K.V.D. sincerely believes in its mission of safeguarding the Soviet citizen's political health; or it attempts as far as possible to conceal from free people the conditions of work in forced labour camps, and to induce them by indirect pressure to break off all relations with their imprisoned relatives; or in this way it is putting power into the hands of camp authorities, which during whole years can squeeze from prisoners the remnants of their strength and health, deluding them with the hope of an imminent visit.

When the relative, usually the prisoner's wife or mother, at last finds herself in the Third Section office of the particular camp, she must sign a declaration, promising not to disclose by even one word, after her return home, what she has seen of the camp through the barbed wire; the privileged prisoner signs a similar declaration, undertaking—this time under pain of heavy punishment, even of death—not to mention in conversation his and his fellow-prisoners' life and conditions in the camp. One can imagine how difficult this regulation makes any indirect or intimate contact between two people who, after many years of separation, meet for the first time in these unusual surroundings; what is left of a relationship between two people if an exchange of mutual experiences is excluded from it? The prisoner is forbidden to say, and the visitor forbidden to ask, what he has gone through since the day of his arrest. If he has changed beyond recognition, if he has become painfully thin, if his hair has turned grey and he has aged prematurely, if he looks like a walking skeleton, he is allowed only to remark casually that "he hasn't been feeling too well, for the climate of this part of Russia does not suit him." Having thrown a cloak of silence over what may be the most important period of his life, the regulations push him back to an already distant and dimly-remembered past, when he was at liberty and an entirely different man, when he felt and thought differently; he is in the unbearable situation of a man who should be free to speak, to shout even, and who is allowed only to listen. I have no idea whether all prisoners keep the promise given before the meeting, but, taking into consideration the high price which they would have to pay for breaking it, it may be supposed that they do. It is true that the closeness of the visiting relative may be some guarantee of discretion, but who is to say whether the tiny room, in which the two live together during the whole visit, is not supplied with an eavesdropping microphone, or whether a Third Section official is not listening on the other side of the partition? I only know that I often heard sobbing as I passed by the house of meetings, and I believe that this helpless, spasmodic weeping relieves their tension and expresses for the wretched human tatters, now dressed in clean prison clothing, all that they may not say in words. I think, too, that this is one of the advantages of a visit, for a prisoner seldom dares to cry in front of his companions, and the nightly sobbing in their sleep in the barrack proved to me that it could bring great relief. In the emptiness which sealed lips create between the two people in the house of meetings, they advance cautiously like lovers who, having lost their sight during long years of separation, reassure themselves of each other's tangible existence with tentative caresses until, at the moment when they have finally learnt to communicate in the new language of their feelings, they must part again. That is why prisoners, after their return from the house of meetings, were lost in thought, disillusioned, and even more depressed than before the longed-for visit.

Victor Kravchenko, in *I Chose Freedom*, tells the story of a woman who, after many attempts and in return for a promise of co-operation with the N.K.V.D., was finally given permission to visit her husband in a camp in the Urals. Into the small room at the guard-house shuffled an old man in filthy rags, and it was only with difficulty and after several moments that the young woman recognised her husband. It is more than likely that he had aged and changed, but I cannot believe that he was in rags. I cannot, of course, make a categorical statement about conditions in the Ural camps, and I can only answer for what I myself saw, heard or lived through in a camp near the White Sea. Nevertheless, I believe that all forced labour camps throughout Soviet Russia, though they differ greatly in various respects, had a common aim, possibly imposed upon them from above: they strive at all costs to maintain, before free Soviet citizens, the appearance of normal industrial enterprises which differ from other sections of the general industrial plan only by their employment of prisoners instead of ordinary workers, prisoners who are quite understandably paid slightly less and treated slightly worse than if they were working of their own free will. It is impossible to disguise the physical condition of prisoners from their visiting relatives, but it is still possible to conceal, at least partly, the conditions in which they live. In Yercevo, on the day before the visit, the prisoner was made to go to the bath-house and to the barber, he gave up his rags in the store of old clothing and received—only for the three days of the visit—a clean linen shirt, clean underwear, new wadded trousers and jerkin, a cap with ear-flaps in good condition, and boots of the first quality; from this last condition were exempt only prisoners who had managed to preserve, for just such an occasion, the suit which they had worn at the time of their original arrest, or to acquire one, usually in a dishonest way, while serving their sentence. As if this were not enough, the prisoner was issued with bread and soup tickets for three days in advance; he usually ate all the bread by himself there and then, to eat his fill just once, and the soup tickets he distributed among his friends, relying on the food which would be brought by the visitor. When the visit was over, the prisoner had to submit all that he had received from his relatives to an inspection at the guard-house, then he went straight to the clothing store to shed his disguise and take up his true skin once more. These regulations were always very strictly enforced, though even here there were glaring contradictions which could at once destroy the whole effect of this comedy staged for the benefit of free citizens of the Soviet Union. On the first morning of a visit the relative could, by raising the curtain in the room, catch a glimpse of the brigades marching out from the guard-house to work beyond the zone, and see the dirty scrofulous shadows wrapped in torn rags held together with string, gripping their empty mess-cans and swooning from cold, hunger and exhaustion; only an imbecile could have believed that the scrubbed, neat man who had been brought to the house of meetings the day before in clean underwear and new clothes had avoided the fate of the others. This revolting masquerade was sometimes comic despite its tragic implication, and a prisoner in his holiday outfit was greeted by jeers from the others in the barrack. I thought that if someone would fold the hands of these living dead, dressed in their tidy suits, over their chests, and force a holy picture and a candle between their stiffened fingers, they could be laid out in oak coffins, ready for their last journey. Needless to say, the prisoners who were forced to take part in this exhibition felt awkward in their disguise, as if ashamed and humiliated by the thought that they were being made use of as a screen to hide the camp's true face for three days.

The house itself, seen from the road which led to the camp from the village, made a pleasant impression. It was built of rough pine beams, the gaps filled in with oakum, the roof was laid with good tiling, and fortunately the walls were not plastered. We all had occasion to curse the plaster with which the barrack walls in the camp were covered: water from melted snowdrifts, and urine made by prisoners against the barracks at night, disfigured the white walls with yellow-grey stains, which looked from a distance like the unhealthy pimples of acne on a pale, anæmic face. During the summer thaw the thin plaster peeled off the walls, and then we walked through the zone without looking to right or left—the holes corroded in the brittle crust of whitewash by the climatic scurvy seemed to remind us that the same process was corrupting our bodies. If only because of the contrast, it was pleasant to rest our weary eyes by gazing at the house of meetings, and not without cause (though its appearance was not the only reason) was it known as "the health resort". The door outside the zone, which could be used only by the free visitors, was reached by a few solid wooden steps; cotton curtains hung in the windows, and long window-boxes planted with flowers stood on the window-sills. Every room was furnished with two neatly-made beds, a large table, two benches, a basin and a water-jug, a clothes-cupboard and an iron stove; there was even a lampshade over the electric-light bulb. What more could a prisoner, who had lived for years on a common bunk in a dirty barrack, desire of this model *petit bourgeois* dwelling? Our dreams of life at liberty were based on that room.

Every prisoner was given a separate room, but the prison rules broke that intimacy brutally by making clear distinctions between the privileges of free men and the obligations of prisoners serving a sentence of forced labour. The visiting relative was at liberty to leave the house at any time of the day and night to go to the village, but always alone: the prisoner had to remain in the same room during the whole visit, or else, if he so wished, he could return to the zone for a few minutes after first being searched at the guard-house. In exceptional cases the permission was burdened by an additional provision which confined the visit to the daytime: the prisoner returned to his barrack in the evening, and came back to the house of meetings at dawn (I could never think of a reason for this cruelty; some prisoners believed that it was a form of deliberate persecution, but this was not confirmed by general practice). In the mornings, when the brigades passed the house of meetings on their way to work, the curtains in its windows were usually drawn slightly aside, and we saw our fellow-prisoners inside with strange, free faces. We usually slowed down and dragged our legs in a slightly exaggerated manner, as if to show the "people from over there" to what life behind barbed wire had brought us. We were allowed to give no other sign of recognition, just as we were forbidden to wave to passengers on passing trains as we passed by the railway tracks (the guards had strict orders to drive their brigades into the forest, away from the railway tracks, whenever they heard the sound of an approaching train). The prisoners in the windows of the house of meetings frequently smiled at us and sometimes greeted us by fondly embracing their visitor, as if in this simple and touching way they wanted to remind us that they were human, with well-dressed relatives, free to touch intimately those "from the other side". But more often tears stood in their faded eyes, and painful spasms passed through the haggard faces; perhaps it was our own wretchedness which thus moved those more fortunate prisoners who saw us through the window of a warm, clean room, or perhaps it was only the thought that tomorrow or the day after they themselves would be back in the brigades, hungry and cold, marching off for another twelve hours in the forest.

The situation of those free women who after surmounting countless obstacles have at last succeeded in reaching the camp for a visit is no more enviable. They feel the boundless suffering of the prisoner, without fully understanding it, or being in any way able to help; the long years of separation have killed much of their feeling for their husbands, and they come to the camp only to warm them, during three short days, with the embers of their love—the flame could not be rekindled from the spark hidden in the warm heart of ashes. The camp, distant and barred off from the visitor, yet casts its shadowy menace on them. They are not prisoners, but they are related to those enemies of the people. Perhaps they would more willingly agree to accept the prisoner's burden of hatred and suffering than to suffer in silence the humiliating and equivocal situation of borderland inhabitants. The camp officials treat them politely and correctly, but at the same time with almost undisguised reserve and contempt. How can they show respect to the wife or the mother of a wretch who begs for a spoonful of soup, rummages in the rubbish heaps, and has long since lost any feeling of his own human dignity? In Yercevo village, where every new face left no doubt as to its owner's purpose in the town, visitors to the camp were cautiously avoided. One prisoner told me that when his daughter visited him in the camp she met an old friend, now the wife of one of the camp officials, in the village. They greeted each other with pleasure, but after a while the official's wife drew back anxiously. "What a coincidence, meeting you here! But what are you doing in Yercevo?" "Oh," answered the girl, "I've come to visit my father. You can imagine how unhappy we are!" and added: "Of course, he isn't at all guilty," as if hoping that after breaking the ice she would succeed in obtaining some consideration for her father in the camp. But the other woman left her coldly, saying: "Good, you should write a complaint to Moscow, they will look into it there."

Although, or perhaps because, these visits were so rare and so difficult to obtain, they played a large part in the life of the camp. I became convinced, while I was still in prison, that if a man has no clear end in life—and the ending of his sentence and his final release were too distant and uncertain to be seriously taken into account—he must at least have something to anticipate. Letters were so rare, and their language so commonplace and restricted, that they had no attraction as an object of expectation; only the visits were left to the prisoners. They waited for them with anxiety and joyful tension, and often reckoned the time of their sentences or their lives by those short moments of happiness, or even its very anticipation. Those who still had not been informed of a definite date for their visits lived on hope; they possessed something to occupy them, and perhaps even more, a quiet passion which saved them from utter despair, from the fatal consciousness of their aimless existence. They fed their hope artificially, wrote requests and applications to Moscow, bore the heaviest work manfully like pioneers building their own future; in the evenings they talked to their more fortunate comrades, repeatedly asking what ways there were of hastening that wonderful event; on rest-days they stood outside the house of meetings, as if to make sure that their rooms were reserved and only awaiting the arrival of the guests, quarrelled among themselves in advance over the choice of rooms, and endlessly cleaned and darned their best clothes. Lonely prisoners and foreigners were naturally in the worst position, but even they were able to draw some benefit from the visits, sharing as they did in the happiness and expectation of others, or recognising them to be their only source of information about life outside, at liberty.

Men isolated forcibly, or even voluntarily, from the rest of the world, idealise everything that occurs beyond the frontiers of their solitude. It was touching to hear prisoners, before the expected visit, recalling the liberty whose mere taste they were about to enjoy. It seemed that never before in their lives had they experienced either important events or bitter disappointments. Freedom for them was the one, blessed irreplaceable. At liberty one slept, ate and worked differently, there the sun was brighter, the snow whiter, and the frost less painful. "Remember? Remember?"—excited voices whispered on the bunks. "I remember, at liberty, I was stupid and wouldn't eat brown bread." And another would take up: "I wasn't satisfied with Kursk, I wanted Moscow. Just wait till my

wife comes, I'll tell her what I think of Kursk now, just wait till I tell
her . . ." These conversations sometimes dragged on till late into
the night, but they were never heard on bunks where a prisoner who
had recently returned from a visit lay. The illusion had come face to
face with the reality, and the illusion always suffered. Whatever the
reasons for their disappointment—whether the freedom, realised
for three days, had not lived up to its idealised expectation, whether
it was too short, or whether, fading away like an interrupted dream,
it had left only fresh emptiness in which they had nothing to wait
for—the prisoners were invariably silent and irritable after visits, to
say nothing of those whose visits had been transformed into a
tragic formality of separation and divorce. Krestynski, a joiner
from the 48th brigade, twice attempted to hang himself after an
interview with his wife, who had asked him for a divorce and for his
agreement to place their children in a municipal nursery. I came
to the conclusion that if hope can often be the only meaning left in
life, then its realisation may sometimes be an unbearable torment.

Younger prisoners suffered additional and, at least as far as their
neighbours on the bunk were concerned, by no means intimate
sexual anxieties before visits from their wives. Years of heavy
labour and hunger had undermined their virility, and now, before
an intimate meeting with an almost strange woman, they felt,
besides nervous excitement, helpless anger and despair. Several
times I did hear men boasting of their prowess after a visit, but
usually these matters were a cause for shame, and respected in
silence by all prisoners. Even the urkas murmured indignantly
whenever a guard, who during his night duty at the guard-house
had relieved his boredom by listening, through the thin partition, to
the sounds of love from the other side, derisively shared his
observations with other prisoners in the brigade. Unbridled sexual
depravity was the rule in the zone, where women were treated
like prostitutes and love like a visit to the latrine, and where
pregnant girls from the maternity hut were greeted with coarse
jokes. Yet the house of meetings, in this pool of filth, degradation
and cynicism, had become the only haven of whatever emotional
life memory had brought into the camp from liberty. I remember
our joy when one of the prisoners received a letter, telling him of the
birth of a child conceived during a visit from his wife. If that child
could have been given to us, we would have looked upon it as our
common child, we would have fed it, going hungry ourselves, and

passed it from hand to hand, even though there were plenty of brats conceived on a barrack bunk. That, for us, was the most important difference: they had been conceived on a barrack bunk in the zone, not in the house of meetings with a free woman and on clean sheets. . . . In that way only did life allow us, dead and forgotten men, to feel a slight bond with freedom despite our incarceration in that earthly tomb.

What else can I say about our house of meetings? Perhaps only that, as a foreigner, I never expected to see anyone there, and possibly that is why my observations about the behaviour of my fellow-prisoners, whose joys and disappointments I shared only involuntarily, are so objective and so indifferent even to pain.

CHAPTER 7

RESURRECTION

THE camp hospital was something like a refuge for the ship-wrecked. Few prisoners could pass the well-built barrack with large windows without sighing inwardly at the thought of two or three weeks in a bright ward, on a clean bed, being looked after by a kind, comforting nurse and a polite doctor, with other prisoners who seemed to be transformed, more human somehow and sympathetic. We longed for a visit to the hospital and dreamt of it, at work and during the night, although the object of our longing was not the short rest which it gave, but rather the return to humanity, the transitory, impermanent revocation of our former ideas of life and of men which, even a short time before death, restored our self-respect and the consciousness of our human dignity. A prisoner went to the hospital, as to the house of meetings, to see his reflection in the mirror of the past. And, as from the house of meetings, he returned to the barrack more dispirited than before: that was the price of his brief return to humanity.

Legends have been handed down of inspired fanatics who gave their lives in a vain quest for even the briefest glimpse of absolute beauty, and the desire which made them put their signatures to the suicidal bond we regard as the source and spring of humanity's ceaseless progress. So prisoners who dared to revive the standards and conceptions of their past paid for their shortlived resurrection, after leaving the hospital, by an agonising relapse into the slow process of death. The most fortunate died in the hospital, and not in the mortuary, on their bunks in the barrack or at work; they had glimpsed and caught the world's better aspect before they finally went out of it.

Life in a prison camp is bearable only when all criteria, all standards of comparison which apply at liberty, have been completely obliterated from the prisoner's mind and memory. A new arrival in the camp was encouraged by older prisoners with the traditional saying: "It's nothing, you'll get used to it." "Getting used to it" meant forgetting how he had once thought, how felt, whom and why he had loved, what he had disliked, and to what he

97

had been attached. From this point of view the perfect prisoner does not exist, but there are men who, after several years behind barbed wire, can control their memories far better than their primitive instincts; a relentless discipline of oblivion has erected an impassable barrier between their past and their present. Most prisoners, however, are unable to impose this rule upon their minds, and seek in memory release from the hideous present. Those who force themselves to forget are stronger, and at the same time weaker, than the rest. Stronger, because they submit to the laws of camp life without hesitation, accepting them subconsciously as normal and natural; and yet weaker, because the slightest breach in their defences, the most trivial event which stimulates the imagination, lets loose a flood of repressed memories which nothing can hold back. They submerge brain, heart and body, with greater or lesser violence in proportion to the length and depth of their incarceration in the sombre dungeons of artificial amnesia.

People of simple faith found life in the camp somewhat easier to accept, for they looked upon it as the natural culmination of their previously hard existence and with humbleness in their hearts awaited heavenly reward for their patience in suffering. But intelligent men, gifted with a richer imagination and a store of accumulated experience, were as a rule more vulnerable, and unless they were able to arm themselves with a veneer of cynicism, helplessly gave themselves up to their memories. It was characteristic of the camp that the kulaks and the habitual criminal prisoners who had fully "got used to it" went to the hospital unwillingly, preferring a few days' dispensation from work in the barrack, as if afraid that, having once been reminded of liberty, they would never be comfortable in slavery again. The others, all those who, despite the warnings of instinct, had no desire to forget, sought escape in the hospital and welcomed the illness which sent them there. When they returned to the barrack afterwards, their faces were drawn and shrunk with pain; they had caught a glimpse of the past, which had given them delusive hope for the future, and then they had been dragged away from the wall surrounding their present.

The hospital was the only barrack in the camp, besides the house of meetings, which was built and maintained as well as the dwellings of free men in Yercevo village. Within, on either side of a wide corridor, were wards with two windows and at least eight beds each. It was neat and clean everywhere, and this was the more striking when one first entered, with the filth of the barracks still fresh in one's mind. Only the improvised sleeping-places on the passage floor, where the sick had to wait, sometimes as long as several days, for a free bed, were peculiar to our hospital; otherwise it resembled in every respect a modest but efficient hospital in a small provincial town on the Continent. At the end of the corridor was a small duty-room for doctors and nurses, where medicines and medical instruments were kept in two glass-fronted cupboards against the walls; the large table there served in emergencies as an operating-table.

The director of the hospital was a free doctor from the village, who came to the zone every other day to inspect the sick in the medical hut. Three camp doctors—Loevenstein, Tatiana Pavlovna, and a russified Pole called Zabyelski—were directly under his orders, and his decision was final in all matters of dispute. The free senior doctor was not concerned with dispensations from work or recommendations to the hospital, which were given out in the medical hut, but only supervised the treatment and decided when a patient was ready to leave. This was officially considered to be sufficient control over the camp doctors to prevent any possible abuse of their authority. The junior doctors, like all the nurses, were themselves prisoners, and in theory they could take advantage of their positions to improve the lot of others. In practice, however, every camp doctor observed the regulations very strictly, for he knew that if the slightest infringement were discovered, he would immediately be sent back to work in the brigades. The sick were freed from work with a temperature of over 100 degrees, and sent to the hospital when it rose over 102·2 degrees, besides accidents and wounds received at work. The doctors had some opportunity of infringing the regulations over the dispensations from work, but even there they were afraid of denunciation by their assistants, whose only qualifications for this position were frequently their contacts with the N.K.V.D., or by the prisoners, whom the Third Section sometimes sent to test the doctors' loyalty by attempting to bribe them. It was always better to err on the side of strictness; a prisoner who was freed from work without the required temperature could end the doctor's medical career for good, but no blame was attached to the doctor for refusing to give a dispensation, whatever the temperature. The explanation of this imposed strictness is very simple and even logical: the camp authorities' view was that it would have been foolish to interfere with the prisoners when they were doing harm to each other, but they had to be prevented from helping each other. This attitude would have been reasonable if men in slavery tended to help rather than to harm each other; unfortunately this condition did not apply to Soviet labour camps. Apart from that, labour camp legislation foresaw a certain maximum percentage of unproductive sick prisoners (I believe that it was five per cent of a camp's total number), which was under no circumstances to be exceeded. There were times when the doctor could exempt only those who were seriously ill, sending the slightly sick out to work with a promise of compensation in the future, so that the number of absentees should not formally be called into question at the guard-house.

Hospital treatment for all diseases consisted mainly of a short rest and excessive doses of drugs to lower the temperature. The camp dispensary was so poorly supplied that the prisoners knew the names of the medicines most frequently used, and asked for them without waiting for the doctor's diagnosis. It was also clear that the doctors' efforts, in accordance with the secret instructions of the camp authorities (of which I learnt from one of my medical friends), aimed at the speedy recovery only of prisoners who had not completely lost the capacity to work. For old men, for prisoners with incurable heart disease, protracted pylagra, or tuberculosis the hospital was only a temporary resting-place before death or removal to the mortuary. The doctors' duty in such cases was to see that incurable patients should, after a short rest, be strong enough to walk on their own feet to the adjoining mortuary, releasing a badly-needed bed in the hospital. No attempt was made to cure complete physical exhaustion, various forms of hunger dementia, night-blindness, and advanced vitamin deficiency which resulted in ulceration of the body and loss of hair and teeth—these qualified directly for the mortuary. Thus only a prisoner who was still strong enough to be regenerated by a short rest alone could be certain that his week or two in hospital would be more than just an escape from the reality of the camp into dreams of the past.

Conditions in the hospital, by comparison with those in the rest of the camp, verged on unbelievable luxury. Every patient was sent to the bath-house before going into hospital; on entering the ward he gave up his rags and received fresh linen, and was shown to a bed made with clean sheets and flanked by a small bedside table. What ever his norm had been in the zone, here he invariably received the third-cauldron ration, as well as some raw vegetables for vitamin deficiency and a large daily portion of white bread; those suffering from pylagra were also given two lumps of sugar and one lump of margarine of the same size. It was all so unusual and so incredible that prisoners who came to the hospital to visit sick friends would take off their caps at the door, and did not dare to step inside until encouraged by a nurse's polite invitation.

It is impossible to write of Soviet labour camps without paying tribute to the kindness and helpfulness of the hospital nurses. Perhaps because, at least in the daytime, they lived in more human conditions, although they returned to the barracks at night, or because the hospital was the only place in the camp where it was still possible to help human suffering—whatever the reason, the nurses treated us with such tenderness and devotion that we looked upon them as beings from another world, whom only some absurd trick of fate had forced to live with us and share all the hardships of our slavery. The human atmosphere of the hospital also affected free men. The camp chief, Samsonov, always exchanged a few words with each patient during his inspections, and the severe voice of Yegorov, the free head doctor (it was said that he too had once been a prisoner) became warm and gentle whenever he stopped by a sick man's bed.

*   *   *   *   *

My own observation of the hospital in Yercevo, as well as the stories and recollections of other prisoners, have led me to the conclusion that a definite "hospital cult" must exist in Soviet Russia. Even in the worst labour camps, even during the "pioneer" period when the proizvol flourished, the hospitals were as if excluded from the system of Soviet slavery and retained a different character. There was something incomprehensible in the fact that the moment a prisoner left the hospital he became a prisoner again, but as long as he had been lying motionless in a clean bed all the rights of a human being, though always with the exception of freedom, had been accorded to him. For a man unaccustomed to the violent contrasts of Soviet life, camp hospitals seemed like churches which offer sanctuary from an all-powerful Inquisition; to break the code of behaviour which prevailed in them was equivalent almost to desecration; and although man was not worshipped in them, he was at least respected within the limits which allow him to distinguish punishment from torture in prisons.

It is not surprising, then, that the prisoners strove by every possible means to obtain admission to the hospital. During the pioneer period this was most frequently procured by self-mutilation at work, and I saw many prisoners with fingers missing from one or both hands; Dimka paid for three months in Nyandoma hospital in 1937 with his wooden right leg, although he also had it to thank for the comfortable job of a barrack orderly. In 1940 the camp authorities, shocked by the high number of casualties, guessed the cause, and from that time "accidents at work", unless confirmed by a detailed and plausible account of the circumstances, were included in the category of "sabotage", and "self-inflicted wounds" were punished with an additional sentence of ten years. Even so, in December 1941, I saw a young prisoner, who two days before had been discharged from the hospital despite his protests and pleading, being brought back to the zone from the forest without a foot.

When self-mutilation was prohibited, other ways were found of ensuring a visit to hospital. At our low level of physical resistance a little dirt, rubbed into a small scratch, resulted in blood-poisoning, which sometimes caused only a slight fever, but occasionally sent the temperature up to the required degree. A method popular among the urkas was the injection of melted soap into the penis; the ejaculations it produced simulated venereal disease, and they were freed from work at least during the period when they were under observation. I myself, having one day become so hot at work that my shirt stuck to my sweaty body, stripped to the waist in a temperature of thirty-five degrees below freezing point. The next day—it was in February, 1941—I was sent to the hospital for two weeks.

In the large ward a nurse showed me to my bed, between the German prisoner S. and the Russian film actor Mikhail Stepano-vich W. During the first few days we lay side by side without exchanging a word. The hospital day dragged slowly on, and the nights, after I had satisfied my great need of sleep, had in them something of life outside the laws of time. I lay back staring at the ceiling or at the frosted window-panes, beyond which extended the unfathomable darkness. I tried to prevent myself from falling asleep, in order to prolong my stay in the hospital by wakefulness. I could now realise, with an intensity which bordered on pain and joy at the same time, the whole degradation and misery of prison life. But simultaneously I underwent a resurrection in the silence and the solitude, and I dreamt of being transferred to a single, solitary prison cell. After midnight, Nurse Eugenia Fyodorovna walked round all the wards and, without switching on the lights, laid a cool hand on every patient's forehead. I would pretend to be asleep in order to avoid her questions, though I remember once seizing her hand without a word and putting it to my fever-parched lips. She looked at me with astonishment and instinctive fear, though from that time she greeted me with a smile whenever she came into our ward. The hospital was the only place, in camp and prison alike, where the light was extinguished at night. And it was there, in the darkness, that I realised for the first time in my life that in man's whole life only solitude can bring him absolute inward peace and restore his individuality. Only in all-embracing loneliness, in darkness which conceals the outlines of the external world, is it possible to know that one is oneself, to feel that individuality emerging, until one reaches the stage of doubt when one becomes conscious of one's insignificance in the extent of the universe which grows in one's conception to overwhelming dimensions. If this condition savours of mysticism, if it forces one into the arms of religion, then I certainly discovered religion, and I prayed blasphemously: "O God, give me solitude, for I hate all men." The resurrection of my personal individuality was also the extinction of all that bound me to other people. I forgot the camp, forgot the prisoners outside, forgot my family and my friends; I thought only of myself. I was dying, then, during my resurrection. Every day I thought with increasing hatred of the prisoner who would take my place in the hospital. I had pushed open my tombstone, only to emerge into a barren desert—it was a bitter triumph. Those moments when the night laid the cool rose of darkness on my parched lips, when in the silence I heard the beating of my own heart pacing out infinity, gave me back the certainty of my own existence, and deprived me too of my respect for the existence of others. I was like a blind man who miraculously regains his sight only to find himself in an emptiness full of mirrors, which reflect only his own solitude.

This psychological condition lasted as long as my temperature was very high—about five days. Afterwards I regained my strength sufficiently to sit up in bed and attempt to talk with my neighbours. The more sociable of the two was Mikhail Stepanovich W., a wonderful old man with a pointed white beard and a shaved head, who before his imprisonment had played the parts of Tsarist boyars in Soviet historical films. The popularity which all film actors, including the extras and the bit players, enjoy in Russia proved useful to him in the camp, and he was made night-watchman in one of the stores at the food supply centre, and allowed to leave the zone without a guard, after only a year's work in the forest. He lived quite comfortably, for free officials at the supply centre would frequently press a cigarette or a piece of bread into his hand, and he seemed to be completely satisfied with his lot. He talked about himself in a deep, slightly mannered voice, so typical of men who have approached acting, however vaguely. I have described him here rather broadly, for he was the only man that I met in the camp who looked upon everything that he had suffered since the moment of his arrest as a completely natural sequence of events. He had the humility of a man brought up to obey and respect all authority; his was the social discipline of a model citizen. He was arrested in 1937 because he had unduly emphasised the nobility of one of the boyars who served Ivan the Terrible; he told me this without the slightest smile, and his expression was as serious as if he had committed a real crime. "That's how it is, Gustav Yosifovich," he would say, "that's how it must be." I tried to explain the stupidity, the inhumanity of his sentence and of the system which had imprisoned him for a bad performance, but he listened absent-mindedly, looking gently in front of him and stroking his silky beard. He was convinced that the highest distinction which an honest man can attain is approval in the eyes of the authorities, and the greatest shame the dissatisfaction of his superiors. He was indifferent to the fate of his fellow-prisoners, saying: "They must have deserved it," though sometimes he would unexpectedly add, with pain in his voice: "Poor souls, those poor souls." I believe that he was of that type of citizen who first, with a spontaneity which excludes all suspicion of hypocrisy, welcomes the overthrow of tyranny, but who will not dare to raise a hand against it himself as long as it is firmly established in its authority. Fundamentally, two dominant feelings lay in him side by side: deep-seated rebellion against injustice, and an instinctive conviction that the definition of the standards of justice and law is invariably the prerogative of those who rule.

Mikhail Stepanovich was ashamed of the offence which had earned him his sentence, although I believe that at heart he regarded it as rather ridiculous. He had something of the "old order" in him that aroused my sympathy and affection, some vestigial and now anachronistic conviction that prison was a method of meting out well-deserved punishment and prisoners were proved criminals. His brain could not conceive of a situation where an innocent man is deprived of his freedom. Gradually he came to believe in his own guilt, or at least he pretended to believe in it; he spent hours convincing us that he had unintentionally read too much into his part, and by an actor's over-playing misrepresented the whole tendency of the film. There was nothing I could do but listen to him seriously, and sympathise with him in his tragic error. Fortunately, he soon returned to good health, and two days before leaving the hospital he was posturing dramatically in the middle of the ward with a hospital cloak thrown over his shirt, reciting to us the verses of his beloved Pushkin. I can still remember a line from Pushkin's "Song of Oleg" which he would repeat frequently, emphasising each word with theatrical intensity:

"O tell me, prophet, darling of the gods, what life has in store for me . . ."

My other neighbour, the German S., was usually silent, if only because he spoke Russian very badly. Although he was not a communist, he had come to Baku in 1934 as an oil-drilling expert, under the provisions of an agreement whereby technicians from all branches of industry were lent to Soviet Russia by Germany. He was arrested in 1937 and accused of espionage. Of all the prisoners that I knew in the camp who had been sentenced for various improbable crimes S. was the only one in whose guilt I was ready to believe. He was one of those men who call attention to themselves and awaken suspicion by their very appearance and behaviour. In a pale face, ravaged by years of prison and illness, his eyes blazed contempt for his surroundings and revealed also the penetrating intelligence of a bloodhound. His thin, compressed lips expressed only hatred, cruelty and the ferocity of a trapped animal. He asked everyone short, pointed questions which struck immediately at the heart of the matter, and after a few days I was certain that he knew more about each of us than the N.K.V.D. He treated

Mikhail Stepanovich with undisguised disdain, and could hardly control his anger when listening to the naïve stories about the ill-fated film; "Gott wie gross ist dein Tiergarten" he once whispered to himself, lifting up to heaven his thin, emaciated arms.

S. was suffering from pylagra; he had been in the hospital for two months when I met him, and I am certain that, but for the Russo-German pact of 1939 and the fact that he was no mere German born in Russia but, nominally at least, a full German citizen, he would have been allowed to die long before then. Once he leaned over to me and whispered: "In half a year's time the war will break out and then these bastards will be made to pay for everything." The war broke out rather earlier, but it was S. who paid first. On June 23rd, although he was in the last stages of the disease, he was thrown out of the hospital without even a medical inspection, and sent with a detachment of Germans, dismissed from their posts in the camp offices, to the penal camp of the Second Alexeyevka. I saw him at the guard-house when the transport was being formed, as he stood, supported by two Volga Germans, in torn rags, his boots carelessly tied with string, shivering with cold, pale and frightened, all his old self-assurance and contemptuous superiority vanished. Advanced pylagra, besides its physical effects —the loss of hair and teeth and putrefaction of the flesh—brings about psychological changes: depression, melancholia, a continual state of terror and persecution mania. S. looked like a heap of human scraps hastily collected and tied with rags, and I could have sworn that if his companions had taken their hands from under his arms, he would simply have disintegrated before our eyes. Later I learnt that he never even reached the Second Alexeyevka. The transport, driven on foot over the distance of twelve miles, abandoned him in the forest after five miles' march, together with an old German from the camp accountants' office and one of the escorting guards. Neither of the Germans were ever seen again, but the other prisoners of the convoy later asserted in the Second Alexeyevka that, after they had walked another half-mile, they heard two consecutive single shots, which echoed through the forest like a sudden thunderclap. . . .

*   *   *   *   *

There were, and doubtless still are, camps where certain exceptional privileges accompanied the position of a doctor.

Apart from the possibility of taking bribes for dispensation from work, the camp doctors had free entry to the hospital kitchen and to the dispensary. Every woman in the camp desired nothing more than to be admitted to hospital, eat a little better than the other patients and in return visit the doctor at night in the small duty-room; every urka, who had acquired a small fortune by robbing the politicals was ready to pay the highest price for a drop of alcohol from the dispensary, a little valerian which was made into spirit with dried bread, or some chloralhydrate which, taking the place of hashish, opium and morphine, could give the camp drug-addicts a short period of numbness. In such camps the doctors were a social *élite* unequalled in its style of life, its opportunities and even its orgies, and the efficiency of a camp medical mafia was improved by the participation of the free head doctor, who usually had himself been a prisoner, and who appropriated a major share of the spoils.

Among the free men employed in the administration of labour camps there were many former prisoners: mostly doctors, engineers and clerks who, when their terms of imprisonment ran out, at once received either a second sentence or a proposal to stay in the camp and take up well-paid duties, with which as a rule went two- or three-roomed flats in the near-by village. This form of compromise was of advantage to both sides, and only rarely was it rejected by the prisoner. After many years of life in the camp the average prisoner becomes so unaccustomed to the idea of liberty that he begins to dread the prospect of having again to live—"at liberty"—in a state of unceasing watchfulness, followed and spied on by friends, relatives and colleagues, exposed to suspicion by the very fact that he has just finished a prison sentence. The camp, too, has to some extent become his second life; he is familiar with its laws and its customs, he moves freely about the zone and knows how to avoid danger; the years behind barbed wire have blunted his imagination, and his conception of freedom is based not so much on his native Kiev or Leningrad, but simply on the open plain beyond the zone and the small village where lights gleam in the evenings and children play in the snow during the day. If no one is waiting for him outside, if during those prison years his family has abandoned him, then the decision is easy and he does not hesitate. The camp gains a conscientious worker, well acquainted with the life and habits of prisoners, loyal because his own prison experiences have made him wiser, now chained for ever to his galley. The N.K.V.D. also has its reasons for approving these contracts of employment between the victim and his persecutors: the practice facilitates the localisation of the camp infection within a radius of several miles, provides them with experienced informers, and gives the camp the appearance of a normal corrective institution, in which every prisoner can see one of his former companions being rewarded for years of hard work with freedom and the status of a full citizen of the Soviet Union.

But for us, looking at it from a different position, the presence of free ex-prisoners in the camp was a painful reminder that there was no escape from it at any time. The whole world suddenly shrank to the limits of the camp. We looked at these former prisoners with the same emotion as a Catholic would experience if he suddenly, with his own eyes, beheld indisputable proof that life beyond the grave differs in no respect from his present existence: that it, too, is an unbroken sequence of suffering, torment and disappointment. And yet, with the exception of foreigners, who could never accustom themselves to the idea of permanent slavery, any prisoner, faced with the necessity of choice between a return to full liberty and the position of a free camp official, would break down before the threat of a return to the past and choose the half-freedom which promised less than the other but also held less danger of disappointment.

Contrary to expectation, former prisoners treated us with even greater ruthlessness and severity than the truly genuinely free officials. Whether it was their own past which they saw and hated in the prisoners, whether they wanted to gain the confidence of their superiors by this exaggerated conscientiousness, or whether the long years spent in the camp had instilled a habit of cynicism and cruelty into them—enough to say that we would in vain have tried to seek any consideration from those who had once shared our bunks. There was, however, one aspect of camp life in which these ex-prisoners showed not only leniency, but also their own willingness and aptitude: in collusion with the brigadiers and camp doctors, they took advantage of every opportunity to squeeze all possible profit from their privileged positions. All forms of bribery depended on the co-operation of former prisoners: the universal toufta in the calculation of norms was possible only if the foreman was one; the rest in hospital could be prolonged if the senior doctor was one. Similarly the camp doctors' organisations, drawing great profits from bribes and the sale of alcohol substitutes to the urkas and turning the women's wards into private harems, depended on the tacit approval of the free doctor, who in his own prison days had learnt to look upon the camp as the rule of lawlessness sanctified by the right of the strongest.

All this, however, could not be said of Yegorov, our free doctor, who in 1939 had finished an eight-year sentence in Krouglitza camp section, and was then appointed director of the hospital in Yercevo, the central section of the Kargopol camp. Yegorov—tall, slim, taciturn, with a hard face, a cold glance and slightly nervous movements—was either very discreet or else incorruptible. He was never seen to eat or drink in the zone, treated the camp doctors distantly and the patients severely but with occasional sympathy and tenderness. Whenever he appeared on the road leading to the hospital, in his long fur greatcoat, his tall lambs'-wool cap and his leather gaiters with metal press-buttons, the duty doctor hastily checked the temperature charts, and Eugenia Fyodorovna paled with emotion. It was said that she was Yegorov's only link with his past as a prisoner, for he had known her before his release from Krouglitza, where he had been her camp husband, and that he had accepted his present position only on condition that she was transferred to Yercevo. Whatever the true story was, Mikhail Stepanovich told me that she had arrived with a transport from Krouglitza two months after Yegorov's appointment, and had been directed straight to our hospital.

Their liaison was something unusual in the camp, for it was based on genuine feeling, even on loyalty. A free official could have any woman prisoner that he fancied for a slice of bread, but it was unthinkable that he should dare or even wish to give this momentary transaction a permanent character. Women came and went like the succeeding waves of transports, and what invariably remained was the possibility of possessing them without the slightest difficulty. A young and unmarried official could not even count and retain in his memory all the faces and bodies which had passed through his small wooden office in the zone. But in the case of Yegorov love, or at least its primitive form, played a part, and though the camp authorities, the prisoners in the zone and the prisoners working in the hospital had no doubt as to the nature of the relationship between these two people, yet Yegorov and Eugenia Fyodorovna behaved as if privacy and discretion were necessary to make their feelings permanent.

Eugenia Fyodorovna would sometimes come into our ward in the evenings and, sitting down on the old actor's bed, talk to us about herself. Her father was Russian, her mother an Uzbek; she herself was quite exceptionally lovely—her face was small and olive-skinned, her eyes beautiful by their sadness, her hair combed back and fastened behind in an old-fashioned bun; although she must have been about thirty, she had preserved in her figure and her movements the youth and freshness of a schoolgirl. She had studied medicine at Tashkent University until 1936, when she was arrested for "nationalist deviation". She did not really know of what her deviation had consisted, but from her remarks and her freely-expressed opinions I gathered that she had objected to the Russi-fication of Uzbekistan, although through her father she was Russian and only through her mother could she feel any distant emotional bond with her adopted Asiatic country. Her opinions were an odd mixture of European progressiveness and Asiatic conservatism: she claimed to believe in free love, freedom of behaviour in marital relations, but she would not allow a word to be said against the traditional subjection of women in Central Asia. She never mentioned Yegorov while she talked to us; once only, when she was describing her hard beginnings in Krouglitza, she betrayed herself unintentionally by telling us that when she was at the end of her endurance, our doctor, then still a prisoner, saved her from further work in the forest and obtained a position in the medical hut for her. Her tone as she said this led me to believe that the mystery surrounding her relationship with Yegorov was caused not only by a need for privacy: I felt that Eugenia Fyodorovna hated free men, and that she was in some way ashamed of her infringement of prison solidarity. She always tried to behave with perfect indifference in Yegorov's presence, but whenever she walked into the ward after she had spent a few hours in his room, she avoided our looks, lowering her swollen eyelids over her heavy eyes. It appeared, then, that Yegorov loved her because he had once been a prisoner and did not want to, or perhaps could not, forget it; if she returned his feeling, it was from the same motives. "It can't last for ever," I would often say to Mikhail Stepanovich. "It must be humiliating for her. Yegorov visits her like a prostitute, and then returns beyond the zone to another, free life."

A month after I had left the hospital I went to call on Eugenia Fyodorovna on one of the days when Yegorov was not coming to the zone, and found her with Sergei K., an engineering student from Leningrad, who had been arrested in 1934 in connection with the assassination of Kirov, then released before time in 1936, and re-arrested in 1937. He was sitting with Eugenia Fyodorovna on a small couch used for the examination of patients, and they were looking at each other in a way which excluded all doubt. In her voice, previously so controlled and determined, there was now a tremor of boundless devotion, and her burning eyes showed a happiness which is seldom seen in the hard faces of prisoners. After that, I used to see them together in the zone on summer evenings; Sergei was said to be "running after her with his mess-can, out for what he can get," but I saw it only as love, the purest love which I had seen in the camp. I was not the only one, for Mikhail Stepanovich described the change which had occurred in the behaviour and appearance of our nurse with the word "resurrection". This must have been an exaggeration, though in one respect it was accurate enough: rather than a return to life in the silence of the hospital ward, the word "resurrection" described her return to an emotional independence, a return so violent that she was willing to risk her life for it. There was no doubt that one word from Yegorov was sufficient to place Eugenia Fyodorovna in the ranks of a forest brigade, lining up for the morning roll-call with the others.

Yegorov, however, did not seem to realise what was happening behind his back. As before, he came to the zone every other morning and, as before, he walked slowly back to the village in the evening. And although there was nothing which could cause me to sympathise with him, yet from sheer perversity, or by some emotional intuition, I felt that I was on his side in this quiet drama. It seemed to me that he was suffering not only the loss of the woman whom he loved, but also a break with the camp to which he had, in such a curious way, become attached. It was said that his wife had left him after five years of his sentence had passed. Since then, everything that still bound him to life had become centred on the road leading from Yercevo-town, across the wires, to Yercevo-camp. Could he, who seemed to be fascinated by his slavery, tied like a dog to the spot where he had spent the hardest eight years of his life, could he ever have lived in true freedom again?

Towards the end of the summer Sergei was quite unexpectedly included in a transport for the Pechora camp—a sign that Yegorov was fighting back. But the next day Eugenia Fyodorovna asked to be transferred from Kargopol to another camp, no matter which —a sign that she had no intention of giving in. Her application was refused, but even so Yegorov stopped coming to the zone soon afterwards. I heard that he had asked for leave and had left to work in another camp, but no one knew anything certain about it. We never saw him again, and in January 1942 Eugenia Fyodorovna died giving birth to her lover's child, paying with her life for her short resurrection.

THE AUTHOR'S PHOTOGRAPH TAKEN IN GRODNO PRISON IN 1940,
AND STOLEN FROM HIS DOSSIER ON THE DAY OF HIS RELEASE
FROM THE KARGOPOL CAMP

A PHOTOGRAPH OF ONE OF THE CAMP-SECTIONS OF THE KARGOPOL CAMP, TAKEN ORIGINALLY BY A CAMP GUARD AS A SOUVENIR, AND LATER SOLD BY HIM TO ONE OF THE PRISONERS

A PHOTOGRAPH OF THE HANDKERCHIEF MADE AND EMBROIDERED BY
MISS Z.

!GANOV'S POSTCARD

AN EXTRACT FROM THE AUTHOR'S DIARY, KEPT AFTER HIS RELEASE FROM THE CAMP

CHAPTER 8

THE DAY OF REST

MONTH after month passed and we worked every day without a break, deceived by the hope that we should soon be given·a "rest-day". According to regulations, prisoners were entitled to one whole day's rest for every ten days' work. But in practice it transpired that even a monthly day off-threatened to lower the camp's production output, and it had therefore become customary to announce ceremoniously the reward of a rest-day whenever the camp had surpassed its production plan for the one particular quarter. In quite exceptional cases the rest-day was given on the basis of the average monthly output, but only if that was high enough to exclude the possibility of a sudden falling-off in the following two months, which would have lowered the output for the quarter. Naturally, we had no opportunity to inspect the output figures or the production plan, so that this convention was a fiction which in fact put us entirely at the mercy of the camp authorities. As in many other cases, the camp authorities followed the spirit rather than the letter of the instructions from the Central Office of Camp Administration in Moscow (GULAG), and usurped for themselves the right of settling administrative details. The demands made on the camps by GULAG and by the industrial trusts which placed orders with it according to the intake of slave labour were so high that they turned all regulations for the administration of the camps into so much waste paper. I have heard of camps with a rest-day once in every three or four weeks; during the whole year and a half which I spent in Yercevo we had only ten of them, one—as in all Soviet camps without exception—on May 1st; but I have never met a prisoner who could boast that in his camp the brigades remained in the zone on one day in every ten.

This system had its good and bad aspects. The prisoners were near complete exhaustion, but then all the greater was the excitement with which they waited for the short day of rest. In my opinion the utter boredom of life in slavery is usually underestimated; this boredom is so all-embracing and so hopeless that every variation in our lives increased in importance the longer we

113

had to wait for it. We were free every day to expect the proclamation of a rest-day, but when it finally came, and passed more quickly than we could have thought possible while waiting for it, our lives again became so empty, so futile, that we needed some fresh hope to fill them. The first few weeks after a rest-day were always the hardest to bear, for they followed too soon after something that was already in the past, and could not yet contain the promise of the future. How painful is the discovery that the object of our longings and expectations is trivial and insignificant when it is at last realised. It is better to wait for something quite unattainable than to know that one has realised only the shadow of one's dreams. Several times I saw prisoners just after they had received rare food parcels from home: they placed a tiny scrap of pork fat on a piece of black bread and, munching the bread slowly, pushed the fat away farther from their mouths, so as to avoid touching it even with their teeth—the last bite was the realisation, but the real joy came from the artificially prolonged moments of expectation. It was the same with the rest-days, and indeed with everything which was worth waiting for in the camp.

This aspect of a prisoner's psychology must have been a source of great profit to the camp administration. By postponing the rest-day they increased its value, saved time and spared themselves the expense of an unproductive day, and redoubled the prisoners' efforts at work in pursuit of the highest limit of that mythical production plan. All rulers who have little to offer their subjects should start by depriving them of everything, and every small favour that they grant afterwards will become the most generous of concessions. If one day the camp authorities had suddenly announced that we were returning to a biblical week, with six days of work and one of rest, we would probably have agreed that Soviet labour camps were the embodiment of our highest conceptions of the humane treatment of prisoners; but the next day, under better conditions, we would just as probably have rebelled against imprisonment itself.

We usually heard on the evening before the great day, at the guard-house or from our brigadiers, that a whole twenty-four hours of rest was before us. The prisoners walked to the kitchen with a livelier step, greeted each other warmly on the way, made appointments for the next day, and became suddenly more human and friendly. By eight o'clock the zone had assumed an almost festive aspect. On the paths, in front of the kitchen, and all over the small square before the guard-house, animated groups were talking, and from some barracks came the first sounds of singing, of accordions, mouth-organs and guitars. Musical instruments were the most precious and the most sought-after objects in the camp. The Russians love music quite differently from Europeans; for them it is not a mere distraction, or even an artistic experience, but a reality more real than life itself. I often saw prisoners playing their instruments, plucking the strings of a guitar, delicately pressing the keys of an accordion, drinking in music from a mouth-organ hidden in the grasp of both hands—full of great sadness, as if they were exploring the most painful places of their souls. Never has the word "soul" seemed so understandable and so natural to me as when I heard their awkward, hastily improvised compositions, and saw other prisoners lying on the bunks, staring vacantly into space and listening with religious concentration. The surrounding silence seemed to emphasise the power of that music and the emptiness in which it resounded like the sharp, sorrowful tones of a shepherd's pipe on a deserted mountainside. The player became one with his instrument, he pressed it hard to his chest, stroked it with his hands and, hanging his head reflectively, gazed with misty despair at the inanimate object which, at one dexterous touch, spoke and expressed for him all that he could never put into words. Sometimes these musicians were asked to stop: "It tears one's soul." And then immediately a guitar or an accordion would break out into the familiar strains of a Ukrainian ballad or a prison song. Various voices joined in with increasing confidence, and soon the whole barrack was full of the sound of singing, sending out into the darkness strange verses about the prisoner who "burst into tears" on his way to work, or the men who met at night to "elect a secret committee", or that prisoner who at the New Year greeted his friends from "the darkness of OGPU dungeons, which move men to tears and to laughter".

The atmosphere of excitement continued in the zone and the barracks until midnight. We never counted our holiday as beginning on the previous evening; that was only a form of restful preparation for the day itself, which would follow with all the tried excellence of a strict ritual of activities, distractions and small pleasures. The ceremonious observance of the rest-day ritual was significant, for it was the only day which, except for a few hours in the morning, we were free to plan and spend according to our private desires and inclinations. No prisoner ever welcomed a day when he was dispensed from work by the doctor so much, for then he was enjoying an individual privilege, not sharing the common gladness. Despite everything that they had suffered and experienced, it is evident that the instinct of fairness and justice was more deep-seated in the prisoners than in those who had herded them behind barbed wire in the name of justice: even this one day's peace from the inhuman struggle for self-preservation was sufficient to bring it out.

＊ ＊ ＊ ＊ ＊

The prisoners talked until late into the night, lying or sitting on the bunks, and some even sat round the tables with their mugs of hot water, giving to their conversations a happy, domestic atmosphere. At every step, in every corner of the barrack, the approaching holiday could be sensed. I could never understand how so much politeness suddenly appeared from under the shell of indifference and mutual hatred. As they talked, the men showed each other so much courtesy and friendliness that, looking at them, I could almost forget that I was in prison. There was a stench of bad breath and sweat in the barrack, clouds of steam seeped in from the door and the faces seemed to blur in the murky light, but despite all this there was so much life and happy excitement there, so much hope and feeling . . . It was impossible not to be moved when, returning to their own barracks or settling down to sleep, the prisoners left each other with a gentle and sincere "good-night". Good-night, good-night, excited voices whispered all around, sleep well, tomorrow is our holiday, tomorrow is a day of rest . . .

The next morning we were woken a little later than usual, and after breakfast we returned to the barracks to prepare for the search. That was the only event which disturbed the peace of our rest-day. Three junior officers of the camp garrison visited each barrack; one stood in the door, the other two walked inside and herded us out. In the door-way every prisoner spread out all his personal possessions, opened his box, and helped to shake out his palliasse (if, during many years in the camp, he had managed to make one with rags and straw), then gathered up everything that had been inspected and went outside. Meanwhile, in the empty barrack, the other two officers were tapping all the bunks and walls, looking under loose planks, inspecting the vertical beams, overturning tables, benches and empty buckets. We had to wait in the snow for two or three hours while they searched, but I seldom heard prisoners complaining about it: to most of us it seemed a natural procedure, rather like a spring cleaning. The guards were looking for sharp instruments, knives, razors, small objects of personal use, crucifixes, rings, books other than from the camp library, all, in fact, that every prisoner should have given up in prison during the first search after his arrest. Despite their thoroughness, it was always possible to hide such objects even during many years; if they were found the officers confiscated them, though no one was punished. When the search was over, and we were allowed to go back into the barrack, there was little time left to tidy it again before lunch, which for the majority of prisoners consisted of hot water. This was really the beginning of the holiday, for the rest of the day belonged exclusively to us. Time sped incomparably quicker in the zone than it did at work.

One of the greatest attractions of the rest-day was the fact that every prisoner was free to spend it differently, individually. With the exception of those who were too tired to move from their bunks even on that free afternoon, each one of us observed his personal ritual, which was so invariable that one could almost infallibly say who was where and what he was doing at every hour of this exceptional day.

After the midday hot water I usually walked over to the camp shop, a small hut by the guard-house. Only on very rare occasions, once in every few months, stakhanovites like myself, who had the exclusive use of the shop, could purchase, at a nominal price, a length of horse sausage and a pound of bread; nevertheless, the shop was open every evening and during the whole of the rest-day. For us it was a comedy in a small theatre without props. The dark little room was always crowded, and Kuzma, the lame old "shopkeeper", stood behind the counter smiling politely, half turned towards the empty shelves which he had decorated with a whole collection of boxes, tins and bottles, all empty. Standing there in the close air and the tobacco smoke, we talked, as if we were meeting in a village wine-shop after Sunday-morning service, discussing the weather, the work, the news from other camp sections, our favourite dishes and the price of alcohol. We would ask Kuzma about the contents of the empty boxes, and he answered gravely, limping along the counter, talking to us, welcoming and greeting each prisoner. He knew us all by name, and it was part of his duties to exchange a few pleasant words with every one of us. The friendliness and conviviality were a convention, seldom exposed by a sudden burst of laughter and proving how strong is the need for theatrical artificiality, even among men who in their limited lives can find few subjects fit to be imitated by art. Our comedy contained also some subconscious masochism, but, for an unknown reason, its effect on us was encouraging and reviving. After two hours of conversation, jokes, greetings, questions and replies shouted across the room, we began to lose our sense of reality, and little was needed to make us start clinking empty glasses and stumbling out into the zone with a hesitating step—at the peak of excitement our conversations took on the sharp and belligerent accents of a drunken brawl. I usually left the shop late in the afternoon. That comedy was not a fantastic fiction but, on the contrary, a substitute for life down to its smallest details.

It was twilight in the zone. Before the barracks stood small groups of prisoners, talking in low voices. The young men moved off towards the women's barrack to call out girls whom they knew. Couples passed on the paths, there was laughter everywhere, prisoners stopped on their way to exchange a few words with others and invite them to their barracks. The evening sky hung over the camp like an opaque membrane, and from the direction of the forest blew a small blizzard, carrying whirls of snow which it swept into undulating drifts. On the horizon the first lights were being lit in the village. Sometimes we stopped by the guard-house, looking at them without a word, lost in thoughts of that other world which lived its own life, observed all the unchangeable laws of day, evening and night, and seemed not to know that only a mile away it was being watched by many envious eyes. What did those people, who were now switching on their lights beyond those windows, think of us? Did they hate us as they had been taught to do, or did they perhaps sympathise with us secretly, looking through their frosted windows at the columns of smoke rising from that small scrap of earth where two thousand prisoners were trying to find some consolation? Would they have believed that we were still alive, if they could have seen our dead faces and touched our dried, ulcerated bodies, if they had glimpsed our hardened hearts? We ourselves were near to doubting it as we looked each other in the eyes, then how could those unintentional abettors of our suffering think that we lived?

I walked round to the barracks where I had friends among the prisoners. At this time of the evening almost everyone was writing letters home or reading over old letters from home. They sat round the tables and on the bunks, leaning over the paper which was spread out on their wooden boxes, lost in thought, their faces flushed with the effort of writing and marked with an expression of longing. In every corner groups of prisoners discussed with excitement the composition of letters to the outside world, what could be said and what had to be concealed from the camp censors and from the recipients. Those who could write walked slowly up and down between the bunks, loudly offering their services to the illiterate for a piece of bread. Prisoners who knew that they would get no letters from home, who had no relations in the area covered by the Soviet postal system, joined the groups where letters were being read aloud. We all felt the troubles and sorrows of our companions, and the barrack really became one large family. There is no need to say how much those moments meant to me, deprived as I was of contact with my own family, able only to share the family news of my friends in the camp.

Letters home were usually almost identical and their style was a compromise between the limitations which the camp censorship imposed on correspondence and the prisoners' need to express their true feelings. "I am in good health, I'm working and thinking of you, and I wish you the same"—that was the formula which satisfied the authorities. "Time passes slowly, and I'm counting the days until I see you again"—so wrote prisoners, trying in one short phrase to give their families some approximate idea of their agonies. "I've been in hospital, but I'm quite well now"; or "Send me some onions, for they're very rare here in the north"; or "As you know, I've never worked in the forest before, so I have to learn everything from the beginning"—these outwardly indifferent sentences were the source of all information about life in the camp for those outside who could read between the lines.

In the foresters' barrack I knew a Don Cossack called Pamfilov who used to read me letters from his son. Out of them grew a curious story, the more interesting because in the middle of 1941 it found an unexpected climax in the camp itself.

The old Cossack had a son in the Red Army, a young lieutenant in a panzer division, whose photograph stood, in a silver paper frame, by the father's bunk in the barrack. I knew that in 1934 the collectivisation of land had robbed old Pamfilov of a large farm near the Don; he had been sent into so-called "voluntary exile" in Siberia, where he had worked as an agricultural instructor until his arrest in 1937. His wife died in Siberia, and the son was conscripted into the army at the age of eighteen. Pamfilov was a real kulak, of the kind seldom met in Russia these days: stubborn, arrogant, avaricious, distrustful and hard-working. He hated the system of collective farms with all his heart, was full of contempt for the Soviet régime, and deeply attached to memories of the land which had once been his. Even so he worked as few prisoners in his brigade could, with as much devotion and concentration as if it was his own forest that he was clearing. The camp authorities often singled him out as an example to the rest, forgetting that the secret of his hard work lay in a rare combination of two factors: first, he was incredibly strong—his knotted, sinuous body, covered with hard skin from which, it seemed, a knife dropped from above would have slid off, might well have been carved out of the oldest and toughest oak; and second, he wanted above all to see his son again before he died. Pamfilov loved his Sasha with inhuman devotion. Often, after work, he lay down on his bunk and gazed for hours at the photograph by his side, stroking it with his gnarled fingers, with so much longing and nostalgia in his stare that, if roused suddenly, he would wake as if from profound sleep. Suppressing his native suspiciousness, he believed that hard and conscientious work would finally earn him the reward of a visit from his son.

His love was not weakened even by the knowledge that it was not being fully returned. Sasha's letters—we knew them almost by heart, so many times had Pamfilov read each one aloud to us—were short and restrained, and recalled fragments of ready-made political propaganda. Usually, Sasha was glad that his father was well and working hard, wrote of his promotions and his hopes of a military career, added a few remarks on the subject of the happiness of life in the Soviet Union, and recommended his father to the justice of our "Socialist Fatherland". Old Pamfilov read slowly the first and the second paragraphs, skipped with irritation through the third, and was always delighted by the last, carefully weighing every word. "You see," he would explain eagerly and with slight embarrassment, "that is what he has to write, but this comes from the heart. I like that—'the justice of our Soviet Fatherland'! It is to God that he recommends me, Sashenka, my only son. They can't change the boy's soul, even if the devil goes to work on him. I brought him up, I, Pamfilov, a Cossack from the Don, master of my own land." He was known in the camp as "that old yeoman Pamfilov", and about fifty prisoners at least must have known Sasha from letters and reminiscences. But few of them shared the father's certainty about the boy's soul; other prisoners had letters from home without a word about "our Socialist Fatherland". Pamfilov himself must have felt that it was not so simple, for after every letter he sought assurance in our faces. "Of course they won't change his soul, Pamfilov," we would say despite our private apprehensions, "of course they won't. A good seed will never breed a bad crop."

But Sasha's letters were all very old, for they dated mostly from the year 1939. The last one, written in November 1939, had reached Pamfilov in March 1940, well before my arrival in the camp. Then there was a long period without news, but Pamfilov filled in the gaps by re-reading the old letters. He found an attentive listener in me, for I was like a man who has started reading a serial in the middle and listens with interest to the previous instalments. That is how our friendship grew: thanks to me the old letters became fresh once more.

Re-reading the stained and crumpled pieces of paper, Pamfilov lost some of his feeling of time and once, looking over his shoulder, I caught him altering the dates. But he was unable to hide his anxiety, which increased as he gradually realised that month after month was passing and not once had the name Pamfilov appeared on the letter-list by the posting-box. Prisoners in a camp may receive an unlimited number of letters, although their own correspondence is restricted to one a month; Pamfilov did not miss a single opportunity to write and ask his son for a letter—the only thing which gave his own life any meaning. And though he tried to justify Sasha's behaviour, as if not only his feelings but also his family honour were at stake, we were not as blind as he. We looked in silence at his tired face and red, dry eyes; his hands trembled as they plunged into the little bag hanging round his neck in which he kept his son's letters, like those of a miser who is no longer able to distinguish real jewels from fakes. We knew that by disregarding his intuition he was shielding himself from what he knew to be the truth.

At last, in March 1941, Pamfilov had another letter. It had taken over a year to reach him, for the date—February 1940—had been but indistinctly crossed out by the censor and was just readable. Sasha wrote that urgent affairs would not allow him to write for some time. The stereotyped phrases about the power of the Soviet Union and our Socialist Fatherland were unusually full of fire, and the letter ended with a sentence in which the son justified and even praised his father's imprisonment as a "sign of historical necessity". Pamfilov closed his eyes and his hands fell to his knees, still holding the paper. We were all silent, for what could we have said? Pamfilov, who knew what the earth was and what fatherly love was, could never have understood a conception so difficult as that of "historical necessity". A few tears trickled out from under his closed eyelids. Then he dropped down on the bunk and quietly whispered: "I've lost my son, my son is dead."

The next day Pamfilov did not go out to work, and was punished by three days' solitary confinement on bread and water in the camp prison. This broke his resistance and he returned to the forest, although he no longer worked hard there. In the evenings he would come back silent and morose, and would not speak to anyone. His neighbours on the bunk told me that one night, as he sat by the fire very late, he got up from the bench, took the little bag from his neck, and threw it into the flames.

In April a transport of officers and soldiers from the Finnish front who had been sentenced to ten years for surrendering to the enemy passed through Yercevo. I was out at work that day, but when we came back to the zone towards morning Dimka told me with excitement that among them was Sasha Pamfilov. He had arrived in the morning, enquired where old Pamfilov was living, and lain down on his father's bunk. Other prisoners must have told him what effect his last letter had had on his father, for when the old Cossack returned to the barrack after work, Sasha jumped down to the ground and backed against the wall. Pamfilov went pale, trembled, dropped his empty mess-can, and advanced on his son with a mad gleam in his eyes. "Come on, Pamfilov," the prisoners cried from their bunks, "give him a taste of his father's fist!" But Pamfilov suddenly sat down on the bench, his head drooped as if he was fainting, and in the deep silence he whispered: "My son, my own dear son. . . ."

All night they talked quietly on the father's bunk, and the next morning Sasha was taken away on a transport for Nyandoma. Afterwards we saw old Pamfilov every day, working hard and patiently as before, as if he wanted to show his gratitude to the camp for at last uniting him with his son.

*   *   *   *   *

Toward the evening of the rest-day, when the time of our main meal was approaching, we dispersed to our own barracks and seldom went out again. The last hours of the day were spent in conversation. We lay on the bunks closer to each other than usual, listening to someone's story or talking in the atmosphere of intimacy which common imprisonment creates when the daily struggle for existence does not put barriers of distrust and instinctive hostility between the prisoners.

At that time of the evening our barrack became warm and homely, and the atmosphere was almost domestic. Boots and rags were drying on the chimney breast over a roaring fire, whose flames cast wavering shadows on the prisoners' rugged faces. Round the tables they played draughts or dice, and the sounds of guitars or mouth-organs cut across the chatter of a hundred voices. Even hunger seemed to be resting on that one day. On all faces one saw only peace, and the sudden swirls of the blizzard, which lifted whirls of snow into the air and hurled them violently at the roof, heightened the feeling, if not of absolute peace, then at least of temporary rest, in the barrack below.

During several rest-days in succession, at least half our barrack listened, with rapt attention and without the slightest signs of boredom, to the repeated story of Rusto Karinen's unsuccessful attempt to escape from the camp in the winter of 1940. Karinen was a Finn from the 42nd (porters') brigade who had come to Russia illegally in 1933. As a qualified steel-worker, he had at once found well-paid work in Leningrad, where he lived comfortably, having learnt to speak Russian quite well, until the purge which followed the assassination of Kirov. Then he was arrested and accused of bringing secret instructions from Finland to the assassins. It would be difficult to think of a more improbable accusation, for all the investigations in the Kirov case—even though they originated a whole wave of arrest and imprisonment, and some students of Soviet problems consider them to be the starting-point of the Great Purges—never led to a public trial, and it is most probable that Nicolayev, the Leningrad student who shot Kirov, did so from purely personal motives. Karinen, an intelligent worker with some education and a wide experience of life, realised after the first few months of uninterrupted nightly hearings that the technique of Soviet inquisition is intended primarily not to ascertain the truth, but rather to achieve a compromise whereby the accused allows himself to be convicted by choosing the most convenient fiction from a number of fictitious crimes. He therefore agreed to play the part of an emissary from a foreign terrorist organisation, on condition that they would not require details about his superiors in Helsinki and his Leningrad contacts. His confession thus confirmed the indictment without giving any further details, and he declared that he had not carried out the mission with which he had been entrusted. But although his reasoning was on the whole accurate, Karinen miscalculated that small move. What for him was a compromise, a fiction designed to spare him further suffering in a situation from which there was no way out, after a few days became for the examining officer a scrap of truth extracted with difficulty from the accused and only the starting-point for further investigations. But this time Karinen would not go a step further, and, what was more, he began to retract his first confession. In January 1936 he spent three weeks in the condemned cell, and in February, quite unexpectedly, a sentence of ten years' hard labour was read out to him. He came to Yercevo in the middle of 1939, having spent three years in the Kotlas camp.

His attempted escape at the time of the Russo-Finnish war had become a legendary exploit in the camp. Every prisoner "plans" his escape from the camp in periods of self-confidence, and tries to include his best friends in the attempt. But these plans contained more naïve self-deception, more desire for an illusory hope of life, than any chance of success or even definite preparation. Projects of escape were especially popular among Polish prisoners, for besides suffering the agonies of camp life, we were also tormented by the thought of our own idleness while somewhere far away, on battle-fronts with exotic names, the war was being fought without us. We would often meet in one of the barracks, an intimate group of Poles, to discuss the details of the plan; we collected scraps of metal found at work, old boxes and fragments of glass which we deluded ourselves could be made into an improvised compass; we gathered information about the surrounding countryside, and the distances,

climatic conditions and geographical pecularities of the north—and
we were not discouraged by the knowledge that we were like
children, fighting their battles with tin soldiers. We all felt that our
preparations were ludicrous, but we did not have the courage to
admit it to each other. In the nightmare land to which we had been
brought from the West on hundreds of good trains, every grasp at
our own private day-dreams gave us fresh life. After all, if membership of a non-existent terrorist organisation can be a crime punished
by ten years in a labour camp, then why should a sharpened nail
not be a compass-needle, a piece of wood a ski, and a scrap of paper,
covered with scribbled dots and lines, a map? I remember a junior
officer of the Polish cavalry who during the worst periods of hunger
in the camp found enough strength of will to cut a thin slice of
bread from his daily ration, dry it over the fire and save these scraps
in a sack which he concealed in some mysterious hiding-place in the
barrack. Years later, we met again in the Iraq desert, and as we
recalled prison days over a bottle in an army tent, I made fun of his
"plan" of escape. But he answered gravely: "You shouldn't laugh
at that. I survived the camp thanks to the hope of escape, and I
survived the mortuary thanks to my store of bread. A man can't
live if he doesn't know what he's living for."

The Finn's story was not very instructive as far as technical
details of escape were concerned, but we always listened to it with
bated breath, as if the contemplation of his brave step would give
us strength for further survival. In the corner of the barrack where
he sat talking, with his legs hanging down from an upper bunk,
complete silence reigned, interrupted only by impatient questions
and cries anticipating the events before they occurred in his
narrative. We knew the whole thing almost by heart, and yet we
listened to it again and again with unflagging interest. Karinen
talked slowly, in fluent Russian with a hardly perceptible foreign
accent, gesticulating and breaking off every few minutes to swallow
a sip of hvoya. His small, swollen eyes seemed to be re-living the
epic, looking for the way in his lonely wandering through the snowbound Archangel forests.

He first decided to escape when the Russo-Finnish war changed
from a short armed expedition into a prolonged tactical war. He
could not say what caused him to make up his mind, whether it was
some vestigial patriotic response or the hope that military activities
had weakened the watchfulness of the frontier guards even on the

Russian side. He knew the frontier country, for he had crossed it to reach Russia, and he planned to steal through the forests in the daytime, sleeping in wayside villages; it was a journey of several hundred kilometres, from the White Sea to the southern shore of Lake Onega, and from there to the northern shore of Lake Ladoga, which leads in an almost straight line to the Finnish frontier. Only the other four prisoners of his team in one of the forest brigades knew of his intentions. He set off during the lunch break, unnoticed by anyone except his companions. If the guard did not notice his absence until the evening, when he checked the numbers as the brigade marched back to the zone, Karinen would have gained about five hours, when he could be three miles away from the forest and six from the camp. He had dressed with particular care that morning, and under his wadded prison outfit he wore all his underclothes and the suit which he had brought with him into the camp, in which he intended to show himself in the villages. He carried a small sack with a few dried slices of black bread, a piece of fat contributed by one of the prisoners in whom he had confided, a bottle of vegetable oil purchased from a free official for a pair of shoes, and some onions; in his pocket he had three boxes of matches and about two hundred roubles (although he refused to tell us where he had obtained the money, it is most likely that he had smuggled in and hidden some foreign currency when he first came to the camp, and later exchanged it for roubles with one of the camp officials). Instead of a compass he had a deep conviction that "it's enough to keep walking west—in the morning with your back to the sun, with your face to it in the evening."

He walked fast during the first few hours, not stopping even to quench his thirst, but as he walked he gathered handfuls of snow from the trees and moistened his parched lips. Towards evening he heard the distant, muffled sound of several rifle-shots, and he guessed that the guard had discovered his absence and was giving the alarm, though he doubted whether the shots could be heard in the camp itself. He had the whole night before him, for the pursuit would not start out until morning. But when darkness fell he lost his sense of direction, and could not go on. He found a place in a large hollow, dug a hole in the snow, covered the top thickly with branches and spent the whole night curled up inside. At the very bottom of his lair, between his outstretched legs, he lit a small fire and kept it going all night, blowing at it with all his strength and sheltering it from above with his frozen hands. He did not sleep that night, but he did not feel as if he was awake. The winter that year was hard and frosty; he inhaled the air into his lungs with painful gasps, but the thick layer of snow outside the hole, the roof of fir branches, the small flame of the fire, his double clothing and finally his own breath provided him with the minimum of heat necessary for survival. And though he was at liberty for the first time in five years, he did not feel free as he crouched tensely in his lair, listening to every noise of the mysterious forest, while his back froze to the wall of the hole. He dozed feverishly for short periods, and woke at the sound of his own shouting, as if he was turning on the hard planks of a prison bunk. Several times he raised himself lightly in his place to stretch his body and beat his chilled hands against his sides. At one moment, probably towards dawn, he suddenly thought that he heard voices and the barking of dogs. He tensed his whole body to jump out and run, but everything was quiet again. All around him was the night—thick and impenetrable, icy and menacing—a night without end and without hope. Huge lumps of snow fell from the trees, hitting the ground with a thud which made him think that he was being pursued. He felt terribly lonely, and for a while even thought of returning to the camp.

At dawn he crawled out of his hiding-place, washed his face with snow, waited until the sky was light enough to see the sunrise, and then started off in the opposite direction. He walked slowly, for his bones were aching, his body was painfully hot, he felt fever and hunger alternately. About noon he took a piece of bread from his sack, poured a little vegetable oil on it, and cut a tiny morsel of fat with his penknife—that was the daily ration which he had decided on before setting out, estimating that his whole stock of food would last thirty days. The day was bright, and the sun, whitish-pink from the frost, seemed to be bringing the forest back to life. He walked more briskly, inhaling deeply, looking at the green outlines of branches under thick layers of snow. He passed clearings where enormous northern fir trees, torn up from the earth by the Arctic winds, protruded up into the sky, their thin roots spread out and covered with frozen mud, as if they were stretching their hands from the very depths of the earth hideously bared from their rotting bodies. With a long stick he felt in front of him to avoid wolf-traps and hollows in the ground. Every hour he stopped to hear if the pursuit was catching up with him. He supposed that the police-dogs had lost his scent, for when he trod lightly his felt boots left almost no trace in the dry, powdery snow.

That evening his heart was full of hope, and having dug another hole in a snow-covered hollow he lit a larger fire than the night before. For the first time since his escape, about midnight, he fell sound asleep, and woke only at dawn. He intended to approach no human habitation until he had covered a distance of at least fifty miles from the camp, after a week's march. On the fourth evening, as he was digging his usual hole and covering it with cut branches, he noticed a glow on the horizon, then the lightning-stroke of a searchlight pierced the night and vanished immediately. He was terrified, for it meant that there was a camp near by. That night he did not light a fire and almost froze to death, sitting in the snow with his jerkin drawn over his head, his hands inside the sleeves and his legs resting on a branch. In the morning he rose with a great effort of will from his snowy arm-chair, stretched himself with difficulty, and slowly began to rub snow on his frozen hands. He started walking a little later, hoping that he was passing the most westerly of the Kargopol camp sections, at a distance of about thirteen miles from Yercevo, perhaps Nyandoma. But he could not dispel his feeling of anxiety, and forgetting his original rule to follow the sun he turned off to the side, away from the place where he had seen the searchlight beam, and made his way north-west. He was walking slowly now, falling and stumbling on the way, had difficulty in swallowing his daily ration, and often had to rub snow on his burning forehead. He was near breaking-point, and though he did not remember this exactly, he thought that tears were streaming from his eyes although he was not crying. All around there was silence, his every step resounded and echoed infinitely. He was so frightened by his solitude that he started talking to himself in Finnish, for the first time in six years. Soon he ran out of subjects and words for this monologue, and he could only repeat a few phrases, even dimmer and longer unused—a prayer remembered in his childhood.

In the evening, as he could see no glow in the sky, he lit a larger fire and slept the whole night through, waking whenever the flame died down. He woke up with a sensation of strange discord within himself: he was and he was not himself, he remembered that he had escaped and yet he fancied that he was going out to work, he felt fever and numbness in his whole body, he knew what he had to do but could only stumble ahead like a sleep-walker. One thing is certain, that he forgot his principle of orientation that day, and simply walked on. In the afternoon he sat down under a tree and immediately fell asleep. He woke up in the middle of the night, suddenly frightened, and shouted loudly. He thought that he heard an answering call, jumped up and began to run, but after a few steps tripped and fell with his face in the snow. He lay like that for a while, then rose slowly and tried to marshal his thoughts. One idea recurred persistently in his brain: he must light a fire at all cost. It was the sixth night of his escape. By the fire he thawed a little, and decided that at dawn he must find some human settlement where he could rest and get better. The next morning he ate a piece of bread and fat, and started off again, without any idea where he was going. Late in the afternoon he saw, far beyond the forest, several pillars of smoke rising into the air. He walked faster and impatiently, but it was not until evening that he saw lights gleaming on the edge of a clearing. Without taking off his prison clothes, he walked into the first hut that he came to and there, on a bench by the fire, he lost all consciousness.

The village which Karinen found after seven days' wandering in the forest was only eight miles away from Yercevo. The peasants drove him back to the camp and there the guards took him to the internal prison, where, still unconscious, he was beaten so cruelly that for three months he was near death, and even after his life had been saved he had to remain in the hospital for another two months. It was said that Samsonov had never sent out a pursuit, knowing that Karinen would either die in the forest or come back to the camp. He had come back. "You can't escape from the camp, my friends," so Karinen always ended the story, "freedom isn't for us. We're chained to this place for the rest of our lives, even though we aren't wearing chains. We can escape, we can wander about, but in the end we'll come back. That's our fate, our accursed fate." "Don't worry, Rusto Petrovich," the prisoners would comfort him, "it was worth it, after all. You had a week's freedom and five months in the hospital." "That's true," he would answer sadly, "but you still can't escape. Our life is here, brothers, this is where we shall end. When freedom itself is against us, how can we escape?"

"Let's go to sleep," the prisoners would say, looking at each other immovably. "The rest-day is over. Back to work tomorrow."

And after a moment, from bunk to bunk, from mouth to mouth, passed these whispered words, like a message sent through the cells in prison, whose horror no one who has not known a Soviet camp can understand: "Back to work tomorrow."

PART II

CHAPTER 9

HUNGER

FROM what I observed in the camp it appears that men bear physical and sexual hunger far better than women. The simple law of camp ethics laid it down that those who were in a position to break down a woman's resistance by depriving her of food satisfied both her fundamental needs when she finally gave in. If the recollection of all that happened in Europe during the late war is to have any meaning at all, we must forget the principles of every-day morality on which the life of our grandfathers and fathers was founded in the second half of the nineteenth century and the first decades of the twentieth century, that period which seemed to realise before our eyes the positivist myth of progress. An orthodox Marxist would say that there is no such thing as absolute morality, since individual experience is conditioned by material surroundings. This means that every epoch, every country and every social class creates its own morality, or that all these three factors together create something which we may call the unwritten law of behaviour in one particular place. The experiences of the past twenty years in Germany and Soviet Russia support this theory to a certain extent. There it has been proved that when the body has reached the limit of its endurance, one cannot, as was once believed, rely on strength of character and conscious recognition of spiritual values; that there is nothing, in fact, which man cannot be forced to do by hunger and pain. This "new morality" is not a code of decent human behaviour, for its standard is expediency in action towards men, and though today its fangs are sharp and dangerous, its tradition reaches back to the Spanish Inquisition on which it cut those teeth. We must not dismiss this fact lightly. The old morality of the Catholic Church and the new morality of the Soviet system share the fundamental conviction that man without faith—faith in the revealed system of spiritual values in the one case or in the enforced system of material values in the other—is a shapeless heap of rubbish. Lysenko's revolution in genetics reversed basically-related principles of the Catholic Church. In the latter, man is lost in the whirlpools of sin and damnation if he is not saved by the light

131

of supernatural grace; in the materialist creed he becomes what artificially developed conditions make him. But both systems deprive man of his will, and it only depends on which formula of the aim of human life is adopted whether the heap of rubbish will bring forth the required specimen of biological cultivation or the blessed flower of the human soul. I myself belong neither to those whom their experiences of the horrors of war have forced into acquiescence in the "new morality", nor to those who see in these horrors further proof of man's impotence when faced with the power of Satan. I became convinced that a man can be human only under human conditions, and I believe that it is fantastic nonsense to judge him by actions which he commits under inhuman conditions —as if water could be measured by fire, and earth by Hell. But the trouble is that a writer who wishes to describe a Soviet labour camp objectively must descend to the depths of Hell where he should not seek human motives behind inhuman deeds. It is from there that the faces of his dead and perhaps still living friends look up at him, and their lips, blue with hunger and frost, whisper: "Tell them the truth about us, tell them what we were brought to."

In defence of women it should be said that the camp morality, like any other system of values, created also its own hypocrisy. Thus, for instance, no one would dream of blaming a young boy who, in order to improve his conditions, became the lover of the elderly woman doctor, but a pretty girl who from hunger gave herself to the repulsive old man in charge of the bread store was, naturally, a whore. The regular monthly denunciations to the Third Section, by means of which almost all brigadiers and technical experts settled their personal accounts, were never questioned as immoral, but a woman who left the zone at night to sleep with the camp chief was dubbed a prostitute, and of the worst type, for she broke the solidarity of prisoners against free men. It was natural for a newly-arrived prisoner to hand over to his brigadier the remnants of his civilian clothing in order to obtain a good rating of his working capacity (for that decided the amount of rations for each prisoner), but there were some who were shocked when a penniless girl, bending under the weight of an axe in the forest, gave to the same brigadier on her first or second evening in the camp her one remaining worldly possession—her body. A prisoner who was found stealing bread from another would probably die as a result of the punishment meted out to him by the urkas, who were the highest law-givers and judges of camp ethics; but among the Poles there was a certain priest who disguised his pastoral dignity under a prisoner's rags, whose fixed price for confession and absolution was 200 grammes of bread (100 grammes less than the old Uzbek who read fortunes from hands), and who lived among his parishioners in an aura of sanctity.

The cause of this complex and obscure phenomenon is the subconscious desire, which exists in every larger community, to drag under the censure of "public opinion" offenders who have been caught red-handed, in order to whiten one's own conscience at a small price. Women were fitted for the part of scapegoats not only because they seldom had an opportunity to trade with anything but their own bodies, but also because they brought with them, even to the camp, the burden of the conventional morality of the outside world. which rules that every man who possesses a woman after only a few hours of flirtation and acquaintance is a dashing seducer, and that every woman who gives herself to a newly-met man is a wanton. Individual moral outlook, and consequently hypocrisy, varied according to the circumstances of a prisoner's life before imprisonment. The problem did not really exist for the Russians, accustomed to "five-rouble marriages" and copulation practised in public conveniences according to immediate physiological needs, and their attitude to it was expressed by the mockery with which they greeted the institution of legal equality for women under the new régime. Foreign prisoners, including veteran communists, frequently shook their heads over "the general decline of morality in Russia". Anyway, it is true that hunger, more frequently than anything else, broke down the resistance of women, and once it was broken, there was no obstacle to stop them on the downward path which led them to the very depths of sexual bestiality. Some gave in not only with the hope of improving their conditions or finding a powerful protector, but also with the hope of maternity. This must not be taken too sentimentally. Pregnant women in camps are freed from work for three months before and six months after the baby's delivery. Six months was the period considered sufficient for the suckling of a child until it was old enough to be taken away from its mother and transported to some unknown destination. The maternity barrack in Yercevo was always full of women who with pathetic gravity pushed the burden of their swollen bellies in front of them as they walked to the kitchen for their soup. But it is difficult to talk of feelings, of genuine human feelings, when we were forced to make love before the eyes of our fellow-prisoners, or at best in the store of old clothing, on piles of sweaty and stinking rags. After all these years one retains a memory of disgust like rolling in the slime left behind at the bottom of an empty fountain, and a deep distaste for oneself and for the woman who once seemed so close. . . .

In January 1941, when I had been at the camp several weeks, a young Polish girl, the daughter of an officer from Tarnopol, arrived with a transport. She was really lovely: slim and supple, with a girlishly fresh face and tiny breasts whose outline could only just be guessed at behind the blue blouse of her school uniform. An informal jury of urkas rated the "young mare" very highly and, doubtless to whet their proletarian appetites, called her "the general's daughter". The girl, however, held out very well; she walked out to work with her head raised proudly, and repulsed any man who ventured near her, with darting, angry looks. In the evenings she returned from work rather more humbly, but still untouchable and modestly haughty. She went straight from the guard-house to the kitchen for her portion of soup, and did not leave the women's barrack again during the night. Therefore it looked as if she would not quickly fall a victim to the night hunts of the camp zone. There was also little possibility that she would be broken by hunger, for she was assigned to the 56th brigade, made up of women and invalids, which patched torn sacks and sorted vegetables at the food supply centre, and though the prisoners of the 56th did not have the same opportunities for theft as we had in the porters' brigade, yet the work was comparatively light. I was not then familiar enough with camp life to foresee the outcome of this silent struggle, and without hesitation I accepted the proposition of the engineer Polenko, supervisor of the vegetable store at the food supply centre, and bet him half a loaf of bread that the girl would not give in. This wager excited me particularly from a patriotic point of view—I wanted to see the red-and-white colours of Poland flying, so to speak, from the mast-head of triumphant virtue. After seven months of prison and camp I was so exhausted physically that I had as yet no desire for women, and I was ready to believe the warning of my first interrogator—"You will live, yes, but you won't want to sleep with a woman." But taking advantage of the position which I enjoyed as a porter friendly with the urkas, I decided to cheat Polenko and, introducing myself to her as a student from Warsaw in order that she should not be able to plead the excuse of a misalliance, I proposed to the girl a fictitious marriage, which would have given her some protection according to the peculiar *ius primæ noctis* of the camp. I no longer remember the exact words of her answer, but it must have been something like "How dare you!", for I gave it up. But Polenko, while she was working under his supervision at the vegetable store, took special care to see that she did not steal even a single rotten carrot or salted tomato from the barrels. About a month after we had agreed on the bet he came one evening to my barrack, and without a word threw a torn pair of knickers on my bunk. Carefully, and in silence, I cut half a loaf of bread and gave it to him.

From that time the girl underwent a complete change. She never hurried to get her soup from the kitchen as before, but after her return from work wandered about the camp zone till late at night like a cat on heat. Whoever wanted to could have her, on a bunk, under the bunk, in the separate cubicles of the technical experts, or in the clothing store. Whenever she met me, she turned her head aside, and tightened her lips convulsively. Once, entering the potato store at the centre, I found her on a pile of potatoes with the brigadier of the 56th, the hunchbacked half-breed Levkovich; she burst into a spasmodic fit of weeping, and as she returned to the camp zone in the evening she held back her tears with two tiny fists. I met her again in 1943, in Palestine. She was already an old woman. A tired smile on her wrinkled face revealed the holes in her yellow, decayed teeth, and her sweaty cotton shirt was bursting under the weight of two enormous hanging breasts like those of a nursing mother.

A similar episode was well-known in Yercevo, not because in itself it was anything but usual and commonplace, but because its heroine had also put up a long resistance by camp standards. It concerned Tania, a black-haired singer of the Moscow Opera, who, according to custom, had been invited with other artistes to a ball given for the foreign diplomatic corps, where she had disobeyed the preliminary instructions of the N.K.V.D. by dancing more than the prescribed amount with the Japanese Ambassador—the suspicion of espionage earned her a sentence of ten years in the labour camp. As a "political suspect" she was immediately assigned to the foresters' brigade. What could that filigree princess with thin, delicate hands do in a forest? Throw twigs on the fire, perhaps, if she had the luck to be under a human brigadier. But, unfortunately for her, she was desired by Vanya, the short urka in charge of her brigade, and she was put to work clearing felled fir trees of bark with a huge axe which she could hardly lift. Lagging several yards behind the hefty foresters, she arrived in the zone at evening with hardly enough strength left to crawl to the kitchen and collect her first cauldron (needless to say, the urka had assessed her working capacity below the 100 per cent norm). It was obvious that she had a high temperature, but the medical orderly was a friend of Vanya's and would not free her from work. This went on for two weeks, a record of endurance under the conditions of the forest brigade; then one evening Tania quietly entered the foresters' barrack, and not looking Vanya in the face, dropped heavily on to his bunk. She had a lucky instinct, treated the whole thing light-heartedly and became something like a brigade mascot until the lustful hand of some camp chief dragged her out by the hair from the rubbish-heap and placed her behind a table in the camp accountants' office. Later, we heard her singing pretty Russian songs at a camp concert in the barrack of "self-taught creative activities", while threatening murmurs of "Moscow whore" could be heard in the foresters' corner. What would happen when she no longer pleased her chief and had to return to the "forest boys"?

Hunger. . . . Hunger is a horrible sensation, which becomes transformed into an abstraction, into nightmares fed by the mind's perpetual fever. The body is like an over-heated machine, working at increased speed and on less fuel, and the wasted arms and legs come to resemble torn driving-belts. There is no limit to the physical effects of hunger beyond which tottering human dignity might still keep its uncertain but independent balance. Many times I flattened my pale face against the frosted glass pane of the kitchen window, to beg with a dumb look for another ladleful of "thin" soup from the Leningrad thief Fyedka who was in charge. And I remember that my best friend, an old communist and the comrade of Lenin's youth, the engineer Sadovski, once, on the empty platform by the kitchen, snatched from my hand a canful of soup and, running away with it, did not even wait until he reached the latrine but on the way there drank up the hot mess with feverish lips. If God exists, let him punish mercilessly those who break others with hunger.

Only the porters, when the supervision at the food supply centre was relaxed, and those prisoners who, armed with special passes, left the camp zone to work outside without a guard, had any opportunities of satisfying their hunger. But even beyond the zone the situation was just as bad. From the guard-house we could sometimes see queues in front of the small wooden hut at the end of the village outside the zone. The whole garrison and administrative staff of the camp were entitled to buy there, above their normal rations, two kilograms of black bread and a length of horse-sausage every day, and once a week half a litre of vodka. Within the village there was, it is true, another shop, called the "speclarok", but that one opened its doors only to ten specified camp dignitaries. At the head of this list came the chief commander of the whole Kargopol camp, Captain of State Security Kolicyn, next the chief of the Third Section in Kargopol, then the officer in charge of the camp food supply, Blumen, the chief of the Yercevo camp section, Samsonov, finally the chiefs of the other six main camp sections. I remember Blumen best of them all, as the whole food supply centre trembled with fear whenever he came round on a tour of inspection. This fat beast, with an enormous gold watch on his right wrist and innumerable rings on the fingers of both hands, was always preceded in the dusk by a faint cloud of perfume. He said little, and then always the same thing: "You must work hard, prisoners, this is not a health resort." I can still see his flushed, angry, fat face when he noticed a rotten carrot hidden in the bosom of one of the women workers and, ripping her blouse open across her breast, slapped both her cheeks with a podgy hand. This incident was the subject of comments whose tendency it was not difficult to guess among prisoners; no one who has not lived in a Soviet labour camp can realise the extent of anti-Semitism in Russia, which becomes increasingly violent and vengeful as it is repressed and eliminated from above. The "fat ten" of the camp command were supplied better than the rest, and often our good-natured guard could not repress a sigh of complaint as we unloaded champagne or confetti for their speclarok. Even the free had their own hierarchies, their petty rivalries and troubles.

*   *   *   *   *

Only in the bath-house was it possible to examine the effects of hunger, for in the barracks the prisoners seldom undressed for the night. The small bath-hut was always full of murky grey light which filtered in through the dirty window-panes, and of steam which rose from a huge vat of boiling water. Before going in, we handed over our clothes to be deloused, and received in return a piece of grey soap the size of a domino counter. When the clothes had been deloused they were brought in, hung on iron rings on a long pole, by an elderly priest who, sloping the pole, let the bundles fall on to the floor of the passage. It was pleasant to feel the hard plasters of heated clothing on a clean body. There was no other way of changing clothes; we went to the bath-house once every three weeks, and these visits were the only time that we really washed ourselves, for usually we just moistened with snow our encrusted eyes, our noses hard as shells, and our cracked lips. A thin, half-naked teacher from Novosybirsk, who looked like a Hindu yogi as he watched us bathing, his eyes covered with a thin cataract, gave us each two pails of water, one boiling, and one cold. Thin shadowy forms, with drooping testicles and fallen stomachs and chests, their legs covered with open sores and joined like two matchsticks to thin hips, bent under the weight of the pails, puffing from exhaustion in the steamy atmosphere of the hut. The Novosybirsk teacher here played the part of a eunuch in a Turkish harem, for his functions were the same when women came to the bath-house. For a pinch of tobacco he would tell us whether their breasts and thighs were beautiful, whether the old ones were flattened like blocks hit with a steam-hammer so that their heads grew straight out of mon-strously widened hips supported on legs like knotted branches, or whether the young ones still retained the vestiges of girlish modesty and the straight line of their shoulders.

One day someone stole my piece of soap from the bench and I swore angrily in Polish. A small, grey-haired old man, standing next to me over his bucket of hot water, raised his gentle eyes towards me and asked in Polish, enunciating each word with difficulty: "Did you by any chance know the poet Tuvim?"

"Not personally, no," I replied, bewildered by this unusual question, "though, of course, I have read . . ."

"Well then, you can wash my back for me."

As I soaped his thin back he explained everything to me, coughing incessantly as he did so. His name was Boris Lazarovich N., a professor who, before the First World War, had studied at the Russian Secondary School in Lodz in Poland, and had gone to

Russia after the Revolution of 1918. From his schooldays he remembered a younger fellow-student, Tuvim, and he had learnt from the press that he had become a well-known poet.   In 1925 N., then Professor of French Literature in the prose class of the Bryusov Institute in Moscow,* arranged for Olga, a young Polish girl from Lodz, to join him in Russia: he married her and placed her at the Polytechnic, and several years later obtained for her a position as electrical engineer at a Moscow factory. In 1937 N. and his wife were arrested and given ten-year sentences for organising a literary salon which discussed exclusively Polish literature. After three years apart they met by chance in one of the Kargopol camp sections, and now they had arrived together in Yercevo, an accident hitherto unprecedented in the annals of Soviet labour camps.

The same evening I met Olga, a young, good-looking woman, who followed every movement of her helpless husband with an expression of sadness and dumb adoration, and the next day the three of us were already the best of friends. The old man had not long before been thrown out of his brigade because of his failing strength; he was given a card for the first cauldron and sent to the mortuary. His wife was assigned to the 56th brigade, and spent her days repairing sacks and sorting vegetables at the food supply centre. N. could not bear hunger and the thought of food became the one obsession of his old age. Sometimes I managed to bring from the centre a few roasted potatoes or a piece of salted treska, and when he had swallowed greedily everything that I had surreptitiously slipped into his hand, he would talk to me about his former life. He had lectured on French prose, chiefly Balzac, at the Bryusov Institute, and he told me of the strange and varying fortunes which Balzac's reputation had suffered in Russia owing to the constant changes in the official political outlook. In the first years after the Revolution Balzac was the widely-worshipped author of *The Peasants;* in the thirties this enthusiasm dropped in face of the cross-fire of Marxist literary criticism, which violently attacked Balzac's royalist position; and just before the Great Purge he became popular again as the unequalled chronicler of

---

* The Bryusov Institute was a school for young writers with courses in prose, poetry, drama, and literary criticism.

nouveaux riches, who then arose from every section of the reigning régime. I remember, too, that N. begged me with tears in his eyes, if I ever left the camp, to read the greatest Russian writer, Goncharov, particularly his brilliant study of Cervantes. Once also, as a proof of his friendship and confidence in me, he brought me an issue of *International Literature* and with great disgust told me to read an article by some English communist called *The Decline and Fall of the British Empire*.

The old professor became very fond of me and even, I venture to say, regarded me as his pupil, while I for my part still look upon him as one of the masters of my youth, even though I could hardly have learnt much from him under the conditions in which we lived then. It sometimes happened that, as I came off the night shift, he would wait for me at the guard-house like an impatient tutor when his pupil is late for a class, and without letting me finish my morning soup, he would drag me off, if the day was sunny, to a small bench near the barbed wire. We would sit together, he trembling with excitement, I half-dead with exhaustion, and looking at the white page of the plain ruled with the long lines of wire, marked off by the clefs of the posts, we rehearsed as if from music our morning exercise. I had to repeat slowly all that I had learnt at previous lessons; whenever I made a mistake the old man corrected me irritably, and when I managed to struggle successfully through wolf-traps bristling with names, facts and his favourite little dicta, he would give me an "excellent", laying the blame for all mistakes on my sleepy eyes and on night work. Occasionally, to my great joy and pride, we exchanged roles, and he listened attentively while I told him of all that had occurred in European and Polish literature since his imprisonment. I remember how his eyes, their fire extinguished by the hopeless struggle with hunger, blazed afresh and his pale cheeks flushed as I told him of Maritain's thomistic theory of art, which I myself had heard at Warsaw University in 1939, just before war broke out. This idyll lasted hardly three months, for in March 1941 N. was sent with a transport to the camp section of Mostovitza—in the nick of time, for a period of terrible hunger was just beginning at Yercevo, and it was becoming increasingly difficult to steal a few potatoes at the centre.

The first signs of this hunger appeared toward the end of winter 1941, and by the spring all life had vanished from the camp. Soup in the kitchens became thinner every day, bread was frequently underweight, and the herrings which were sometimes added, to the great joy of Dimka, to the third cauldron disappeared completely. The effects of this starvation began to be very apparent. The brigades returned from work more slowly; in the evenings one could hardly walk along the paths which were crowded with stumbling victims of night-blindness; in the waiting-room of the medical hut swollen trunk-like legs, covered with festering scurvy sores, were revealed ready for inspection; every night a large sledge brought back to the camp one or two foresters who had fainted at work. Hunger does not relax its hold at night, but on the contrary, it attacks cunningly and forcefully with its hidden weapon. Only Iganov, an old Russian from the carpenters' brigade, prayed till late every night, covering his face with his hands. The rest slept in the oppressive silence of the barrack the feverish sleep of those in pain, sucking in the air with a whistle through half-opened lips, turning restlessly from side to side, gabbling and sobbing in their sleep in a heart-rending whisper. My own dreams assumed a cannibalistic, erotic form; love and hunger returned to their common biological root, releasing from the depths of my sub- conscious images of women made of fresh dough whom I would bite in fantastic orgies till they streamed with blood and milk, twining their arms which smelt like fresh loaves round my burning head. I would wake, exhausted and covered in sweat, usually just as the Moscow-Archangel express passed like an arrow of sound about a mile away from the camp zone. Iganov would still be at his prayers, while Dimka, priest though he was, gazed at him with hatred and contempt, beating out with a spoon his own litany of hunger on the wooden leg stretched out in front of him. Dimka had agreed to help three latrine cleaners for an extra plateful of soup, and he would return to the barrack just before midnight, wet and stinking like a sewer rat. From old habit he would still lift the lid of the rubbish bin, but for a long time now there had been no herring- scraps on its clean bottom. Once he came back looking gay and mysterious, and pulled a piece of bleeding raw meat from the front of his shirt. He roasted it over the dying fire for a long time, and when we were tearing the hard meat with our teeth, he laughed softly: "Let that one pray if he wants to, we'll just go on and finish off this poor little dog who was silly enough to stray into the latrine." "Of course," I answered, laughing, "the heavenly dogs are on chains, guarding the Kingdom of God—they would never stray into a camp." From the two rows of living dead around us sleep forced a weakening sigh, a soft weeping which rose gently like bubbles on the surface of a murky, tainted pool.

It is an old saying that "necessity is the mother of invention", but it took me two months to realise that the flour dropped and swept up after each wagon had been unloaded at the centre could be made into a kind of dough which would serve to fill holes in the stomach. From that time we took small tins with us to the centre, and in the lunch break one of us stood on guard in front of the watchman's hut while we heated the tins and mixed the dough in them with twigs. In the second half of May I perfected this technique, and every day, half an hour before we finished work and returned to the zone, I mixed in a small pan a large piece of soft dough, which I then spread in a thin, even layer over Olga's naked breasts in the darkest corner of the sack-repair hut. Padded like this, Olga passed unscathed through all searches at the guard-house, though we trembled at the thought that the old guard who did no more than gently feel the outlines of the women who passed through the gates might be replaced by the pock-marked wardress Nadyezda Mikhailovna, who would be much more thorough. We would meet after dark in the old-clothing store and divide the food into four portions: one for the store-keeper as payment for the use of the hut, one for Dimka and one for each of us. It happens that even in a labour camp the most fantastic and improbable dreams may come true.

But from Mostovitza came very sad news of Professor N. Prisoners who passed through the transit barrack told me that the old man was dying of hunger, did not wash or shave, never left the mortuary except to collect his food, and, begging on the platform outside the kitchen, frequently had fits of hunger dementia. But once, just before the outbreak of the Russo-German war, Olga received through a prisoner a dirty scrap of paper with a note from her husband. One sentence showed us that his brain was not yet completely destroyed: "Please tell Gustav Yosifovich that at last I can understand what an excellent social-realist Knut Hamsun was."

CHAPTER 10

NIGHTFALL

"We are a beaten lot," they used to say; "our guts
have been knocked out, that's why we shout at
night."—DOSTOEVSKY—*The House of the Dead.*

THE electric light burned in the barracks continuously from dusk
till dawn. Nevertheless, we had a very distinct intimation of the
approaching night.

After work, after the evening soup, we still had two or three
hours' rest left before nightfall. The prisoners spent them in
various occupations: some, sitting on their bunks and swinging
their legs over the sides, mended their worn camp clothing or wrote
letters, leaning on the wooden boxes which contained their possessions; some went out to visit friends in other barracks; the young
men gathered outside the women's barrack; the stakhanovites, who
were allowed to make use of the small shop in the zone, went there
to see if a piece of horse sausage had appeared on the empty
shelves of the dark little room; the sick prepared themselves for a
visit to the medical hut next morning, and the brigadiers hastily
wrote out their statements of productivity norms for the
accountants' office. All these activities had one quality in common
—they imitated the normal occupations of a free life. Our behaviour was a parody of the gestures, habits and responses of our
former existence, observing the symbolic ritual of a dimly remembered routine particularly when the form had lost all meaning
in the conditions of the camp. I frequently heard remarks like: "I
always used to play draughts after supper," or: "My wife always
grumbled because I wandered about propping up other people's
mantelpieces, instead of staying at home and going to sleep. A
habit is a habit, after all, and it's stayed with me all my life." The
subconscious imitation of past freedom saved a prisoner from
despair and made his life in the camp bearable, though he never
stopped to distinguish between illusion and reality. It is difficult to
say how far this instinctive defence mechanism was the natural
behaviour of people who had spent the greatest part of their lives at
liberty, and how far an artificial reaction imposed by the conditions

of slavery. One thing, however, is certain: it is impossible to understand slavery without applying to it even the most deformed
standards of freedom.

The foregoing description, however, applies only to those few
prisoners who made some effort to save themselves from complete
demoralisation. But the majority—a dreadfully overwhelming
majority, of whom I was one at the beginning and at the end of my
imprisonment—left their bunks during the evening only to fill up
the hollowness of their stomachs with a pint or two of the inevitable
hot water. It must be remembered in their favour that after eleven
hours' work on an empty stomach the slightest activity demanded
either an enormous effort of will, or else a temptation strong
enough to conquer exhaustion. The majority of prisoners, who
dreamt of rest throughout the long day and lay on their bunks
motionless after supper, deluded themselves that this suicidal form
of relaxation strengthened the organism of their bodies. In the
camp the normal process was reversed: inertia and apathy hastened
death, while any form of activity postponed it for an unforeseen
period. A prisoner who gave himself up to despair and the thought
of death, without the slightest attempt to overcome it, and who, in
an access of hunger dementia, poured into himself a useless ballast
of hot water, would suddenly die one night, and the dawn revealed
his swollen and monstrously distended body lying on the bunk. If
he avoided that death, similar to the bursting of an inflated bladder,
he would gradually swell out, then return briefly to normal only to
end up in the mortuary by the side of other skeletons like himself.
Prisoners who before dying tried to save themselves by a certain
voluntary exertion lived for several years in relatively good health,
then quite suddenly one day began to swell and died of starvation
swelling when the exhausted heart was unable to go on pumping
blood through arteries so extended.

In the evenings the barrack, with only a few places empty on the
bunks, was a sight oddly reminiscent of a hospital. Some prisoners
lay without moving, having taken off nothing but their shoes, and
begrudging themselves every movement of arms or legs stared
aimlessly at their neighbours; others talked in small groups,
sprawled in untidy positions on the bunks, like patients who speak
only in whispers even in the hours free from the doctor's visits;
guests from other barracks usually sat round the stove or on their
hosts' bunks, and as the only fully-clothed people there, they gave

the impression of being healthy visitors to the bedsides of sick friends. There was over it all an atmosphere of peace, relief, steaming exhaustion and sadness in forced isolation, and the constantly burning light of several electric bulbs underlined the resemblance to a hospital in a lifelike, but not in the least incongruous, fashion. The flames cast dull reflections on the frosted square window-panes, white inside and gleaming outside like black crystals. Looking in from the door, one could easily have mistaken the bundles of rags lying on tiers of bunks for untidy bedding, and the cloth foot-wrappings, now steaming on the clay chimney-breast overhanging the fire and on lengths of string stretched between the beams of the ceiling, for drying linen. It was not, then, the appearance of the barrack which was so terrifying. The appearance of its inhabitants, however, made one realise that this was a ward for incurables as one walked from the door farther into the barrack and saw those eyes in which the shadow of death lay tensely before its flight on the wings of the night. The prisoners who never stirred from their bunks in the evening feared the night with its menace of sudden death, and their pulse quickened as its approach grew more imminent.

On the evening of my arrival in the camp, when I returned for a moment to the barrack from the medical hut, I was struck by the expression on the face of an old man who sat over the fire, half-naked, poking about in the flames with an iron rod. The wrinkled, flabby pouches of his cheeks drooped down almost to the sparse tuft on his chin, exposing the distended, burning eyes of a fanatic. I can no longer remember the expression in those eyes, but even now I cannot explain the feeling I had then that I was looking into the eyes of a man who was dead although he still continued to breathe, who knew that he had been dead for a long time although his shrivelled heart continued to beat in the empty sack of his body. I saw in those eyes not the active despair of a man helpless before approaching death, but the passive hopelessness of one who, despite everything, continues to live. Those who still expect something of the future are free to talk about hope; but how are you to breathe hope into a man who is too weak even to put an end to his own suffering? How could I have convinced this fundamentally religious man, who prayed for a speedy death as for God's greatest blessing, that man's greatest privilege is free will in slavery, that he always retains the right to make his own ultimate choice between life and death? For him everything was finished, all hope had vanished, there was left only the torture of an empty life; and yet his hand, instead of ending the aimless, endless beating of his heart, suddenly dropped the poker and, as if with a flaming sword, traced a broad sign of the cross from the furrowed brow down to the folds of the stomach, and over the hairy chest. In the lives of some prisoners there is something inexplicable, some unsuspected revelation; their final hope seems to be that they will eventually be killed by their own hopelessness, and the silent torment of their lives comforts them with momentary happiness which the thought of death gives them. Their Christianity is not a belief in the mystical redemption of souls wearied with earthly wandering, but only gratitude to a religion which promises eternal rest. They are religious suicides, worshippers of death for whom the release of the grave is the ultimate end, not the means to a life after death. Perhaps the deeply emotional nature of their vision of death explains their hatred of life. They hate themselves and others, if only because, despite their hopes and most fervent dreams, they are still alive. "We should be dead; we're human rubbish, we should die for our own good and for the greater glory of God."

Later, I became acquainted with the old man. He was a farmer from the small, autonomous region of Chechen in the Caucasus; he worked at the food supply centre sorting potatoes. Once, when I gave him a piece of salted fish, he told me something of himself, looking at me distrustfully from under his bushy eyebrows; in the daytime his frenzied, demented stare became merely savage. The other prisoners, including his neighbours on the bunk, he treated with hostility.

Collectivisation had deprived him of his small farm—a few acres of arable land and some pasture—on the slopes of the Caucasus. He was arrested in 1936 for refusing to give up a sack of his wheat and for killing two lambs from the collective herd which had been put in his care and then burying the quartered meat. His family—a wife and three children—were sent into exile to an unknown destination; he did not know what had happened to them. During his interrogation he had stubbornly refused to reveal the hiding-place of the meat and the grain. He was beaten so cruelly that in 1941, after five years, his body was still covered with blue bruises, but he had clung to the idea that silence was the only revenge of which he was capable for the loss of his land and his whole life, and until the end he did not breathe a word. After the last hearing he was carried, unconscious, back to his cell, and several days later—when it had become quite clear that he was willing to die rather than tell where he had hidden the meagre remnants of his own farm—he was sentenced to fifteen years' hard labour and sent first to the Kotlas camp and then, in 1939, to the Kargopol camp. "What is there left for me"—he said—"besides death? I've no family, I'm too old to go back to the kolhoz, I'll never see the mountains again. . . . Every day I pray for death . . ." And every evening the old man drank his soup, spent a few minutes poking the fire, sometimes hiding his face, flushed with the blaze, in his knotted hands, climbed back on his bunk, said a short prayer, and went straight to sleep. And the curious thing was that he, whose guts had been "knocked out", never shrieked or moaned in the night; only occasionally he groaned quietly with the pain as he turned over on his side, or whispered deliriously in his sleep of death and God. . . .

But he was not the type of prisoner that I had in mind when I started writing this chapter. I thought rather of those who are afraid of death and whose terror is transformed into the fear of night, not those who pray for it. It was not until toward the end of my imprisonment in the camp that I understood and experienced the emotions which make up this daily agony.

Every prisoner knew, as he returned to the zone after work, that each day in the camp was costing him whole irretrievable years of health and physical endurance, and that his death was approaching with a speed which excluded the consciousness of dying when it finally caught him. Death in the camp, because it threatened constantly and struck suddenly and unexpectedly, seemed to break the laws of time and acquired a metaphysical inscrutability which placed it outside the rhythm of our material existence. A prisoner, after a time, found himself in that stage of decomposition where he breathed with difficulty, could not control his bowels but performed his natural functions where he lay, wept without cause whenever he was left alone for a moment, gripped his heart, squeezed in an iron band of pain, with a trembling hand, stumbled and tripped on a smooth path, swelled up with alarming speed, and vainly tried to chase fiery flakes from before his eyes. He went to the medical hut, and was told that he was perfectly well, that there was nothing wrong with him; but he knew what was wrong even if it was no disease with a name and symptoms. There is unfortunately no cure for complete physical exhaustion other than good, rich food and a long rest; the medical hut was no kitchen, and admission to the mortuary was given only to prisoners with incurable heart disease, advanced consumption or pylagra, or serious vitamin deficiency which covered the whole body with ulcers. It may, therefore, have been an exaggeration, but every prisoner went to sleep with the thought that death would come upon him in his sleep that very night. He was afraid of its suddenness because he could not know when, how and from what causes he would die.

A second reason of our fear of that death which we imagined as lurking behind the night's dark curtain was the very quality which in normal conditions usually robs it of some of its irresistible terror —its community to all mankind. Every one of us felt helpless in face of the knowledge that on all sides were lying men just as defenceless and just as exposed to sudden attack as ourselves. Why this should be so, I cannot say, though presumably this helplessness divided us instead of bringing us all together. Only healthy men, secure in their own lives, can be moved by a sudden call for help from a dying man. In the barrack, where all prisoners were equally vulnerable, where all hearts were beating with the same difficulty, an agonised cry could only remind us of our own sickness, and passed unheeded. Defoe, in the *Journal of the Plague Year*, has described people who avoid each other for fear of infection. Our behaviour was the same, but without such clear motives. It was almost possible to believe, looking round our barrack at night, that death itself was contagious; we feared the risk of infection from others, carrying the germ in our own blood as we did. The presence of death was so strong and convincing that every prisoner seemed to hide within the brittle shell of sleep from the menace which was stealing towards him across the neighbouring bunks, afraid to remind it of his existence by even the softest sigh. We were united in an egotistical, silent conspiracy of death and we all accepted the understanding without talking about it, but we thought with horror that we would become its victims in our turn. We recalled moments when, without making the slightest movement, we had watched from under drooping eyelids as dead bodies were being carried out of the barrack at night and we knew that our own shrieks for help would fail to rouse the others from their defensive apathy.

Death in the camp possessed another terror: its anonymity. We had no idea where the dead were buried, or whether, after a prisoner's death, any kind of death certificate was ever written. During my stay in hospital, through a window by the barbed wire of the zone I twice saw a sledge taking bodies out beyond the camp. It drove out along the road leading to the saw-mill, then turned suddenly to the left into a rarely-used path which had been trodden out years ago by the first brigades of Kargopol foresters, disappeared on the horizon, rising from the white plain of the snow like a speck of dust whirled into the air by the wind, and merged into the pale-blue outline of the forest. Here the extent of my vision ended and here our borderline between life and death was established. That melancholy funeral *cortège* was probably making for some abandoned forest clearing, whose whereabouts no one in the camp knew except the dumb driver of the hearse. We tried to find out from him where our prison cemetery lay, but the wretched Ukrainian could only shrug his shoulders, nod his head wistfully and, choking with the effort, bring up from his throat a few incomprehensible, meaningless sounds. Those who were familiar with his speech asserted that he was indicating the hunting lodge built a few years before at the place where the first camp road had come to an end, but this was not considered to be a likely possibility, if only because in winter no spade could have broken the frozen earth, while in summer the marshy clearing opened up in the heat, gradually swallowing into its depths the dilapidated hut, the bared roots of the trees and the wooden car track. The certainty that no one would ever learn of their death, that no one would know where they had been buried, was one of the prisoners' greatest psychological torments. It is possible to be an atheist, to deny the existence of life after death, but even then it is difficult to reconcile oneself to the thought that once and for all the only material trace which prolongs human life and gives it a distinct durability in human memory will be wiped out. This aspect of the fear of death, or rather of complete annihilation, became a positive obsession with some prisoners. There were secret, many-sided agreements which laid on the party who survived the duty of informing the others' families of the date of death and the approximate place of burial; the barrack walls were covered with names of prisoners scratched in the plaster, and friends were asked to complete the data after their death by adding a cross and the date; every prisoner wrote to his family at strictly regular intervals, so that a sudden break in the correspondence would give them the approximate date of his death.

All this however was not sufficient to still our anxiety at the thought that Soviet labour camps have robbed millions of its victims of the one privilege accorded to every death—its publicity, and the desire which every human being subconsciously feels: to endure in the memory of others. *

In the evening the conversations on the bunks reached the feverish tension of whispered farewells, and two or three hours later, about ten o'clock, gradually died down, still hissing here and there like burning embers extinguished with a bucketful of water. All was quiet, but sleep would not come to us for a long time. Some prisoners prayed, sitting on the bunks with their elbows on their knees, their faces buried in their hands. Others lay without moving, staring in silence at the faces of those lying opposite. The formless piles of human bodies, rags and blankets, lying only a moment ago in the corners of the barrack, spread out over the bunks like sand dunes formed by the regular ebb and flow of the waves. The light of the bulbs seemed to grow dim behind the clouds of smoke, and the dying fire gleamed alternately with black and red reflections. The white night flattened itself on the windows with icy flowers, the slippery planks of the paths creaked under the footsteps of the last passers-by. Straining one's ears, it was possible to catch the sounds of howling dogs and the clanging of buffers at Yercevo station. The camp was slowly being plunged in sleep.

After midnight the strange nightly progression of noises began: first a snore, then whistling breaths and painful moans, low at first, then growing louder into one almost continuous lament broken only by occasional convulsions of dry, tearless sobbing which shook the prisoners on their bunks. Someone would shout violently, someone else would wake from his sleep and sit up, warding off an unseen attacker with both outstretched hands, then look round with

* Since writing this chapter, I have met in London a former Polish prisoner from Ostrovnoye who was there assigned for a few weeks to work at the death-registration office. He cannot recall the exact daily average of deaths there, but he remembers that in the office stood two cupboards the height of a normal man; one was filled with three vertical stacks of death certificates, the other contained only two and a half such stacks. Dead prisoners were brought into the office, each with his personal data written on a slip of paper tied round his ankle. It was my informant's job to write out, according to these data, the death certificates, of which he made three copies: one for GULAG, one for the camp, and one nominally for the deceased's family, though he knows that these last were never sent off. The bodies were buried in the 7th "sector" of the Ostrovnoye forest, in long trenches which were dug in the summer, since the ground was too hard in the winter, and gradually covered with earth during the year as they were filled up.

an unseeing, oblivious gaze and, regaining consciousness, lie back again with a heart-rending sigh. The sleep-laden, disjointed babblings formed themselves into a sustained chant of "mercy, mercy", a background for the shouts, which mounted to a shrieking crescendo in which appeals to God mingled with the names of distant families. Prisoners tossed and turned anxiously on their bunks, clutched at their hearts in sudden spasms of fear, and their bodies thudded on the hard planks. Only Dimka sat by his bucket unmoved, like the still centre of a tornado, and his faded eyes, long dried of tears, looked with indifference round this tangle of bodies caught in the bonds of the night.

Like a phantom ship pursued by death, our barrack floated out into the moonless sea of darkness, carrying in its hold the sleeping crew of galley slaves.

CHAPTER 11

"THE HOUSE OF THE DEAD"

ONE evening, as the brigades were filing in through the gate into the zone, our attention was caught by a large notice, pinned to the "red table" or list of stakhanovites which was posted up at the crossing of the paths. "Eight o'clock. Film: 'The Great Waltz'. In the barrack of 'self-taught creative activities'." This was the second film to be shown in Yercevo, the first during my imprisonment there. A year before it was the Soviet historical film, "Minin and Pozharsky", when Mikhail Stepanovich had seen himself on the screen, eating a roast from the Tsar's table, as he sat, wiping his red-rimmed eyes, in a place of honour in the front row reserved for the free camp officials. There had been rumours about the new film for several months, but no one had believed them. "Cinema!" the prisoners would say. "A little extra soup, or a hundred grammes of bread, would do us more good." But these words did not express their true feelings; the cinema meant more to them than bread, and if they spoke of it contemptuously it was because they believed that only those desires to which outwardly one pretends to attach no importance can ever come true.

The barrack of "self-taught creative activities" was situated near the kitchen, and when the peresylny was full it was also used to house prisoners in transit through Yercevo. The barrack and all the "activities"—the very rare films and concerts which we always called "shows"—were under the absolute control of the director of the "cultural and educational section", which was known, by its initials, as the "kaveche". Only a free official, or else a released criminal prisoner, could aspire to that high position, and his assistant was chosen from among the bytoviks. The appointment of criminal prisoners was a precaution against the possible contamination of prisoners by seditious literature and any anti-Soviet allusions ingeniously concealed in the amateur concerts which were organised from time to time. The precaution was unnecessary, and there was no danger of contamination. What the kaveche was pleased to call a library contained only many copies of Stalin's *Problems of Leninism*, several foreign-language propaganda works issued by the State Publishing House, a few sets of Russian classics, and several hundred pamphlets with the texts of speeches and resolutions made at the sittings of the Supreme Soviet. During my whole time in the camp I read the *Collected Works* of Griboyedov once, and Dostoevsky's *The House of the Dead* twice, and both these books had been lent to me in secret by other prisoners; in order to keep up appearances, however, I borrowed Stalin's *Problems of Leninism, The Folklore of the Komi Republic,* and the speeches of the Spanish revolutionary leader Dolores Ibbaruri (Passionaria), from the kaveche library. I remember that in Passionaria's book I came across and underlined in pencil a sentence dating from the period of the defence of Madrid: "Better to die than to live on your knees". From that time the book enjoyed great popularity in the camp until a N.K.V.D. commission of inspection from Vologda withdrew it from circulation. Apparently those proud words, which I had first heard at a meeting of my high-school communist group in Poland, had a different ring in captivity, and had to be suppressed.

The camp authorities' anxiety about the theatrical performances was also unjustified. Even if there had been any intention of smuggling anti-Soviet allusions into a camp concert, there was virtually no material in which they could be concealed, for all conversational or dramatic interludes were forbidden and the show could consist only of musical items. But regulations had to be obeyed, and Kunin, a Moscow thief released after serving three years for larceny, was the director of our kaveche, assisted by old Pavel Ilyich, who, when I knew him, was serving the eighth year of a sentence for the murder of his brother.

The kaveche office occupied a small hut near one of the barracks, and was reached by a rarely-used path next to the barbed wire. Inside Pavel Ilyich sat by the iron stove mending damaged books, or cutting out decorative patterns of coloured paper, or inscribing in beautiful handwriting the names of stakhanovites for the red table, spread out before him. A prisoner who entered would instinctively assume a humble posture at the door: "Pavel Ilyich," he would say, "what about a little book?" "What sort of book?" the old man would ask without lifting his head with its snow-white hair from his work. "I leave it to you, Pavel Ilyich, as long as it is interesting." "You must talk to the director about that," our librarian would say, scratching his head in uncertainty.

Kunin lived in the village, but took all his meals in the zone. Tall, slim, dressed in a cap with an upturned peak, a linen blouse and high boots, he moved about the camp with the ease and familiarity of an experienced prisoner. It was said that the sentence which he had completed in Yercevo in 1939 had been his third, though he himself never mentioned it. He would walk through the zone with a lively, energetic stride and pay frequent visits to the barracks, talking with the prisoners for several hours at a time, and though this was in a sense part of his duties, we could feel that he was thinking with nostalgia of the days when, in a ragged jerkin, he lay on an upper bunk among his friends, peering round the barrack with his rat-like eyes to see what else he could win at cards or to find a box which he had not yet inspected. "You must lead cultural lives, prisoners," he would repeat, smiling with superiority at the word "prisoners"; that must have been one of the sentences which he had learnt by heart two years before, when he had first been entrusted with the task of educating the prisoners. His attitude to Pavel Ilyich was in a way extremely moving. Once they had shared a barrack bunk, and now they ate their soup from the same can, Kunin shared his cigarettes with him, and would usually bring him half a loaf of bread or a little vodka from the village. Pavel Ilyich returned this friendship with blind obedience and devotion, and though we supposed that in private they called each other by their Christian names, in front of us he would never have dared to address Kunin as anything but "Citizen Director". Kunin liked this title and obviously attached more weight to it than to all his "cultural and educational" activities. He could not have lived away from the camp, but he did not intend to forgo the dignities which, after so many years of prison life, had raised him above the scum and the enemies of the people. Older prisoners who remembered him from those days said that he was making up for his unfulfilled hopes of becoming a brigadier. Late in the evening Kunin would send Pavel Ilyich back to the barrack and receive his prisoner-mistresses in the kaveche office. He changed them as frequently as he had done when a prisoner, and there were jokes among the prisoners about his "educational and cultural activities" with newly-arrived girls, or about the "little school" which he could have started with the children that had been born to him on the hard bunks of the camp maternity barrack.

The kaveche's entire activities consisted of lending books from the library and organising occasional shows. Kunin had probably never read a book in his life, but he knew the principles of their issue in the camp. The first question that was asked of a prisoner who went to the library was: "Section?" It was the section of the penal code under which they had been sentenced that was meant, for the politicals could read Stalin's book and the propaganda pamphlets only after a preliminary talk with Kunin, while criminal prisoners had access to political publications without limitation. This system satisfied the majority of those concerned: the criminals seldom felt the need to read anything except the announcements on the red table, while the politicals had a quite understandable aversion to studying the theory responsible for their imprisonment. From time to time, however, we would feel it necessary to see Kunin and ask for a copy of the *Problems of Leninism*, and then the conversation with our instructor took the following course: "Soviet justice does not deprive those who have erred of the right to understand their own mistakes. What political problem interests you most?" We would answer: "Collectivisation of the countryside," or "The problem of socialism in one country," or "Industrialisation." "Ah, Comrade Stalin gives an excellent exposition of that subject in the essay entitled . . ." Doubtless, Kunin had learnt by heart a guide to the *Problems* without knowing the book's contents, and he avoided all detailed discussion of it; neither would anyone have dared to embarrass him by a question concerning a "political problem" which Comrade Stalin had not touched upon. We all knew of Kunin's good relations with the Third Section, and for that reason we all wanted to be included in his list of readers of the book which, not unjustly, is regarded as the Bible of Soviet Russia.

The procedure of book-lending, as so many other camp customs, was probably a vestigial reminder of the regulations drawn up in Moscow in the days when the camps were really intended to be corrective, educational institutions. Gogol would have appreciated this blind obedience to an official fiction despite the general practice of the camp—it was like the education of "dead souls". Kunin, however, had greater ambitions; he had dug up somewhere a statute about the necessity of eradicating illiteracy in the labour camps, and he set about trying to organise evening classes for the prisoners. It was easy to imagine, as one saw him running round the barracks recruiting pupils, that, like Gogol's Chichikov, he was building up a fortune with the captured souls. But this was too much for the prisoners. It was one thing to go to the kaveche once in every few months, take out the first likely-looking book which they could not read anyway, and leave it, untouched, under the rags which served for a pillow; but only the bayonets of the N.K.V.D. could have induced them to learn reading and writing while struggling with hunger, exhaustion and death itself, and fortunately the evening classes were not compulsory. All prisoners solemnly assured Kunin that they had mastered the difficult art of reading and writing while they were at liberty, but on one of our rest-days it was still difficult to escape the numerous requests to write the prisoners' letters home for them. Meanwhile Kunin probably wrote in his reports to the authorities that in "his" camp illiteracy had been completely exterminated. . . .

The concerts were the only activity of the kaveche which could count on the full and enthusiastic support of the prisoners. Among those freed from work by the doctors, Kunin was sure to find a sufficient number of volunteers to make decorations of coloured paper and hang them round the barrack of self-taught creative activities. The prisoners, especially the older men, did this with pleasure, as if they were adorning a church. When they came back to the barracks in the evening, they told us with excitement how the "theatre" would look, asking the foresters to bring a few fresh pine branches home with them and the saw-mill workers for sawdust to spread on the floor. On the day of the concert the "cultural" barrack looked really festive: the walls were decorated with paper patterns, green pine branches gleamed between the beams of the roof, and the planks of the floor were shining from energetic scrubbing and polishing. The prisoners took their caps off at the door, shook the snow from their boots in the passage outside, and took their places on the benches with ceremonious anticipation and almost religious awe. Then could be seen only long rows of shaved heads and folded hands like grey knots. In the barrack of self-taught creative activities politeness was obligatory, and women who came in late had seats in the first rows of the benches offered to them. There was never enough room on the benches for all the prisoners, and large groups of them stood in the doorway and against every wall. A short while before the beginning the conversations died down, and from all sides of the barrack impatient voices called out: "Quiet, they're going to start." The entrance of

Samsonov, surrounded by his staff, was the signal for Kunin to open the proceedings.

He walked forward to the front of the stage, welcomed the officials with a bow, and silenced us with a gesture. "Prisoners"— so began his traditional preface—"Soviet justice is capable of forgiveness, and it knows how to reward honest work. The production plan set for the camp has been achieved. As a reward you are about to see . . ." (here came details of the show). "This act of lenience should encourage you to even greater efforts for our Soviet Fatherland, whose full citizens you yourselves will one day become." A murmur of satisfaction passed through the audience: the theatre was indeed like a foretaste of liberty.

The first show that I saw in the camp was, as I have said, the American film based on the life of Strauss called "The Great Waltz". It was preceded by a short Soviet film about a group of Moscow students, all members of the Communist Youth Organisation, who work on the land during their summer holidays. It was full of propaganda, speeches, declarations and songs in praise of Stalin, but it contained some beautiful camera work and a humorous episode which made the prisoners laugh till the tears rolled down their faces. One of the students, a Jew judging by his appearance and his accent, could not manage his spade on the first day of work, and folding his hands on the handle said: "A spade isn't for me. With me, it is the head that works, not the hands." The audience roared with laughter. "Look at the cunning Jew," the prisoners shouted. "He'd like to command, would he? And who'd do the digging then? Send him to the camp for a year or two, that would teach him!" But the film ended with the triumph of righteousness, the clumsy student came first in their socialist competition of work and with blazing eyes delivered a speech glorifying the State where manual labour had been raised to the highest position of honour. The audience of prisoners heard it in silence, unconsoled by its sentiments. Silence was the only weapon at our disposal, when every careless word could sound like a cry of rebellion.

"The Great Waltz", on the other hand, moved us deeply. I would never have believed that an average American musical, full of women in fitted bodices, men in tight jackets and frilly cravats, shining chandeliers, sentimental melodies, dances and love scenes, could reveal to me what seemed to be the lost paradise of another epoch. I held back my tears, my heart beat faster, my throat was choking, and I cooled my feverish cheeks with my hands. The prisoners watched the film spellbound, without moving; in the darkness I saw only wide-open mouths and eyes absorbing passionately all that was happening on the screen. "How beautiful," voices were whispering all around me. "So that's how they live outside." Filled with naïve admiration, barred from that outer world, they forgot that the action of the film was taking place over half a century ago, and these images of the past became the forbidden fruit of the present. "Shall we ever live like men again? Will the darkness of our tomb, our living death, never come to an end?" I heard these words by my side, so distinctly that someone must have whispered them in my ear, and though against the background of prison slang the exaggerated language was unusual, at that moment I felt no astonishment. The decorated barrack, the figures weaving on and off the screen, the music, the concentration in the faces around me, the sighs which suggested an inner thawing, all pushed us back into the past and released the long-frozen sources of emotion.

It was my neighbour on the bench, Natalia Lvovna, who had whispered these unusual words to me. I had known her for a long time, but only very slightly. I knew that she was employed in the camp accountants' office, even though her lack of any personal beauty should rather have qualified her for one of the forest brigades. In her middle twenties she looked already exceptionally old and ugly—she had large, protruding eyes, sparse hair, flabby cheeks which were sometimes covered by a rash of brick-red spots, and a heavy, awkward figure. She was one of a small group of prisoners who were known in the camp by the abbreviation KWZD. These were the initials of the East China Railway, which was sold by the Soviet Government to Japan, or (officially) to the Government of Manchukuo, on March 23rd, 1935. All the Russians who had lived before that date in the territory traversed by the railway and who chose to return to Russia after the sale were at once arrested and sent to labour camps with ten-year sentences. The name of the East China Railway thus became a convenient abbreviation for the particular section of the Soviet penal code under which they had been convicted. Similar sets of initials (KRD—counter-revolutionary activity; KRA—counter-revolutionary agitation; SOE—socially dangerous elements; SP—

social origins; PS—industrial sabotage; SChW—agricultural sabotage, etc.) created an unofficial jargon which allowed prisoners to learn quickly, without prolonged questioning, the nature of the offences of newly-met comrades. Those of the KWZD section differed from other Russians in that, although of the same nationality, their mental reactions and habits of thought were closer to those of foreigners than of their own compatriots, as if the greater part of their lives had been spent beyond the frontiers of the U.S.S.R.

It was said that heart disease was responsible for Natalia Lvovna's post in the accountants' office. She had never confessed this to anyone, but her slow, careful step, the movements of her body, always controlled by a tense watchfulness, and her drawling speech, all suggested that she was concentrating on some inner suffering which, like a badly-healed wound, would be aggravated by any violent movement. But there must have been another reason why, even with heart disease, she was not sent out to heavier work and did not finish her life in the hospital after a few weeks of it, for she had nothing to offer except her kindness, goodness, patience and humility, all qualities of small value in the camp. I believe that, paradoxically, she was saved by her ugliness. No one was sufficiently interested in her to attempt to force her into submission by torturing her with work. In her own fashion she disarmed and gained the sympathy of all, even the urkas, by her great courtesy, her disinterestedness, and her readiness to perform small services for anyone. In the camp human feelings most frequently revived when compassion satisfied the remnants of self-respect. Natalia Lvovna seemed to be so insignificant that her death, like her sad life, would have passed unnoticed.

When the film ended, a crowd of prisoners tumbled out of the barrack. The night was beautiful, white, brilliant with stars—the sky seemed to have been suddenly raised higher, as if a pair of giant hands had pushed it up and spread it out above the camp; in the frosty air our voices sounded almost gay, and our feet trod the fresh snow into the paths. From the barrack where we had watched the film, the ground fell in a gentle slope towards the barbed wire and rose again on the other side, on the horizon, in a hill beyond which, at midnight, we could hear the violent clatter of railway trucks and the piercing whistle of a passing train. The prisoners did not go straight back to the barracks, but stood in small crowds on the paths, with excitement recalling scenes from the film, arguing about the slightest details, imitating the gestures of the actors, and at the same time looking beyond, toward the hill which concealed the railway track from view, as if they had only suddenly realised that beyond it lay the liberty of which a fragment had been revealed to them on the screen. So little is needed to make one enjoy oneself in a human fashion! It seemed as if there would be no end to these discussions, whose every word contained more meaning than the whole film. "Citizen Director!"—the prisoners cried out as Kunin walked through the crowd—"Thank you for the show! It's made me want to live again. . . !"

Natalia Lvovna was crying. I walked beside her, embarrassed, slowly so as not to outstrip her and quietly so as not to frighten away her outburst of emotion. So far I had known her only by sight and by hearsay—I could not know why she was crying. I thought that every woman in the camp must be crying at that moment, having seen so many dresses, dances, and love scenes at once. But at the bend of the path, where it turned off to the women's barrack, she stopped and, holding back her tears with an effort, asked: "Do you think that I'm crying because I long for that other life?" I looked at the ugly face, the fleshy cheeks now lined with thin wet streams, the enormous eyes, which behind the misty veil of tears were almost pretty, and hesitated. Then, meaning to please her, I said: "Why yes, Natalia Lvovna, you must have enjoyed dancing once." "Oh, no," she answered quickly, "I have never danced in my life. But I have been here in the camp for five years, and I still can't control myself whenever I think that it has all happened before, years ago . . . that for centuries we have been living in the same house of the dead . . ." She looked at me carefully; I did not know what to say, for I was afraid that one careless word might graze her most personal feelings. Suddenly she said: "Please wait here, I want to bring you something," and walked to her barrack with a faster step. After a moment she returned, puffing with the effort, hiding something under her jerkin. "Please read this"—her voice trembled—"but don't tell anyone where you got it from. It is banned these days—especially here," she added with a smile. I took a ragged, disintegrating book from her hand and looked at the cover: Dostoevsky, *The House of the Dead*, Petersburg 1894.

Two months passed; during that time I read *The House of the*

Dead twice, but I saw Natalia Ivanovna only from a distance in the zone, and greeted her always with a friendly wave of the hand. She looked at me with anxiety, as if she wanted to see from my expression whether the book had made the expected impression on me. I avoided talking to her, though I would always regret my decision as I watched her walking slowly to her barrack, greeting everyone who passed with a polite nod.

I avoided her because, from the moment when I read the first few pages of the book until I closed it for the second and last time at the final paragraph: "Yes, with God's blessing! Freedom, new life, resurrection from the dead . . ." I lived in a state of trance, as if I had woken from long mortal sleep. The thing about the book was not Dostoevsky's ability to describe inhuman suffering as if it were a natural part of human destiny, but that aspect of it which had also struck Natalia Lvovna: that there was not the slightest break between his fate and ours. I read the book in the evenings, at night, and also in the daytime, robbing myself even of sleep. My heart beat like the clapper of a bell and my head hummed with a tumult which increased like the infinitely repeated echo of countless drops of water, which fall at regular intervals on to the same spot of the skull, and seem to crack it every time with the resounding blow of a hammer. It was one of the most difficult periods of my prison life. I read the book at night under cover of my jerkin, and in the daytime concealed it in the safest place on the bunk, under a loose plank near the head. I hated it and loved it, as a victim can become attached to the instrument of his torture. After my return from work I always looked anxiously to see if it was still in its place, but on the way to the barrack I subconsciously longed for it to disappear without return, that I might be free once and for all from this nightmare of life without hope. I did not know then that a mental condition of full consciousness is more dangerous in slavery than hunger and physical death. Until then I had lived like other prisoners, instinctively avoiding the necessity to come face to face with my own existence. But Dostoevsky, with his modest and rather slow story in which every day of hard labour drags on as if for whole years, swept me along with the tide of a black river of despair making its way through subterranean channels into eternal darkness. In vain I tried to swim against the overpowering current. I felt that I had never really lived before, I forgot the faces of my family and the landscapes of my childhood. On the stone walls of the cavernous labyrinth, dripping with water and gleaming in the darkness, I saw in a fever of the imagination only the long rows of names: those who had been here before us, who scratched the traces of their existence in the rock before they were finally swallowed up, with a hardly audible bubbling, by the slimy darkness. I could see them, on their knees, desperately gripping the slippery curves of the stone, rising for a moment and falling back again, calling for help in voices which broke out of them and vanished at once in the dead silence of the chasm, catching with bent fingers at every projection in the rock with a last attempt to jerk themselves out of the stream which relentlessly carried everything and everybody towards the dark sea of predestination. And when, submitting at last, they fell to the bottom, the black wave brought others in their place, who stumbled as they had done under the burden of suffering, and struggled to escape from its fatal whirlpools—and I knew that we were the new victims, that we too were being swept away. . . .

The greatest torment of my state of half-sleep was the inexplicable fact that the laws of time ceased to apply to it—between the engulfment of our predecessors and our own struggles there was no pause, the stream was continuous. That is why it assumed the character of something inevitable—of destiny in which, for those who stand by and watch, eternity is the batting of an eyelid, and for those condemned to our fate the batting of an eyelid becomes eternity. The most trivial details repeated themselves with nightmarish accuracy: the prisoners of the *House of the Dead*, at the end of a free day, also whispered with terror: "Back to work tomorrow." I could not have gone on living in the camp for long with this feeling of endless fate haunting me. The deeper I drank of the poisoned source of *The House of the Dead*, the greater consolation did I find in the thought which first came to me that year: the idea of escape by suicide.

Fortunately, Natalia Lvovna turned out to be an even more addicted reader of Dostoevsky than I was, for after two months she came to my barrack one evening, called me out into the zone, and said quietly: "I must have the book back, I can't live without it. I have no one in the whole world, and it means everything to me." Then, for the first and last time, she told me something of herself; before, I had only heard from other prisoners that her father had been shot by a firing squad immediately after his return to Russia from the territory sold to the Japanese. I went back into the barrack and took *The House of the Dead* from its hiding-place under the loose plank. I regretted having to give up this book, for it had opened my eyes to the reality of the camp, even though what I now saw had every appearance of death; at the same time I was secretly glad at the thought of release from the strange and destructive spell of that prose, so full of despair that life in it had become merely the shadow of an interminable agony of daily death.

"You were quite right, Natalia Lvovna," I said, helping her to conceal the book under her jerkin.

She looked at me with gratitude, and over her ugly face passed the shadow of almost happy excitement.

"Do you know that from the moment when I got that book, here in the camp, my life acquired new meaning? Can you believe that? It sounds strange—to draw hope from Dostoevsky! . . ." and she laughed nervously, forcibly.

I looked at her with astonishment. Somewhere in the corners of her large, unhealthily swollen eyes lurked a hardly perceptible gleam of madness. Her lips, trembling with cold, were twisted in a puzzling grimace, not a smile, nor yet a spasm of pain. She brushed away from her forehead the thin locks of hair, stuck together with snow and slightly frozen. I thought that she would burst into tears again, but she continued talking in a calm, even voice.

"There is always room for hope when life becomes so utterly hopeless that nobody can touch us, we belong to ourselves . . . Do you understand? We become absolute masters of our lives. . . . When there is no hope of rescue in sight, not the slightest breach in the surrounding wall, when we can't raise our hand against fate just because it is our fate, there is only one thing left to us—to turn that hand against ourselves. You probably can't understand the happiness which I found in the discovery that eventually one belongs only to oneself—at least so far that one can choose the method and the time of one's own death. . . . That is what Dostoevsky has taught me. In 1936, when I first found myself in prison, I suffered greatly, for I believed that I had been deprived of freedom because I had in some way deserved it. But now I know that the whole of Russia has always been, and is still, a house of the dead, that time has stood still between Dostoevsky's hard labour and our own, and now I am free, completely free! We died so long ago, though we still won't admit it. Just think: I lose hope when the desire for life awakens within me; but I regain it whenever the longing for death comes upon me."

I turned round at the barrack door in order to be able to remember her as she walked away. She walked through the zone slowly, her arms folded across her chest as if she was pressing her precious book, old and yellow like her own prematurely aged face, to her diseased heart. She squared her shoulders and stepped gently in her gum boots, and the snow covered her footsteps as she walked away.

*   *   *   *   *

Of the next show, this time a concert given by the prisoners, we learnt earlier and not so suddenly, for they had been preparing it in the zone for several weeks beforehand. "They" were only three people, and Pavel Ilyich would come round the barracks as Kunin's envoy, to collect his small cast and take them off for a rehearsal at the kaveche office. Thus we knew roughly what the programme of this second camp spectacle would be. Tania, the one-time prima-donna of the Moscow Opera, was to sing Russian folk songs; Vsevolod Prastushko, a Leningrad sailor from the saw-mill brigade, would follow with a group of sailors' songs; and Zelik Leyman, a Jewish hairdresser from Warsaw, who in March 1940 had crossed the River Bug into the Russian sphere of occupation, would end the concert with a violin recital. Of this concert trio two, "our Vsevolod" and Leyman the hairdresser, merit a closer description.

The first was known as "our" Vsevolod because he was to some extent the camp favourite. In every barrack which he chose to visit in the evenings he was always greeted with friendly shouts and invitations to "share a bunk". He made himself at home everywhere, and walked about in a sailor's vest with blue stripes, joking with the prisoners and smiling under his toothbrush moustache. Vsevolod had a whole repertoire of favourite sea-going reminiscences; moreover, he thought of himself as a great baritone, but would not allow himself to be persuaded to sing on any occasion, for he valued his talent highly, and preened himself like a spoilt actress. "No, brothers, I don't sing when you like, but when I like. My voice isn't at anyone's disposal." He would be interrupted by laughter. "Then tell us a story, Vsevolod, you've travelled and seen a bit of the world. And then show us the circus, Vsevolod, dear soul. Show us the circus!" the prisoners asked in pleading tones.

Vsevolod willingly talked about himself, always starting from his early youth. His accounts were highly-coloured and exaggerated, but there were certain permanent elements which for lack of something better could be taken as the core of truth in his stories. He came from Minsk, and as a child of the streets he wandered about the country as a bezprizorny from his earliest years; when he was eighteen he was conscripted into a Leningrad regiment of marines. Then he was transferred to the merchant service, and spent three years travelling and seeing the world. He bragged about his voyages to distant lands, and it seemed that in every one of them he had had some unusual adventure, though frequently he muddled both places and events. One thing, however, was certain: he owed his imprisonment to a romantic escapade in Marseilles. He stole away from his ship, spent the night in a port brothel, and did not return until dawn. This was not his principal offence, for the ship's captain could always have ignored or hushed up the episode, but six months later a postcard from Marseilles, addressed to Prastushko, turned up in Leningrad. The prostitute with whom he had slept that night was probably a communist, and could not resist this opportunity of maintaining contact with someone from the Socialist Fatherland. Our Vsevolod paid twice over for his foreign contamination in Marseilles: with ten years' hard labour, and with syphilis. But the most astonishing thing was that he did not consider his punishment either unfair or undeserved. He would always finish the story sententiously: "Life, brothers, is like an ocean wave. If you stick to the crest, it will always take you to a safe shore, but if you allow yourself to be submerged, it will carry you farther out to sea."

Vsevolod's "circus" was something quite exceptional. His chest, shoulders, stomach, and thighs were tattooed all over with a little assembly of acrobats, clowns, dancers, hoops and obstacles, lions, elephants, and horses with splendid plumes on their heads. When, coaxed by the prisoners, he had undressed completely, he sat down on a bench by the fire, and by dexterously flexing the muscles on his stomach or his thighs, on his chest or his biceps, contracting and relaxing them in turn, he brilliantly brought to life the most realistic circus performance: the lions jumped through their hoops in mid-air, the horses leaped over obstacles, the elephants stood up on their hind legs, the dancers twirled with frenzied twists of the body, the clowns in their tall caps and baggy trousers turned somersaults, and a whole pyramid of acrobats walked carefully along the tight-rope. Vsevolod was a real artist; he became absorbed in his performance and forgot everything else, moved his arms rapidly like a virtuoso at the final chords of his cadenza, rolled his flesh frenziedly, and his short, stocky body seemed indeed to become a circus ring trampled in a fantastic orgy by men and animals. After ten minutes he would fall back exhausted, wipe the sweat off his body with the striped vest, and look round at us triumphantly with his small cunning eyes, bristling his moustache under his flattened nose like a beetle. The barrack rang to the sound of applause, for the prisoners loved Vsevolod's circus, and after the performance gave him articles of clothing and even pieces of bread. "An artist," they would say, "a real artist. He has a whole kaveche in his pants."

Zelik Leyman was an altogether different type of artist. We all knew him from the hairdressing hut next to the bath-house, where he worked with the old Yercevo barber, Antonov. Although he had been born in Warsaw and had spent his whole life there, he would never talk to us in Polish. Antonov confidently described him as an informer, and this seemed probable, as Leyman had miraculously avoided the fate of other Jews from Poland, who were driven in hundreds to a slow death in the forest.

After the defeat of Poland in September 1939 the Jewish youth of the northern suburbs of Warsaw and the Jewish quarters of small towns and villages occupied by the Germans set out like a cloud of birds in the direction of the River Bug, leaving their elders to the German crematoria and gas-chambers, and seeking safety and a better life in the "fatherland of the world's proletariat", which had suddenly approached so closely to Warsaw. During the winter months of 1939-40 the Bug, along its whole course, was the scene of fantastic events, giving only a foretaste of what was inevitably approaching to plunge millions of the inhabitants of Poland in a five-year agony of lingering death. The Germans did not try to stop the escaping crowds, but with clubs and rifle-butts gave them a last practical lesson in their philosophy of the "race myth"; on the other side of the demarcation line the Russian guardians of the "class myth", dressed in long fur greatcoats and peaked caps, and with fixed bayonets, met the wanderers fleeing to the Promised Land with police dogs and bursts of light-machine-gun fire. During the months of December, January, February and March, the crowds of Jews camped on the neutral no man's land of a mile on the eastern bank of the Bug, sleeping under the open sky, covered with red eiderdowns, lighting fires at night or knocking at the doors of near-by peasant huts to beg for help and shelter. In the farm-yards small barter markets sprang up—clothing, jewellery, and dollars were given for food and help in getting across the river to the other side. Every peasant hut along the frontier became a small smuggling centre, and the populace of the neighbouring countryside prospered rapidly, blessing its unexpected good fortune. Every cottage was besieged by a crowd of shadows, peering in through the windows and tapping on the glass, and then returning, shrivelled and empty of hope, to their family camp fires. The majority returned to German-occupied Poland, and were swallowed up almost entirely during the next few years by the concentration camps of Auschwitz, Majdanek, Belsen and Buchenwald. Some of them, however, did not give up and remained on the banks of the river, waiting stubbornly for an opportunity to cross. Sometimes, at night, one would break away from the shapeless human mass, run several hundred yards across the snowy plain, and then, caught in the beam of a Soviet searchlight, fall on his face, hit with a machine-gun bullet. Then piercing wails mixed with outbreaks of spasmodic crying, hands were raised like the thin flames of the fires, angrily threatening the sky, then everything died down again into the silence of waiting.

During these months many refugees managed to cross through gaps in the line of soldiers, and the once Polish, now Soviet, towns of Bialystok, Grodno, Lvov, Kovel, Luck, and Baranoviche filled up suddenly with young Jewish communists who, despite everything that they had gone through on the frontier, seemed to be rapidly regaining the dreams of a country free from racial prejudice which had caused them to immigrate. The Russians assumed indifference at first, then started recruiting for voluntary settlement in the depths of Russia, giving the Jews the choice of a Soviet passport or return to their original place of domicile. And then an extraordinary thing happened—the same crowds who only a few months ago had risked their lives to enter the Promised Land now started a mass exodus in the opposite direction, back to the land of the Pharaohs. The Russians looked at this too with indifference, but they must have remembered the reactions of these candidates for Soviet citizenship to their first test of loyalty. In June 1940, after the defeat of France and the fall of Paris, the purges started in Eastern, Russian-occupied Poland, and hundreds of goods trains transported the Jewish lumpenproletariat of Polish villages to prisons and labour camps in Russia. Inside the camps they became the most bitter enemies of Soviet communism, more uncompromising in their hatred than old Russian prisoners and even the other foreigners. They exaggerated their hatred, as once they had exaggerated their love for it, with unequalled passion. They went out to work only to avoid being shot, but in the forest they sat warming themselves by the fire all day, working just hard enough to qualify for the first cauldron; in the evenings they rummaged in rubbish-heaps for something to satisfy their continual hunger, and died rapidly in the severe climate of the north with Biblical curses on their lips and the angry look of cheated prophets in their eyes. In Kargopol, they were usually all transported to the "penal" camp of the Second Alexeyevka, leaving in Yercevo only humble and obedient prisoners like Zelik Leyman. Zelik had drawn away from his bitter co-religionists and had decided, with similar exaggeration, to start life afresh in the camp. It was natural that he should be an informer, for he had obtained the hairdresser's job after barely two weeks in Yercevo, but, although it amused us while we were being shaved, we felt that it was unnecessary to treat us to speeches in praise of Stalin and the achievement of the October Revolution; doubtless he was promising himself an early release for his zeal. He was hated by the prisoners but they could not touch him, for as an informer he was protected and dangerous, and he seldom left the little room next to the barber's shop which he shared with Antonov. He was also saved from their revenge by the fact that he could play a violin beautifully. Many times, in the evenings, we would gather outside the windows of his room, to see Zelik standing before the mirror, leaning his large head, with a pale face, protruding ears and glassy colourless eyes, on the belly of the violin, and producing from it strangely beautiful and sad music. He saw us in the mirror and looked at our reflections with hatred and contempt. Sometimes we caught sight of our own faces in the mirror, and there was something moving, even tragic, in this exchange of our looks.

I went to the concert with Natalia Lvovna and Olga. Although the camp was passing through its worst period of hunger, the barrack of self-taught creative activities was full, and the prisoners' faces, though grey and swollen, contained a flicker of interest. But this time Kunin's inaugural speech was greeted with silence. Hunger breeds scepticism and disbelief, and the promise that we would one day become "full citizens of the Soviet Union" was repulsive and irritating when we could not know whether we would be alive to receive that privilege. We heard Kunin out calmly and with outward attention, holding back our shouts of protest. During the fiercest hunger (it must be understood that we were always hungry, but "real" hunger we called that condition when one looks upon everything around as something to eat) both sides—the prisoners and the jailers—lived in a tense atmosphere of instinctively increased watchfulness. Any careless reaction of anger might provoke an outbreak, so that we kept our hands over our mouths, and the guards theirs on the triggers of their rifles. It was like a savage war-dance in which the two warring groups, divided by the barrier of fire in the middle, sway for hours to the rhythm of a drum, staring at each other with distrust and gradually increasing fury.

All three of us had, besides hunger, other sorrows to distract us. Olga, a month ago, had said good-bye to her husband, Professor Boris Lazarovich N., who left with a transport for Mostovitza, knowing that she was seeing him for the last time; Natalia Lvovna knew that, with "reductions" in the camp administration, the day was approaching when she would be forced into general work; for me, it was also only ten days since Misha Kostylev's tragic death. We decided to see the concert as it was such an unusual occasion, and because we knew that it was necessary to follow at any price the set routine of camp life as long as possible. Even Natalia Lvovna, who had avoided me since our last conversation about Dostoevsky, now let herself be persuaded, and came to the theatre accompanied by Olga.

The lights went out in the barrack, and the stage was lit by three lamps in place of footlights. This was Kunin's innovation, and we welcomed it with a long sigh of admiration. The audience, plunged in darkness and silhouetted indistinctly against the light from the stage, looked like a team of miners in a flooded shaft. The waxen masks of their faces gleamed yellow against the background of ragged clothing and black fragments of the walls, and the half-open mouths seemed to be struggling with asphyxiation or calling for help rather than a concert. The air in the barrack was stifling; the stench of urine and excrement mingled with the peculiar, sickly-sweet odour of suppurating scurvy sores and rotting soaked clothes. Eyes red with exhaustion and blazing with hunger stared at the stage, fascinated. The concert began.

The first to appear was Tania. She looked lovely in a white ruffled dress bordered with lace which Kunin had borrowed beyond the zone for the occasion. She held a coloured handkerchief in her right hand, and waved it during the songs or caught it with an agile movement of both hands as she accompanied the words with gestures. Her small face, with a little snub nose and enormous eyes, surrounded by a thick line of black hair, was again, as once on the stage of the Moscow Opera, gay and radiant with laughter. She opened with an enchanting Russian song about "full stops" whose whole charm lies not in its story but in the wonderfully rich verbal variations and word-play of which it really consists. She had not sung more than the first few bars when the foresters' brigade started hissing from their corner and loudly shouting: "Moscow whore!" Tania stopped and looked at the audience, panic-stricken; tears stood in her lovely eyes and we thought for a moment that she would run off the stage without finishing even that one song. Then, as if she had come to some desperate decision, she resumed the song, but her slight voice tried in vain to drown the two burning, stubbornly and rhythmically repeated words. "Tania, Taniushka," I heard Natalia Lvovna whispering next to me, and then Samsonov turned round in his seat in the front row, looked towards the shouting group, and everything was suddenly still and quiet again. Tania sang on, though she could not recover the freedom with which she had started the first song. The audience heard her out to the end with indifference, and when Tania finally curtsied, lowering her head on her bosom with a theatrical gesture, there was only scattered and very timid applause. Poor Tania! That failure must have hurt her bitterly, for it was her first appearance on a stage since 1937; but she had to pay for preferring a free man to a prisoner. . . .

Vsevolod made close contact with his audience from the moment that he ran on to the stage energetically, wearing his sailor's vest and a sailor's cap with a ribbon and the gold lettering of "Red Fleet," the latter also borrowed beyond the zone. He stood still and putting his right hand to his forehead, began to look round the audience, as if trying to see the outline of distant land on the horizon from a crow's-nest. At this there was applause and laughter, and the prisoners shouted gaily: "Bravo, Vsevolod, a fine sailor, a wonderful sailor." Vsevolod bowed low and proceeded to "tune" his voice, snorting, coughing and feeling his throat with two fingers of his left hand. Evidently convinced that a true artist never sings without preliminary exercises, he always carefully went through all his professional ritual. The prisoners looked at each other and then back at the stage, shaking their heads in admiration: "Vsevolod knows what he's about, there's no doubt."

The barrack walls suddenly trembled when Vsevolod started on his first song, from the Soviet film "The Children of Captain Grant". He roared splendidly, gesticulating with his hands and throwing his whole body into the performance, bristling his moustache and rolling his eyes so that they shone from the distance like two silver buttons. The prisoners held their breaths and listened with sincere appreciation. After the song "Smile, Captain, Smile", he sang several others, also songs of the sea, whose subject or names I have now forgotten, but each of which was rewarded with tumultuous applause. Finally he asked for silence with the gesture of a real actor and announced, for his finale, the song "The sea spreads wide and far". From the expression on his face I guessed that, unlike the previous songs, this would be a sad one. In the deep silence Vsevolod took up a position, turned sideways to his audience, stretched his hands out before him, and after a moment sang in a voice heavy with tears:

> "We shall follow the waves that play
> On the sea which spreads far and wide.
> Comrade, we are sailing away
> Far, far from Russian soil."

When he had finished the verse and was about to repeat the refrain, he suddenly turned round to us and lifting his hands like a prison prophet, invited us to join in with a quick "All together now." And from several hundred throats burst a song, a cry of despair:

> "Comrade, we are sailing away
> Far, far from Russian soil."

The prisoners stood up as if at a given signal and, watching Vsevolod's hands beating time, repeated as if enchanted those two powerful lines. All the faces were full of emotion, in some eyes I even saw tears. And though the words sung with such feeling were like a curse flung by galley-slaves chained to the "Russian soil", yet the singing itself was full of a boundless nostalgia . . . nostalgia and longing for the land of suffering, hunger, death and degradation, the land of great fear, of hearts hard as stone and eyes seared with tears, the barren desert of human longings. Then, as never before, I realised, if only for a short moment, that Russian prisoners live beyond the bounds of their Russia and, hating it, long for it and recall it with all the strength of their choking feelings.

We had not completely recovered from Vsevolod's performance, and Natalia Lvovna was sitting next to me with her face buried in her hands, when Zelik Leyman, dressed in a dark suit which he had saved from liberty, came on to the stage. His bow was a trifle too stiff and superior, but as soon as he placed the violin against his shoulder, laid his head on it, and raised his bow with one hand, gripping the neck with the other, his features and his gestures became gentle and a shadow of sadness smoothed out his face. I can no longer remember what it was that he played, for my head began to ache intolerably, I felt the pangs of tormenting hunger, and hiding my face in my hands like Natalia Lvovna, I fell into a state of feverish indifference. I know only that Leyman's recital must have lasted a long time, for listening to the sounds of the violin, reaching me dimly as if through a padded wall, I had time to dream through the whole of that period of my life when, as a young boy, I stood in the street of my native provincial town in Poland and listened to the melodious laments and wailings for the destruction of Jerusalem which on every Judgment Day came from the smoky window-panes of the dilapidated synagogue. Zelik Leyman was so Jewish himself, he seemed to sob with his violin, he glorified himself and then suddenly relapsed into humility, he was afire with vengeance like a burning bush, angrily sweeping the bow over the strings, he prayed zealously with his face turned towards that quarter of the world where, on the ruins of Jerusalem, the Promised Land was to flourish again with olive groves: he sang his own fate and that of his nation, a fate which drew no distinction between love and hatred.

I came to, half-conscious, when I heard the sound of applause.

Zelik Leyman was bowing mockingly, and his thin, tight lips were smiling with contempt. The prisoners began to get up from the benches, and, still applauding, made their way towards the door. I turned to Natalia Lvovna, but her place was empty, and someone told me that she had felt weak and had left the theatre at the beginning of the violin recital. Dragging our legs heavily, we crowded in the foul air towards the door, and into the spring night which had already lit all the stars and brought a sharp, refreshing breath of thawing nature.

*   *   *   *   *

Several weeks after this memorable concert, shortly before the outbreak of the Russo-German war, there was a sudden rumour in the camp that Natalia Lvovna had tried to commit suicide by cutting her veins with a rusty penknife. Her neighbour on the bunk gave the alarm to the guard-house in time, and Natalia Lvovna was taken to the hospital, where she spent over two months in slow and unwilling return to life. After leaving the hospital, she did not go back to the camp accountants' office, but worked for a time in the kitchen, though she was soon dismissed for taking food out to prisoners. Then she was assigned to the supply centre, where she darned torn sacks, but by that time I was already working at the timber depot. I saw her often in the zone, and greeted her as usual from a distance, but we never exchanged another word. There are secrets which unite people, but there are also secrets which, in case of failure, separate them.

CHAPTER 12

"IN THE REAR OF THE WAR FOR THE FATHERLAND"

> "As for telling tales in general, it is very common.
> In prison the man who turns traitor is not ex-
> posed to humiliation; indignation against him is
> unthinkable. He is not shunned, the others make
> friends with him; in fact, if you were to try and
> point out the loathsomeness of treachery, you
> would not be understood."
> —DOSTOEVSKY—*The House of the Dead.*

1. A GAME OF CHESS

THE outbreak of the Russo-German war was responsible for some essential changes in my life: on June 29th, together with other foreigners and Russian political prisoners, I was taken off work at the food supply centre and sent to the newly-created 57th brigade, which was to work at haymaking in the forest clearings during the summer, and in the autumn and winter to help in the saw-mills and with the loading of felled trees on to open railway trucks.

The last week which I spent at the centre, however, allowed me to observe the effects of the German surprise attack, and the un-disguised psychological anxiety with which the camp's garrison and administrative staff met the news of the outbreak of war. The first reaction was a mixture of astonishment and fear; only Mr. Churchill's declaration, from which we gathered that "England is with us, not against us", brought some relief. The guard attached to our brigade greeted the news with a loud "urra", throwing his fur cap and his rifle—with bayonet fixed—into the air, and began to assure us excitedly that "England has never yet lost a war," clearly forgetting that only a few days ago England had been a "little island" which the Germans "could cover with their hat." A similar change of attitude, although of course in a much more intelligent form, was noticeable in the tone of the Soviet radio. News bulletins and political commentaries, which until recently had welcomed every German success in the West with wild ac-clamations, now overflowed with anti-German propaganda and cooed gently whenever they mentioned England or the occupied countries. So, externally at least, appeared the change of dancing partners. But actually we had already heard and recognised earlier the murmurs of the approaching storm. We did not ignore the meaning of the communiqué which Tass, the Soviet Press agency, issued during the first days of June. It was a "categorical denial of rumours, current in the West, that several Siberian divisions had been moved from the Far East to the banks of the River Bug" (which was then the boundary between Russian- and German-occupied Poland). The agency report calmly reassured its listeners that the army movements in question were made within the frame-work of normal summer manœuvres, and that the good-neighbourly relations of Germany and the Soviet Union, cemented by the pact of August 1939, could not be destroyed by the shameful intrigues of Western warmongers. The engineer Sadovski, once the friend of Lenin and Dierzhynski and vice-commissar for light industry in one of the Russian post-revolutionary governments, bent close to me and whispered in my ear that the denials of Tass are to intelligent people in Russia what positive newspaper reports are in England or France. The outbreak of war itself did not surprise Sadovski at all; but he would not make any prophecy as to its further course or outcome until the first month of the fighting had elapsed.

On the day after the first German attack on Russia, we were gathered outside the wooden hut which served as an office at the food supply centre, to hear Stalin's speech on the radio. It was the speech of a broken old man; he hesitated, his choking voice was full of melodramatic over-emphasis and glowed with humble warmth at all patriotic catch-phrases. We stood in silence, our eyes on the ground, but I knew that every prisoner there was suddenly thrilled by a spasm of hope, with that bewildered blindness of slaves for whom any hand which opens the prison gates is the hand of Providence itself. During the first few weeks of the war we talked of the fighting rarely and surreptitiously, but always in the same words: "They are coming!" It is a measure of the bestiality and despair to which the new system of slavery reduces its victims that not only the thousands of simple Russians, Ukrainians and nacmeny, for whom the Germans were the natural ally in their struggle against the hated labour camps, but also almost without exception all European and Russian communists, worldly, educated and experienced men, awaited from day to day with impatience and excitement the coming of Nazi liberators. I think with horror and shame of a Europe divided into two parts by the line of the Bug, on one side of which millions of Soviet slaves prayed for liberation by the armies of Hitler, and on the other millions of victims of German concentration camps awaited deliverance by the Red Army as their last hope.

The only free men whom I had an opportunity to observe, the camp guards, reacted, naturally, in quite a different fashion to the news of the German advance. For them the whole problem was summed up in the question: "Quis custodiet custodes?" They passed from the first instinctive anxiety about the fate of their "Socialist Fatherland"'(which in Russians, in my opinion, has the character of an organic inferiority complex towards the Germans), to uncertainty about closer and more tangible matters, their own particular fate. Their fear was that, to meet the demands of the front, staff reduction might begin in the camp, in other words that they might be forced to give up an easy and secure job in the north to spend their time wandering about in the trenches. After the first two weeks of the war the position was made clear in the most unexpected way. There was something incredible in the arrival at Yercevo of fresh contingents of young and healthy N.K.V.D. soldiers* to strengthen the garrisons of camps on the shore of the White Sea, while at the same time the names of the towns mentioned in the wireless communiqués made it quite clear that the front was rapidly moving eastward. Now brigades of twenty prisoners walked out to work guarded by two armed soldiers,† and the first blood that the camp laid at the altar of its threatened fatherland was the declaration of total war on potential internal enemies. Thus all politicals were removed from responsible technical posts, and replaced by free officials; all German prisoners from the Volga settlements were transferred from camp offices to the forest brigades, where, however, they were treated with great respect by the Russian prisoners, who believed that they would soon rule the country; all foreign and political prisoners were taken off work at the food supply centré, to prevent any danger of poisoning the food destined for co-operative stores outside the camp; the sentences of all who had been suspected of spying for the Germans were doubled, the liberation of political prisoners who were due to be released soon was postponed indefinitely, and several Polish officers, naturally suspected of pro-German sympathies, were

---

* The N.K.V.D. commands a powerful and quite independent army.

† If there were then twenty million prisoners in the camps, this must have cost the Soviet command about a million picked soldiers, who made no contribution to the war effort.

placed in solitary confinement. The camp breathed freely again, and the wave of Russian patriotism, which had receded in the terror and fear of the first weeks, flowed back. The patriotic self-confidence of the camp garrison was doubtless greatly influenced by a certain occurrence which I witnessed during the last day of my work at the food supply centre. We unloaded that day a truckful of Lithuanian pork, packed in jute wrappings stamped with the German import stamp. That load evidently did not reach its original destination, and after long wanderings finally arrived at Yercevo. To commemorate the outbreak of the "War for the Fatherland" the pork was divided equally between the speclarok—the shop supplying the ten highest officers of the camp command—and the modest shop near the camp zone for the administrative staff and the garrison.

A month passed and nothing happened. Once, when we were haymaking, Sadovski was asked for his conjectures of the future. He took a few twigs, two handfuls of hay and some berries of different colours, spread them on the grass, and opened a fascinating lecture. In his opinion, the first four weeks of the fighting would be decisive. While listening to official Soviet communiqués, it was necessary to keep before one's mind the map of Russia in order to determine the speed of the German advance. If the advance was very rapid, it was a bad sign, if only moderately quick—then there was nothing to fear. The defeat of Russia could only be possible if signs of inner demoralisation accompanied defeats at the front. If the Red Army retreated in such panic and at such speed that it could only be held back by the bayonets of the N.K.V.D. Army in the rear, then, finding itself between two fires, it would turn round against its own rulers and start a civil war in Russia itself. But nothing of the kind was actually happening. Soviet forces were retreating in proper order, and could retreat like that right up to the Urals, where for years a reserve centre of war industry had been built up, at the cost of great technical effort and human lives from the Ural labour camps, with just such a possibility in mind. The circumstances of Russia's final victory over the Germans would depend on the military and political tactics of her Western allies.

This view of the situation appeared to me to be quite logical and accurate, and I accepted it as my own. My own position had altered greatly since the signing of the Polish-Russian pact of July 1941, and the declaration of a general amnesty for all Polish prisoners in Russia. I could now desire Russian defeat only from a feeling of revenge, not from any logical reasoning or on the basis of any particular feeling towards the Germans. I found myself among the fifteen or twenty out of the two thousand prisoners in Yercevo who in face of continuous Russian defeats had the courage to believe and say loudly that Russia would not lose the war. Later I had to pay dearly for my opinion when brought before the Third Section of the N.K.V.D.

The situation of Poles in Russia was greatly altered by the Sikorski-Maiski pact and the amnesty. Before the Russo-German war broke out we were regarded as "anti-Nazi fascists", and cowards because we had been defeated so easily by the Germans; from the beginning of the war in June, until the end of July, we were just ordinary pro-Nazi fascists and, since Russia herself was suffering heavy defeats, perhaps not such cowards after all; in August, when the pact was signed, we suddenly became fighters for freedom and allies. The guard of the 57th brigade, who, I was told, before that time had not spared Poles many insulting reproaches for their defeat in 1939, patted me on the back when the news of the amnesty came and said: "Well, my boy, now we'll fight the Germans together." This sudden reconciliation did not please me for two reasons: first, a prisoner can never forgive his warder, and second, it turned against me my fellow-prisoners, both Russian and foreign, who were not fortunate enough to have been born Poles, and to many of whom I had become attached more deeply than to any of my own compatriots. After the amnesty other prisoners became hostile towards the Poles, regarding them from that time as potential allies in the hated task of defending Soviet prisons and labour camps.

In December 1941 we heard Stalin give another and very different speech. I shall never forget that strong voice, cold and penetrating, those words hammered out as if with a fist of stone. He said that the German offensive had been arrested at the outskirts of Moscow and Leningrad, that the day of victory over German barbarism was approaching, and that the thanks for this must go not only to the heroes of the Red Army, to airmen, sailors, partisans, workers and farmers, but also to those who guarded "the rear of the war for the Fatherland". The prisoners, collected in the barracks to hear the speech, listened to it with expressions of helpless despair on their faces, while I thought of Sadovski's theory and the reinforcements of N.K.V.D. troops with which the garrisons of the Kargopol camp had been supplied just after the declaration of war. Yes, even here, we were a part of the "rear of the war for the Fatherland".

*   *   *   *   *

That is the background of the incident which I witnessed during the first days of July 1941 in the technical barrack at Yercevo. This barrack was situated at the turn of the path which led from my barrack to the guard-house, and was inhabited exclusively by prisoners whose professional qualifications made them indispensable to the authorities, who assigned them to special functions in the camp. Most of them were technical experts and engineers with higher education and training, though there were also a few humanists who exceptionally, and only because of their high qualifications, filled minor posts in the camp administration. Assignment to the technical group gave certain privileges in the way of housing, food and clothing, which, needless to say, were not granted to prisoners, even with the highest education, who worked in the labour brigades and lived in ordinary barracks. The technical barrack was more comfortable than the others, with spaces between the individual bunks and a solid table at either end; the "technicals" received waterproof blouses of sailcoth and high jute boots, and the special iteerovski cauldron, equal in amount to the third stakhanovite cauldron, but strengthened with a spoonful of vegetable fat and a portion of "cyngotnoye", chopped-up raw vegetables. In the undeveloped social structure of the camp the technicals were thus an aristocracy of the second degree, without the power over other prisoners which belonged to the urkas who overran the executive departments of the administration, but nevertheless distinctly elevated by their privileges and style of living above the grey mass of the slave proletariat. All the technicals had been sentenced to ten or fifteen years for counter-revolutionary activities, and from the moment war was declared they were "assisted" in their functions by uneducated free assistants. Zyskind, a Red Army lieutenant, who was serving only two years for stealing regimental funds, remained in charge of the solitary confinement prison within the camp zone.

The special cauldron carried with it a tacit condition *sine qua non*, from which only the indispensable experts with very high qualifications were free—the obligation to spy and denounce for the

N.K.V.D. No one was surprised at this and no one was shocked—after all, night always follows day. Every Wednesday evening a handsome Russian woman with a bulging brief-case made her appearance in the barrack—this was Senior Lieutenant Strumina of the N.K.V.D.'s Third Section. Like a priest who visits a lonely, distant village to say a quiet mass, she greeted all passing prisoners with a gentle, polite "zdrastvuytie" which from her sounded like the old country form of greeting, "God be with you". In a small room adjacent to one of the barracks she would instal her travelling confessional.

I had several friends in the technical barrack. Fienin, a well-known hydro-electric engineer, often talked to me with sympathy of conditions in Poland under German occupation; I played chess with Weltmann, an engineer from Vienna; Makhapetian, an Armenian engineer, was my closest friend and like a brother to me; Yerusalimski, a historian who had once carried on a bitter academic controversy with Professor Tarle, the leading Soviet historian, and now would not be parted from his more fortunate opponent's "Napoleon", became my friend through Makhapetian. Only a pair of inseparable friends, Doctor Loevenstein and the Russian airfield-constructor Mironov, treated me with reserve and suspicion. They were known throughout the camp as "the two Gorkists", because they were both serving ten years for—Gorki. Loevenstein, a good-natured, fat man in gold spectacles, had been Gorki's doctor during the great writer's last years, and his presence in the camp seemed to give the lie to all rumours that the old bard of the October Revolution had been poisoned;* Mironov, close and silent, was unfortunate enough to be responsible for the construction of the airfield from which the huge new Soviet plane "Gorki" took off on its trial flight, only to come to pieces in mid-air after a few moments.

Thanks to Makhapetian, I had a standing invitation to the technical barrack at any time of the day or night. I took advantage of this, perhaps straining the laws of hospitality, to visit it almost every evening, so eager was I for intelligent conversation, for the formulas of politeness now so rare, and for that particular atmosphere of sarcastic mockery which accompanies any larger gathering of intellectuals. Exhausted by the absurd nightmare of the Soviet system, I could find a moment of relief and nervous relaxation only

* See Appendix I.

in the technical barrack. Its inhabitants looked on everything which happened to them and around them as a farce in rather bad taste, in which the criminals take the parts of policemen, while the policemen sit handcuffed against the wall. Only in the periods of hunger and increased terrorism the laughter in the barrack died down, and instead could be heard whispers from the wings about the further acts of this already over-long tragi-comedy. This made me wonder just what these men related as information to Lieutenant Strumina—each of them had already whispered enough to his neighbour to have earned him a second sentence if it had been reported.

One stifling July evening we sat playing chess at one of the tables —Loevenstein with Mironov, I with Weltmann. The barrack was still and quiet. Some of the technicals slept, Makhapetian and Yerusalimski were writing letters on their knees, Zyskind read a book lying on his bunk, his legs resting on the ledge of the bunk above. Weltmann would always beat me mercilessly at chess, but he liked playing with me, for, like every bungler, I calculated several moves in advance, aloud and in German, and this gave Weltmann the illusion that he was sitting on a calm Sunday in his "kaffenhaus", carefully studying the chess corner of the "Wiener Zeitung" with a group of friends. Punctually at midnight the wireless loudspeaker was switched on to broadcast the news bulletin. We did not interrupt our game until the barrack door opened with a clatter, and a young engineer, whose name I have now forgotten, staggered into the room, clutching the bunks for support with uncertain hands. The speaker had just finished reading the Supreme Command's Order of the Day, and had started on the communiqués from the front. He had to tell us only that Soviet planes had brought down thirty-five of the enemies', and that the infantry, in a courageous counter-attack, had recovered two villages in the Ukraine. The newcomer listened to this, leaning against a vertical beam, one leg crossed over the other. When the loudspeaker was disconnected, he shook himself all over like a wet dog, and with the reckless daring of the drunk, shouted loudly: "It would be interesting to hear how many of our planes the Germans have brought down!"

The barrack became so still that I could hear the sound of a chessman sliding on the board of the "two Gorkists" and the rustling of Makhapetian's notepaper. Zyskind closed his book violently, jumped off his bunk, and went out of the barrack. The young engineer pushed himself away from the beam, threw himself on to the bench by our table, and laid his head on his folded arms. From the neighbouring board a chessman, shaken by the sudden jerk of the table, fell off on to the floor. Mironov picked it up and quietly hissed: "If you're fool enough to get drunk, stuff a gag in your mouth." The drunk lifted his head for a moment and waved his hand heedlessly. A quarter of an hour later he and Makhapetian were taken away by two junior officers from the Third Section.

We played on as if nothing had happened, stopping only when Makhapetian returned, to hear his story. In a voice breaking with emotion, he told us that, in the presence of Zyskind, he had to verify and sign the text of the words spoken by the accused. Zyskind came back about one o'clock and, without looking at anyone, lay down in his former position on the bunk, his face hidden from us by the open book. Weltmann was just about to mate for the second time that evening, when we heard the sound of a shot beyond the zone, instantly lost in the woolly wrappings of the night. I felt stifled and sick: Weltmann's face looked old and shrivelled with fear.

"A war tribunal," he whispered, holding by the mane a wooden knight ready to jump.

"I resign—your game," I said, scattering the pieces on the board with a trembling hand.

Zyskind read on unperturbed, while our neighbours went on with their game: Loevenstein hanging over the board like a bird of prey, Mironov with his elbows against the edge of the table, his head hunched into his shoulders.

"Check—and mate," Loevenstein shouted triumphantly after a time.

"Oh, but I didn't notice that bishop," protested Mironov, using the German word "laufer", which, as we all knew and as we all understood it then, also means a "runner", or "henchman".

"Well, that's it—mate. One should always keep one's eyes open when playing chess."

Then Loevenstein turned towards the bunk where Zyskind was lying and, wiping his spectacles with a handkerchief, said with a hardly noticeable gleam of sarcasm in his eyes:

"Did you hear the news, Comrade Zyskind? Of us all, only you have the chance of standing soon in the ranks of our country's defenders, and . . ." he hesitated, "I do sincerely envy you. As for those sick in the prison, please bring them round to the medical hut tomorrow after the morning roll-call."

Zyskind lowered his book and nodded his head in agreement.

2. HAYMAKING

The way to work led by a narrow and winding path, round the food supply centre, through a damp clearing near the camp, then by a wooden track through a small copse, then along another path through three new clearings near a ramshackle, rotting hut which had once served as a tool-shed, then across a peat-bog and a wooden bridge over the stream, then by zigzagging paths through another wood, and finally—into an enormous field where, after the snows melted, broad, sharp marsh grass grew towards the sun, reaching up to the waist of a short man.

Dear God, haymaking! Could I ever have dreamed, when, as a young boy, I learnt to scythe for fun in my native countryside, that I would one day earn my keep this way. . . . And yet I remember that summer with great emotion and happiness, for then I felt an intensity, a freshness of experience such as writers call the inner resurrection, which I have never felt again. It was almost a year since I had been out so far beyond the camp zone, and as once I had felt the blades of grass during the only period of exercise which I was allowed in the Grodno prison, so now I touched with beating heart the flowers, the trees and the hedges. Though the road was difficult and long (about three miles each way), I would walk out at dawn with the brigade in single file, with a light and springing step, and in the evenings I returned sunburnt, exhausted, full of fresh air, berries and the beauty of the landscape, drunk with the smell of the forest and of hay—like a gad-fly which stumbles on its thin little legs when the horse's blood has gone to its head.

In command of brigade 57 was the old joiner Iganov, the one who always prayed till late into the night on his bunk, a quiet, calm man, helpful and passionately devoted to farmwork. He never took advantage of the usual privileges of a brigadier; every day, having written on a wooden tablet the names of all his workers, he took up a scythe and stood with the rest of us in the row, and it was only an hour before we packed up that he left us in order to pace out with even strides the area that each of us had mowed.

Every evening he would sit down in the barrack and compare the
work done that day by each prisoner in his brigade with the
officially-prescribed norm; these figures he submitted to the camp
office, where prisoners' rations were allotted according to working
capacity. Both guards usually slept most of the day in the haycocks
by the edge of the field, so that often from where we worked we
could see only the gleam of their bayonets and the tips of the
sharpened poles which strengthened the haycocks with the
traditional branches of red-green sorb placed on top. We lived
quietly and pleasantly. When we marched out at dawn we could
see the last stars twinkling dimly in the opal sky, and the whole
zone was grey. After an hour's walk the sky began to take on the
colour of a pearly shell, pink and blue at the edges and white in the
middle. Sometimes, when entering the field, we surprised a herd of
elks grazing, and long after, as we were replacing with our forks the
hay which they had pulled off and trampled about, we could hear
the sound of their hooves as they raced away. And once Iganov
showed us, at the edge of the forest, a large lair, trodden out in the
moss, with wisps of fur and half-eaten bunches of berries scattered
round it, and putting his nose carefully to the still steaming excrements, told us that not half an hour ago one of the huge Archangel bears had lain there. As soon as the sun rose from behind
the forest, we would spread out across the field like beaters before a
hunt, and with wide sweeps of our scythes begin to cut down the
waving grass, leaving behind us long rows of hay, even as furrows of
newly-ploughed earth. About nine we stopped work for fifteen
minutes; one small whetstone was passed from hand to hand and
its rough underside caressed in a sweeping arc the gleaming edges of
our scythes. When the whistle blew at the saw-mill in the camp at
midday, we dispersed in twos and threes and, lying under the haycocks, we ate bread, which we had saved from the previous day,
with a few berries. Then we went to sleep and slept so deeply that
at one o'clock the harassed Iganov had to shake our legs violently to
wake us.

The northern summer is short, stifling and heavy with the
poisonous exhalations of marshes and bogs. During the afternoon
the sky—crystal-clear at dawn and inflated like a full sail at evening
—wrinkles and shimmers in the heated air like the ashes of tinfoil
held over the flame of a candle. Many times, alarmed by the clouds
of black smoke rising from behind some copse, we ran with our

guards to near-by clearings to put out fires of turf, dry moss and wood chips which the burning torch of the sun had ignited. In the first days of September the northern rains begin, and continue throughout the whole month. I remember the emotion I felt when, on the last day of the haymaking, we all ran to the dilapidated way-side shed to take shelter from the storm of rain and hail which had surprised us. Drenched to our shirts, we stood under the rotting roof on which the hail bounced loudly, while the warm, autumn storm raged outside, and the shutters banged in the wind and turned with a screech on rusty hinges, giving us glimpses of the green clearing, the bent tops of trees and the sky dappled with pink streaks of lightning. I poked the ashes with a stick and I felt that tears were mingled with the drops of rain which streamed down my cheeks and into my mouth. It was sufficient to turn one's back on the two figures with guns to feel oneself quite at liberty. But the hay-making was over, a month had passed since the amnesty of Poles was first announced, hundreds of them were leaving the camps every day, yet I was returning for the last time from the fields and woods where I could feel alive, to the wired camp zone where death shares one's bed.

During the haymaking I made friends with the old bolshevik, Sadovski. I liked him for a certain inner truthfulness, a fanatic solidarity in camp life, and a sharp intelligence which he delighted in using to split the proverbial hair into four. Sadovski despite everything had remained a communist, as a man who is already too old to reconsider his early decisions remains blindly faithful to his old ideals. Like that story-book hero who was granted eternal youth, he was doomed to become a heap of loathsome corruption if he once broke his enchanted vows. "If I ceased to believe in that," he would often say, "I would have nothing left to live for." "That" meant in practice a deep attachment to the tradition of the "old guard", chiefly Lenin and Dierzhynski, and a gleam of hatred in his eyes whenever the name of Stalin was mentioned. He told me that Lenin, before his death, had often warned his old comrades against Stalin—"That cunning Georgian, who likes his lamb shashlyk over-peppered and over-salted, will over-pepper and over-salt the Revolution."* From his meagre hints about his own life I knew only that he had a grown-up son in Vladivostok, of whom he

---

* Isaac Deutscher also quotes this saying, very popular in Russia among the older generation of communists, from Trotsky's *Mein Leben*.

had heard nothing since the moment of his own arrest—in 1937; when asked about his wife, his face twitched painfully and his eyes closed. I suppose that before his arrest he did indeed hold a high position in the Party hierarchy, for he once told me of the faked official statistics which had wiped out of existence several national minorities in Russia, including the Polish. Once he explained to me with excitement how, at the time of an academic breathing-space, when Soviet historians were exhausted by their eternal race to keep up with succeeding changes in official historical orientation, he spent a whole night discussing with "Emelian" the probable trends of Soviet historical thought. When I asked him who Emelian was, he replied simply and with slight astonishment that it was Yaroslavski—the chief of the powerful Anti-Religious League of the Soviet Union. Sadovski was completely in the power of the demon of logical reasoning—all that could be logically proved became automatically just and true for him. Sometimes, in a kind of somnambulistic trance, his own reasoning would lead him to the conclusion that the Great Purges, of which he himself was a victim, were the logical outcome of certain unquestionable dialectic premises of the October Revolution. Suddenly faced with that aspect of the question which concerned him personally, he would start like a sleep-walker waking on the edge of a precipice, and shrug his shoulders with a gentle smile. Doubtless this is how Hegel must have looked, when he replied to remonstrances that his theories did not fit the facts with the words "so much the worse for the facts". But Sadovski could always fall back on his favourite "Japanese anecdote". This related that the Mikado decree ordering the Japanese to take off their hats before officials was substituted first by one forbidding hats and replacing them with caps, then one "forbidding all head-covering"; finally came an order to "cut off the heads of all non-officials so that they shall have nothing on which to wear hats or caps". In a similar way Roman Catholics talk of the doctrine of papal infallibility in spiritual matters, and explain all the human weaknesses of the Church's stumbling servants in secular matters. One has only to see old communists in Soviet prisons to become convinced that communism is a religion.

After the haymaking was over, the 57th brigade was assigned to the timber depot, where until midday we sawed wood into blocks for the saw-mill, and spent the rest of the day loading fir trees, to be made into masts, on to open railway trucks. Then began one of the most difficult periods of my life. My organism, toughened by the dose of vitamins which it had received during the haymaking, instead of strengthening me for further exertions, reacted with a strong attack of scurvy. All my teeth were loose in my gums as if set in soft plasticine, and my legs and ankles became covered with painful festering boils which suppurated so much that my trousers stuck to my legs and I stopped taking them off at night, sleeping with a rolled-up jacket under my feet. I suffered from night-blindness, and in the evenings Iganov had to lead me back to the camp zone. The work at the timber depot seemed to me to be beyond human endurance, even though, after my stakhanovite efforts at the food supply centre, I ought to have regarded it as a rest in its own way. I shivered in the rain and frost, my loose teeth chattered in my mouth, and every few moments I had to stop sawing to clutch at my heart which seemed to be bursting through my ribs. Frequently now I would fall down under the burden of the fir masts, to the quiet and patient despair of Sadovski, who was in front of me. Sadovski did not last long either, though he reacted to his new sufferings not with scurvy, but with hunger dementia. It was at this time that he snatched a tinful of soup from my hands outside the kitchen. I could swear that he did not recognise me then, even though he looked straight at me with distended, matter-encrusted eyes. I forgave him then, and I forgive him now—him, or his mortal remains. He found himself beyond the protection of the magic formula of his youthful faith; in a situation where the logical brain of man can no longer control the animal reflexes of his body.

But all this was as nothing compared to my greatest suffering: the amnesty passed me by as if with some inexplicable obstinacy. Every evening I would stumble through the zone to the transit barrack, where parties of Poles, leaving other camp sections for freedom, would spend the night before their final release. In the daytime I left my work whenever a junior officer of the N.K.V.D. Second Section with a piece of paper in his hand appeared at the depot, and I would try to catch his eye; but I was evidently forgotten, perhaps even by mistake crossed off the list of the living. If it had not been for Makhapetian, I would have broken down completely during those days of torturing uncertainty. Only he never tired of comforting me, he brought me my soup from the kitchen in the evenings, dried my leg-wrappings, listened with unwavering interest to my explanations of the political and military theories which Sadovski had passed on to me, asked for my views on the course of the war, praised the objectiveness with which I summed up Russia's potential military and industrial strength, stroked my shaved head with kindness when I was near despair, or took me over to the technical barrack for a game of chess. Makhapetian was indeed like a brother to me—and even more, a brother and a friend in one person. But even I had to listen to his perpetual stories of the "good old days", when, as the Deputy Commissar for the Aircraft Industry of the Armenian Republic, he had been a friend of "Mikoyan himself".

The autumn evenings are not so dark as those of the winter, so that night-blindness consists of an uncertain stumbling rather than a helpless struggle in the invisible bonds of the night. One November evening I was carefully making my way along the slippery planks of the path to the barrack, when I was stopped in front of the camp craftsmen's shed by a short stocky prisoner. I recognised him even before he led me into his workshop—it was an old Armenian cobbler whom I had seen before with Makhapetian, when, on free days, they whispered quietly together in a foreign language. He was known in the camp as an extremely honest and helpful man, and it was even said that he refused the customary bribes of extra bread for mending the boots of camp chiefs. Having seated me on a low stool, he first looked behind a partition to make sure that there was no one still at work in the tailors' section of the hut, and then considered me in silence for a long time.

"Listen," he finally said, "is it true that you talk in the camp about a Russian victory over the Germans?"

"Yes, why?"

"Well, it's like this," he sat down next to me, "you know that Lieutenant Strumina's office is next to the corner of the barrack where the tailors sit?"

"Yes, I know," I said, and a feeling of foreboding passed over me.

"Well then," the cobbler went on, "a tailor I know has pierced a small hole between the planks in the wall. In the daytime he covers it with a layer of plaster, and on Wednesday evenings he listens to what the informers have to say to Strumina. Yesterday he called me to the hole, but not only because they were talking about you . . ."

"About me?"

"Yes. Strumina first asked the informer what sort of morale

there was in the camp. He answered that, apart from a handful of good citizens of the Soviet Union, who only in the camp came to realise the error of their ways, all prisoners long for a German victory. 'That's understandable,' says Strumina, 'and what about the little Pole?' The man said that he had come specially to tell her that 'the little Pole Gerling' is of a completely different opinion. 'No wonder'—says Strumina—'we have signed a pact with the Polish Government and declared an amnesty for them.' But the informer would not give up there. 'All Poles,' he said, 'even though they are going back to freedom, talk in the transit barrack—in whispers—of the defeat of Russia and desire it just as eagerly as those who remain in the camp.' 'Well, so what?' asks Strumina. 'Well, so this Gerling is certainly not the simple student that he makes himself out to be, but probably a Trotskyist, or else someone very important, one of Colonel Beck's collaborators. For, O comrade Strumina, you don't know how well he can discuss politics.' 'There is the Sikorski pact,' Strumina hesitated. 'Yes, surely, but in every pact there are reservations and special clauses. Just let him get out, and you will see what happens if they send him to America. Wouldn't it be better to take him in a transport to a special tribunal of the N.K.V.D. in Moscow and unmask him as a spy?' 'We'll see,' says Strumina—and that was all."

"Listen," I asked him breathlessly, "couldn't you see who it was through the hole?"

"I didn't need to. I recognised his voice."

"Who was it?" I asked, gripping his arm.

"I wasn't sure if I should tell you . . ."

"Tell me," I shouted furiously, "for Christ's sake tell me!"

And quietly, not looking me in the eyes, he said: "Makhapetian."

CHAPTER 13

MARTYRDOM FOR THE FAITH

TOWARDS the end of November 1941, four months after the general amnesty for Polish prisoners in Russian camps had been announced, when I knew that I should not survive until spring and when I had given up all hope of being released, I decided to go on a hunger-strike in protest.

Only six Poles remained in Yercevo of the two hundred who had been there. Every day dozens of them passed through our peresylny on their way out from all the main sections of the Kargopol camp: Mostovitza, Ostrovnoye, Krouglitza, Nyandoma and the two Alexeyevkas. Yercevo seemed suddenly to have become empty for us, and it looked as if unless we died soon, we would share the fate of the "old Poles" from the Ukraine, who had been cut off from Poland by the outbreak of the 1917 Revolution, and who, until the announcement of the amnesty, had considered themselves to be Russians. We now understood their bitterness when they learnt that the Polish-Russian pact also considered them to be Russians.

My hunger-strike was not so much an act of courage as a desperate step which had every appearance of common sense. I was in the final stages of scurvy, physically exhausted, and according to experienced prisoners I had only six months to live. A hunger-strike was something almost completely unknown in Soviet prison camps, and even in peace-time it was treated as industrial sabotage, punished with a heavy additional sentence or even with death; what is more, I could hardly expect my physical condition to be improved by a period of several days without any food or drink. I recognised all the arguments as well as did the friends who advised me against the step. But what finally decided me was the thought that when I came to die in a few months' time, it would be with the bitter knowledge that I had given in without a struggle. As long as parties of Poles still went out into liberty through Yercevo there was always a slight chance that I would remind the authorities of my existence by a gesture of self-destruction. I risked cutting my life short by a few months, but although even that decision demands a

190

great deal of determination, yet the stake was too high for me to hesitate. A man who is buried alive and suddenly wakes in darkness does not think reasonably, but jerks his body and beats with bleeding fingers on the lid of the coffin with all the strength of his despair.

But it was not so easy to convince the other Poles of the necessity for action, and yet without their participation the hunger-strike would lose the moral force of a solid common effort. During several evenings in succession we met together in the corner of one of the barracks: M., an engineer; B., a teacher from Stanislavov; T., a policeman from Silesia; Miss Z., a bank clerk from Lvov; L., the owner of a saw-mill near Vilna, and myself. Their objections to my proposal wavered between exaggerated fear and undue hope. "Not everything is lost yet, and a hunger-strike, as an offence committed after the announcement of the amnesty, will only serve to make our situation worse, and perhaps exclude us from the amnesty altogether. Besides, for all we know, they may still treat us as Soviet citizens despite the signing of the agreement in London, and you know that hunger-strikes and refusal to work are punished by death. . . . But everything isn't lost yet, our lives are in God's hands. . . . They surely can't keep genuine Poles like ourselves in the camp, and release people who until recently were denying their Polish nationality. . . ."

But they could, however, only too easily. The difficulty of our dispute lay in the fact that both sides had, of necessity, to use entirely irrational arguments. My friends believed in the justice of Divine decrees and in the force of international obligations; I believed in the possibility of escaping our fate by deliberately provoking it. On the evening of November 30th, when I had almost made up my mind to strike by myself if they would not, I went for the last time to our corner of B.'s barrack. The engineer M. sat, as usual, in the darkest corner of the lower bunk, resting his thin, ascetic face on his hands, and looking at me with tentative friendliness. The teacher B., formerly an officer of the reserve, who after the outbreak of the Russo-German war had been locked up in the camp prison and had only recently returned to Yercevo from the Second Alexeyevka, seemed to be looking for a way out of the situation in which he was placed, and was obviously avoiding my eyes. T. and L. played draughts with assumed indifference, and Miss Z., her hands folded across her stomach, was whispering a prayer. In the murky light of the barrack they looked like a group of tourists lost in some rocky mountain cleft while darkness falls, who are ready to risk a dangerous attempt to escape if only their guide will take upon himself all responsibility for its success or failure. I stood before them, seized also with a sudden fear, not knowing what I should do.

"You must remember how I was denounced by Makhapetian," I said at last. "Which of you can be certain that he doesn't owe his prolonged imprisonment to equally absurd accusations which have been made against him by an informer? After the Ribbentrop-Molotov pact of 1939, German communists went on hunger-strike in a Moscow prison. And what happened? Of the six hundred who participated five hundred-odd were released and repatriated, and the fact that I myself, towards the end of January, saw three of those who had been detained in Russia, in our own peresylny, surely proves that not one was taken before a firing squad. . . ."

These two arguments made an unexpected impression, and for a moment I was almost sorry that they had agreed so easily and so readily. But it was now too late to draw back, and we decided that M. should not strike with us as he had a serious heart disease, and he was also the only Pole in the camp besides us, the only man who could hope to be released and whom we could trust to take news of us out to liberty, in case our mutiny should end before an emergency war tribunal. The very same evening we handed in our bread ration and soup tickets at Samsonov's office, though we took the precaution of going there separately, at half-hourly intervals, and afterwards we were careful not to meet or talk in the zone. From the stories of Russian prisoners we had learnt enough about the Soviet penal code to know that the slightest infringement of regulations is treated as the most serious offence if it has any appearance of an organised conspiracy. We had committed ourselves.

The days immediately preceding my decision to strike had taught me some curious things about myself. After the amnesty, when my release seemed to be only a matter of time, I had felt guilty and ashamed before my Russian fellow-prisoners because I was leaving the camp by the simple accident of being a Pole, and not as an ordinary prisoner, leaving it, too, to defend the régime which was responsible for their imprisonment and their suffering. But as the weeks passed without release, and the gates of the camp still barred my way out to freedom, I lost all my generosity and humanity.

Gradually, without admitting it even to myself, I began to hate the Russian prisoners with all my heart, from the very depths of my hopelessness, as if with invisible hands they were holding me back by my ragged jerkin, pulling me down into the quicksand of their own despair, to shut me out for ever from the light of day because their own eyes had for years vainly tried to pierce the obscure night of their existence. I became suspicious, peevish and boorish, avoided even my best friends, and received the expressions of their sympathy with unhealthy mistrust. This psychological condition drove me to my decision as much as any reasoning or sheer despair. I wanted to assert, with my own life if necessary, the existence of the right to an ultimate free choice, a right which they, the eternal slaves, would never have dared to claim for themselves. My behaviour was repulsive and humiliating to me, but I could not defend myself against it as a man cannot defend himself against his own nature. It was the greatest self-degradation of my life, this longing to be revenged on the other prisoners only because I was threatened with having to share for ever their accursed fate.

Among the six Poles who had joined together in a hunger-strike relations were developing badly. Despite the appearance of friendship and solidarity which a common struggle had created, we did not trust each other, and waited only to see which of us would be the first to break down or betray the rest. In our fear of the trial before us, we suspected above all that the hunger-strike might for every one of us become the opportunity to gain freedom at the price of the others' lives. We were like a shipwrecked company, drifting in one lifeboat to some unknown destination; they are necessary to each other, for every pair of hands mans an oar, but not one of them can for a moment forget that every man in the boat must eat until the meagre food supply is exhausted. Although if I had struck alone I would have forcibly isolated myself from the rest of the Poles in the camp, yet to strike together was to assume the dangerous character of an organised action. And, we wondered, what if one of us should break down? Would he save himself by incriminating the others, or would his failure help them to a quicker triumph? We were bound together as human destinies are on earth—every move in the direction of freedom involved someone else's suffering. We saw so clearly what lies hidden in a human heart: the rare gift of nobility in moments of comparative safety, and the seed of failure to live up to it in the face of death. It was our pettiness and our cowardice, not our courage, that held us together. We decided on common action only when that silent distrust could separate us irrevocably or weld us together. And in that atmosphere of tension it was no accident that, when we shook hands in agreement on that gloomy November evening, we decided to exclude M. from the hunger-strike as a pledge of our honesty and good faith in this final test. A snowstorm was raging outside, and on the table by B.'s bunk the yellow flame of a candle-stump wavered uncertainly. M. accepted with a nod of the head, though a bitter little smile passed over his pale face.

When I returned from Samsonov's office to my barrack, I was greeted by silence. All the conversations round the table broke off suddenly, my nearest neighbours on the bunk edged away as if I were contagious, my friends avoided my eyes and answered my questions unwillingly The news of our hunger-strike had already spread throughout the camp, arousing excitement and fear everywhere. The feelings of my Russian friends towards me must have been as embarrassing as mine were towards them. When the amnesty was first announced, they had treated me with reserve, almost with dislike, for the prospect of my miraculous release was for them a break of prison solidarity. But the long months of waiting which followed, while I gradually lost all hope of freedom, had again brought them closer to me, though for the same reason I still kept myself apart from them. I suspected that their sympathy for me was really the comfort which condemned men draw from the despair of others. Their reactions to the news of the hunger-strike were equally complex. They were excited and fascinated by the very fact that we had dared to lift a hand against the unalterable laws of slavery, which had never before been disturbed by one gesture of rebellion. On the other hand, there was the instinctive fear, which they had retained from their former lives, that they might be involved in something dangerous, perhaps a case threatened with a war tribunal. Who was to know whether the hearings would not reveal the "rebel's" conversations in the barrack immediately after committing the offence? Better keep away from him, at least until the Third Section takes up some definite attitude towards his unprecedented case. There were also other, more hidden, reasons for their attitude. Our hunger-strike was a revolt of foreigners. Its failure would prove once and for all that even the people "from over there" cannot force a hole in the prison wall which separates all

Russia from the rest of the world. But if the rebellion were successful, it would show only too clearly that even behind the barbed wire
of the camps different laws exist for foreigners and for Russians.
Our success would increase their despair, for in a situation without
any solution it is better to be certain that there are no exceptions to
the common fate. Nothing comforts a suffering heart so much
as the sight of another's suffering; and nothing deprives one of
hope so much as the thought that only a chosen few have a right to
hope.

I was alone, then. Lying on my bunk, I looked round the barrack
with a feeling of loneliness and fear. The prisoners were preparing
for the night, whispering quietly among themselves and drying their
foot-rags over the fire. Several were boiling, in small tin cans,
potato peelings and rotten parsnips which they had collected from
the rubbish-heap by the kitchen. The period of acute hunger and
food shortage in the camp seemed to be never-ending, but it had
reached the phase when we were almost indifferent to it. There
comes a moment when the hungry man begins to suffer from the
hunger of the imagination far more than from pangs in the stomach.
His thoughts become filled with feverish visions of food, and his
dominant feeling is panic, fear that his body will slowly wither away.
Then the possibility of cheating hunger is more important than a
full stomach. Even snow seems to take on a solid consistency—it is
eaten like porridge. Thus, though the most starving prisoners
detested the actual taste of rotten vegetables boiled into a fluid mess,
they looked upon the acquisition and eating of these scraps as
exceptional luck, for in itself it gave them the confidence that they
were warding off, even momentarily, the inevitable end. Those
evening meals were celebrated with quiet solemnity, and prisoners
invited to share the contents of someone's bowl were honoured
guests partaking of a magnificent feast.

In the sphere of human emotions there exists a strange phenomenon which is something more than mere habit, the almost
suicidal condition of psychological indolence. I mean by this that
at the very depth of human degradation there occur moments when
every possibility of change, even change for the better, appears risky
and dangerous. I have heard of beggars who look upon their
benefactors with increasing suspicion if they receive more from
them than the usual alms, a roof over their heads or work instead of
a few pennies. Below a certain standard of life man develops a

fatalistic attachment to his misery and treats with distrust any prospect of improvement; bitter experience has taught him that change can only be for the worse. "Leave me alone," he seems to say. "All I want is just enough to live on." It is possible to draw from this the conservative conclusion that no one should be made happy against his own will, and this is accurate in one respect: happiness is never the same to him who receives it and to him who gives it. In the camp I almost believed that a man condemned to a certain fate should not rebel against it. I was astonished that night, as I lay on my bunk and looked at my fellow-prisoners with hatred, to find myself suddenly regretting my attempt to escape their life. It was easy to tell from their faces that few of them would live longer than a year, and yet I felt so much safer and less lonely as one of them, even in the face of death, than without them in this last struggle for life. There was some unperturbed resignation about these barefooted men with bristly faces flushed from the warmth of the flames, who sat over their pots, aimlessly poking the fire with pieces of wood, or else lay down on their bunks to wait for sleep, staring with exhausted eyes at the dim light of the bulbs. It was already quiet in the barrack; occasionally a prisoner crawled with difficulty from his sleeping place and, stumbling as if drunk, knocking aside the bare legs which protruded into the passage from all sides, walked over to the bucket of hvoya for a drink. The corner bunk where Dimka used to sit in silence was now empty— our orderly had been sent to the mortuary. The night was approaching. I felt alone, dreadfully alone.

That night I did not close my eyes. I lay on my back on the hard bunk, with my hands folded under my head, and once more attempted to settle in my mind all that had happened. After midnight the whole barrack was asleep, the bulbs became dimmer, and from all sides came the first nocturnal shrieks, babblings and sobbings. It was stifling, and like my neighbours I threw aside my jerkin and greedily inhaled the heated air. Closing my eyes, my imagination brought up the sound of carp plashing in the reeds of an abandoned pond; when I looked round I could see half-open mouths and rotting teeth, which gave out the sweetish odour of decay, discernible even at that distance, and the whites of eyes gleaming in dark sockets. Beyond the windows spread the white night, leaving the frosty imprint of leaves and ferns on the glass. The beams of light from the four corner searchlights, patrolling the night as usual, pierced the barrack at regular intervals, picking out sleeping faces from the half-darkness of lower bunks, and disappeared rapidly like swords cutting the soft curtain of the night.

Far more audacious than the hunger-strike, and far more dangerous, was our refusal to work. In Soviet camps it is known as "otkaz", and is one of the most serious offences against internal camp discipline. For example, the Kolyma camp, which is cut off from the rest of the world by ice and snow during most of the year, is ruled by a cruel régime of internal regulations which are not subject to central control, and there refusal to work is punished by immediate shooting; in other camps the offender is stripped naked and left standing in the snow and frost until he either submits or dies; in others yet, the first punishment is solitary confinement on water and two hundred grammes of bread a day, and if the offence is repeated, the prisoner goes through a second trial and is given a second sentence—five years for criminal prisoners, ten years or death for politicals. In Yercevo "otkazchyks" with a second sentence were after a few months taken away to the central prison beyond the zone, and we never knew what became of them. But from time to time we heard the echoes of machine-gun and rifle fire from beyond the zone, and we had good reason to believe that they came not, as we were told, from the camp garrison's shooting range, but from the walled-in courtyard of the central prison. After the outbreak of the Russo-German war the camp authorities did not attempt to conceal from us the fact that new regulations had come into existence which gave the extraordinary powers of war tribunals—in practice power of life and death over the prisoners—to the "people's courts" in villages near labour camps. The example of the drunken sceptic in the technical barrack proved this sufficiently. Among the gravest offences which could be committed in the camp after June 22nd, 1941, were the spreading of defeatism and refusal to work, which, under the new defence regulations, was included in the category of "sabotage of the war effort". There remained only the vital question of how far the Sikorski-Maiski pact exempted the Poles from the mechanism of Soviet martial law. On this thin thread hung the whole success or failure of our hunger-strike, and I knew that the first hours of the day which was dawning beyond the opaque glass of the windows would give us the full answer to the question. In the pros and cons of our enterprise it was the only unknown quantity, and it would decide whether the sign of equation would point toward us like rifles aimed at our hearts, or stand like the open double gates of the camp.

Towards morning I fell asleep so heavily that I slept right through reveille and was only woken by a sharp tug at my ankle. Zyskind was standing by my bunk and with a gesture of the head ordered me to come with him. I climbed down from the bunk, put my cap on, tied my jerkin into a bundle with a piece of string, and followed him out of the deserted barrack into the zone. Outside, orderlies were shovelling the snow away from barrack doors, broad sweeps of smoke issued from the kitchen chimneys and the bath-house and, spreading over the roofs, bounced off the eaves like rolled-up pieces of paper tossed into the air. The water-sledge rode slowly from the kitchen towards the gates, carrying an empty barrel with Kola, the water-carrier, sitting astride it and prodding his frost-rimed bay with a juniper twig. When he saw me walking with Zyskind he turned round as if to shout something, but after a moment bent over the reins again, tugged them towards him, and hit the horse with the twig. Several sick prisoners were already waiting by the dispensary. The morning was frosty, dry, and sharp. It was the first of December.

Instead of going directly to the internal camp prison, I had to accompany Zyskind while he went round the barracks where the other hunger-strikers lived, and then the six of us walked together to Samsonov's office. He saw us individually, but the interviews were identical. He sat at his desk, behind him on the wall a large map of the Soviet Union, large portraits of Stalin and much smaller ones of Beria, graphs of the production scheme and a plan of the camp; he looked at me calmly from under his fur cap, his reproachful, almost fatherly expression betrayed by occasional flashes of hatred.

"Who told you to strike?"

"No one. It was my own decision."

"Why are you striking?"

"I ask to be released from the camp in accordance with the terms of the general amnesty for Polish citizens imprisoned in Russia, or else to be allowed to communicate with the Polish plenipotentiary to the Soviet Government."

"Have you heard of the special tribunals which in wartime can shoot prisoners for refusing to work? Do you know that a hunger-strike is rebellion against Soviet authority and Soviet law?"

"Yes, I know."

"Sign this declaration to say that you do know."

"I won't sign anything. From the moment that the Soviet-Polish agreement was signed in London, I have been the citizen of an allied country, and I owe no allegiance to Soviet law."

"Silence! Zyskind, lock this Polish bastard up!"

Zyskind ran energetically into the room, crying "Yes, Citizen Chief," and led us outside in front of the barrack. The first hearing was over. We looked at each other in silence, but with relief on our faces, and only Miss Z. went pale, her teeth chattering, while B. wiped the sweat from his forehead with his sleeve.

By nine o'clock we were all in the camp prison, each in a separate cell. The internal prison of Yercevo squatted like a hen-roost by the observation-post in the corner of the zone. It was a small house, with barred windows the size of a human head, and surrounded by a barbed-wire fence so that no doubt might exist that this was the prison within a prison. Prisoners usually avoided it, walking round it at a distance, not even looking in the direction of those grey stone walls, pierced by openings which seemed to breathe out a cold dark emptiness. But sometimes shouting and singing could be heard from the prison, and then prisoners would step on the path, with their backs to its walls and facing the barracks so as not to awaken suspicion, and listen in case those inside were asking for something. The internal prison housed those punished for minor offences committed in the zone, and those who were to be transferred, with a heavier sentence, to the central prison beyond the zone, which was also used for the free citizens of Yercevo. One of every prisoner's most cherished dreams was of escape from the torture of daily work in a labour camp to the blessed idleness of a normal prison, but conditions in the two Yercevo prisons were such that it was indeed a heavy punishment. A prisoner in one of them received only water and 200 grammes of bread a day; the windows in the small cells had neither glass nor even a board over them, so that the temperature was never higher than outside; finally, the prisoner could take with him into the prison only the things in which he went out to work—if he was fortunate enough to possess a palliasse or a few horse-blankets, he had to leave them in the barrack. In some cases, too, the punishment of solitary confinement was limited only to the nights—the prisoner went to work in the daytime as usual, but in the evening he came from the guard-house straight to the prison, and received for this only the "penal" cauldron, 300 grammes of bread and two platefuls of the thinnest soup. The prison therefore was a dreaded punishment, and sometimes prisoners there wept like children, promising good behaviour only to get out.

The window of my cell looked out on the zone, and pressing my face to the cold bars I could see some of the barracks, the kitchen and the bath-house. In the neighbouring cell, on my right as I faced the window, was the Silesian policeman T., a simple and honest man who for reasons unknown to us concealed his real name and profession in the camp, where he passed for a miner, and who was one of the best foresters in the whole of Yercevo. T.'s cell adjoined that of Miss Z., and the other two hunger-strikers were beyond her. On my left was Gorbatov, an electro-technician from Rostov, who was in solitary confinement for insulting a free official in the Yercevo electricity plant. T.'s window, beyond the corner of the prison building, commanded a view of the road leading from the camp to the town, and he could see a few of the houses in Yercevo and the fork of the road which led to the central prison.

My cell was so low that I could touch the ceiling with my hand, and so narrow that with one step I could walk from the wall of T.'s cell to that of Gorbatov's. Half the space was taken up by a two-tiered bunk, made of rough, unplaned wood nailed together, and turned with the head towards the window. It was impossible to sit on the upper bunk without bending one's back against the ceiling, and the lower one could only be entered with the movement of a diver, head first, and left by pushing one's body away from the wood, like a swimmer in a sandbank. The distance between the edge of the bunk and the bucket by the door was less than half a normal step. After some deliberation, I chose the upper bunk, even though a bitter wind blew in continually through the open window, piling up a thin layer of snow on the ledge. I thought that if I walked backwards and forwards, as one does in a prison cell, on a scrap of bare earth measuring a step by half a step, I should soon go mad. I could communicate with both my neighbours through the red-brick walls, and not only by the usual prison method of a knocking alphabet, but even in a loud whisper through chinks in the wall where fragments of dried cement had fallen out. Before going off to lunch, Zyskind once more tested the lock on the door. The key turned in the lock, the judas was raised for a brief moment, and then the quiet tread of felt boots receded, leaving us in dead silence.

The first day I spent looking round my cell and out at the zone through the tiny window above the bunk. It was strange to look at those other prisoners, hurrying to their barracks, stopping on the paths, greeting each other from a distance: I could almost believe that they were free men. But I did not envy them. After so many months of life in a large herd, solitude was again, as before in the hospital, a fresh and reviving feeling. I was terribly cold, but I did not feel any hunger. Somewhere at the bottom of my consciousness was a small spark of pride, as if I had already gained my freedom with difficulty. Thousands of men all over the world fight for various causes, without knowing that even the possibility of defeat, if it can only assume the character of martyrdom, becomes conquest and glory. Men defeated in a lonely struggle for something in which they believe, willingly take upon themselves the burden of martyrdom as the bitter reward of their solitude. But unfortunately there are very few whose physical endurance can live up to the strength of their determination. On the very first evening of my imprisonment, when the bulb was lit in my cell and I heard the usual sounds of mess-cans and pots tinkling in the zone, I was suddenly seized by hunger and fear, and from that moment, even though I refused all drink, I passed water several times every day and night until the end of my hunger-strike.

That night I slept badly, waking frequently, and my dreams were so puzzling, disconnected and intangible that with the greatest effort I could not recall them even a moment after waking. Shivering with cold, I squeezed myself into a corner of the bunk, as far as possible from the window, with my legs drawn up to my stomach, my head almost entirely covered by my jerkin, and my hands in its sleeves. In this position I could lie on one side only for an hour at a time, but because it seemed the most sensible, and because it protected me best from the wind, I did not change it during the whole time that I stayed in the prison. The next morning the hunger had receded, but the feeling of loneliness grew. I climbed down from the bunk and for a few minutes walked about on the small space of floor to warm myself, beating my hands against my sides. When at last I felt my blood running faster through my numbed limbs, I knocked on the wall of T.'s cell.

"How do you feel?" I asked.

Behind the wall I heard a loud noise like the falling of a body,
then a gentle scratching at the cement, and finally T.'s calm voice:

"Bloody cold, but I'm managing. And you?"

"I'm all right. What about the others?"

"They don't answer."

I stepped across to the other wall and knocked.

"How long have you been here, Gorbatov?"

"Five days. And as many more to come."

"How is it going?"

"I'm starving. The scrap of bread they give you here . . .
You're mad to try this hunger-strike, you won't last out. . . ."

"That's none of your business, Gorbatov. . . ."

I sat down again on the edge of the lower bunk, looking aimlessly
at the bucket. Gorbatov turned out to be more sociable than T.
He knocked on the wall:

"Do you know who I've got next to me?" he asked.

"Well?"

"Three nuns, being punished for their faith."

"Impossible!"

"It's true, I can hear them singing and praying. I tried to talk to
them, but they won't answer. Virgins, you see." He laughed, and
at once choked with a fit of coughing.

Vaguely, as through a mist, I remembered the story of the three
nuns of Hungarian origin, which had been whispered about in the
camp though none of us had ever seen them. It was said that they
had been sent to Yercevo prison with a transport from Nyandoma,
where they had been imprisoned since 1938. They had worked well
until the autumn of 1941, when one day they suddenly refused to
leave the zone in the morning, saying that they would not "work
for Satan". The prisoners in Yercevo discussed their case frequently, but in October the whole affair seemed to die down, and I
was certain that the three nuns had either been dead for a long time,
or else were in the central prison. The severity of martial law gave
to their mysterious madness the character of certain suicide.

T. knocked again.

"What's that dripping in your cell? Roof leaking?" he asked.

"No, I was making water."

"Why, are you drinking?"

"No."

"Well, then, what's the matter? Frightened already?"

"No, I must have a sick bladder."

T. laughed and said something else, but I had taken my ear away from the crack. For a long hour I stood in silence leaning against the bunk, feeling my former assurance vanishing and giving place to anxiety, and seeking escape in the contemplation of my daring and ambition. There are moments in the life of every man, particularly after periods when his self-confidence has been inflated by the audacity of his plans and actions, when his legs seem to melt under him and his only desire is to escape, to fly without looking back.

"Do you know who's in here with us?" I asked T.

"Who?"

"Those three nuns who won't work for Satan."

"Still here? What do they want?"

"It's their martyrdom for the faith," I replied without thinking, not even realising then that I had borrowed the phrase from Dostoevsky.

"Just like ours," he answered calmly.

"You're exaggerating, we only want our freedom," I retorted, and immediately knocked on the other wall again.

"Hey, Gorbatov, give our love to the three little nuns—from the starving Poles."

"Have you gone mad? I want to get out of here some time! Quiet, it's Zyskind."

I heard steps on the path in front of the prison and the opening of the main door. Zyskind walked along the corridor for a while; finally the key turned in the lock of my door. He came inside, and without a word placed a whole ration of bread on the upper bunk. He must have done the same thing in the other cells, for I heard the turning of the key and the regular slamming of doors receding down the corridor. I looked at the fresh bread for a long time, but I felt no hunger; and although Zyskind brought me a fresh ration every day at the same time, I greeted his visits with increasing apathy, and the pile of bread grew on the bunk, untouched.

In the evening the door of my cell was again opened. Someone was kicked inside through the door, rolled across the floor like an enormous rag ball, and disappeared in the lower bunk. After about a quarter of an hour the door opened slightly, and Zyskind pushed through first a plateful of steaming soup, then a slice of bread, on the floor. The unknown prisoner jumped up, hit his head on the bottom of the upper bunk, swore, and threw himself on the floor.

He ate loudly and greedily—smacking his lips, gulping down the hot fluid, and rapidly crushing the bread in his jaws. This went on for more than a minute, and then I heard the familiar sound of a tongue licking round the plate, the clang of the empty tin dish thrown on the floor, and an animal grunt of satisfaction.

I suddenly felt the sickly taste of a lump of phlegm in my throat, beads of sweat on my forehead, and a weakness in my whole body like a total loss of consciousness. When I came to, the other was already asleep, snoring and breathing out with a penetrating whistle, and muttering in his sleep. In the morning he was taken away to work, and in the evening brought back again to my cell. And though we spent five nights together we never exchanged a word, and I did not even once see his face. When he ate, I lay on my bunk, seeing only a foot of earth by the door and the bucket, and when he went out in the morning I was either asleep or pretending to be. In the dark light of the evening I saw only for a fraction of a second the cowering crumpled shape of his body, pushed inside with a violent blow which sent him sprawling straight into his bunk. I knew that his function in my cell was that of a tempter, but I became attached to him, for in the stream of time which dragged mercilessly slowly he was the only stable point on which I could fix my starved imagination.

On the fourth day of hunger I was so weak that I could only with difficulty climb down to use the bucket, and the rest of the day I spent without movement on my bunk, dozing restlessly even in the daytime. This feverish, broken sleep brought me a certain relief, a full taste of my loneliness, but it also put me in a strange state of fear and gradually robbed me of all feeling of reality. I was neither hungry nor cold, but I would wake up suddenly to find myself shouting, not knowing at first where I was and what I was doing there. In my rare moments of consciousness I tried in vain to recall my life until that moment, perhaps to draw consolation from a last glimpse of the face which had once borne my name, the man that I had been. I realised vividly as never before the sadness and bitterness of dying, and experienced the process of detachment from one's own personality which is surely the most terrible aspect of death and the one which most disposes to religious conversion. What is left to a man if he does not even believe that somewhere, when his time on earth is up, will occur the miraculous fusion of a body which has been abandoned on the hard planks of suffering with the purpose of life which leaves it as the blood flows from the veins? At those moments I regretted the fact that the camp had hardened me so that I could no longer pray; I was like a barren, parched desert rock which will not stream with living water until it is touched by a miraculous wand.

About midday the door opened and a high-ranking officer of the N.K.V.D. whom I had not seen before walked in, in a uniform crossed by a belt, an unbuttoned leather coat and a red-and-blue cap with a gilded Soviet emblem. Samsonov was looking into the cell over his shoulder, in a fur cap and with his fur greatcoat buttoned up to the neck.

The unknown officer opened his overcoat and I could see his hand resting on his revolver holster. "Name?" he asked sharply.

With difficulty I raised myself on the bunk and slowly pronounced my name, but suddenly I imagined that I saw the officer unbuttoning the holster and taking the black, gleaming handle of his revolver into manicured fingers. My heart beat faster, and all my blood seemed to rush into my unbearably overfilled bladder. I closed my eyes, and heard the next question like the explosion of a bullet:

"Will you stop this strike?"

"No," I answered, shouting hastily and desperately, "no, no!" and fell back on the bunk, drenched with sweat, while my bladder collapsed like a pricked balloon.

"War tribunal for you!" I heard as if in my sleep. The cell door slammed shut again.

I have no idea how long I slept then but it was already dusk when violent knocking on T.'s wall woke me up.

"Miss Z. fainted," he said quickly, "they've taken her to the hospital."

"And the others?"

"I don't know. The communication has broken down because her cell is empty, but I heard many steps in the corridor. I thought that you'd been taken off too, I've been knocking for an hour. Did they threaten you?"

"Yes."

"Are you holding out?"

I thought for a while and then answered: "Yes."

Towards evening Zyskind brought me the daily portion of bread, and instead of leaving without a word as usual, he pressed a scrap of paper into my hands. I crawled over the bunk nearer to the bulb to read the message. It was from B.: "We are all three in hospital. Stop the strike. It won't get you anywhere."

I read it out to T., but he only swore when he heard it. With a feeling of relief I curled up to sleep again, while the other prisoner burst noisily into the cell and greedily threw himself on his soup.

The next morning I awoke with a strange feeling that I was choking. I caught the air into my lungs with difficulty, my hands and legs seemed to be bursting out of my clothes and hanging out in rolls of flesh, and my whole body felt as if it was firmly tied down to the bunk. Without changing my position, I raised one hand before my eyes, and found it so swollen that the wrist joint had disappeared from sight under a layer of flesh, and two soft, fat cushions had formed on either side of the hand. I sat up slowly and looked at my feet, which were bursting out of my rubber shoes above the ankle. So it was true: one did swell from hunger. I unlaced my shoes, freeing my feet from the straps, and with difficulty I began to un-pick the seams of my thickly-wadded trousers. Every movement was a piercing streak of pain, for I had to tear the cloth away with the crust of dried blood and pus, but I did not stop until I saw my two legs naked, red blocks covered with open sores from which a yellow-pinkish fluid trickled slowly. I felt the legs as if they were not mine—the finger plunged into the soft dough of flesh, and bounced off as from an inflated rubber tyre. But to pull off my jerkin I had to get down from the bunk, and when the whole operation was accomplished I sat down on the floor exhausted, with my back against the wall. Now I could swell freely, I had enough living-space. I was not even cold, I felt only sick and giddy. And without noticing it I fell asleep with my head on the cushions of my knees, soft and wet with blood.

It cannot have been later than four in the afternoon, for the light still streamed in thinly through the window, when I heard not so much a knocking, as a violent noise, from Gorbatov's cell. Without changing my position I knocked back and listened.

"They've just taken the nuns away, I'm going out this evening. All the best."

I crawled across the floor to the other wall.

"Look through your window. They've just taken the nuns."

"Right," answered T. "I'll knock later and tell you."

I waited, full of incomprehensible excitement and apprehension.

My head weighed on me like a ripe pumpkin; the sores on my legs had dried while I was asleep, but were itching so mercilessly that I began aimlessly to pick at them, playing with the thin scabs. I was stifling and I felt my bladder burning again, but I had not the strength to get up. I felt a hot wave flowing through my trousers and saw a small puddle forming on the floor.

T. was knocking. "I saw it."

"Tell me what happened."

"They took them out beyond the zone, towards the central prison. I couldn't see very far, it's dusk already. . . ."

"What did they look like?"

"Quite ordinary. Three women with inhumanly tangled hair. Still young, I should think."

"Large escort?"

"Two guards with bayonets."

"Tell me some more. How did they walk?"

"Quite normally. I didn't see anything else, it's almost dark beyond the zone. Good-night."

I climbed up into the bunk, cutting my legs on the rough edges of the planks, and squeezed into my corner. I lay motionless while Zyskind brought the bread, while the ragged body tumbled into the cell and ate its beastly meal on the floor. Time passed quickly now, for I had fallen into a state of sleep-sodden, oblivious numbness. It must have been near midnight when I heard three salvos from the direction of the shooting-range. Like the flash of the shot itself, my brain registered the fact before I was plunged in darkness again.

The next day Dr. Loevenstein, who came to see me in the prison during Zyskind's absence, did not attempt to conceal the truth from me:

"My friend, your heart is quite healthy, but the healthiest heart cannot go on for long pumping blood to legs as rotten and diseased as yours. I advise you to give up your illegal hunger-strike"—here he smiled gently—"and to return to the lawfully prescribed hunger. You will live three months in the peace and warmth of the mortuary, and during that time things may, after all, take a turn for the better."

I shook my head in answer. I was feeling better now, I even climbed down to see the old doctor to the door. But that night— the seventh of the hunger-strike, my sixth in the prison—I felt a sharp pain in my heart and I was suddenly frightened. There is nothing worse than fear without an object, fear of something unknown; a mysterious presence seemed to be lurking everywhere—by my side, at my feet, in my heart itself. . . . The other man stirred in his sleep underneath me and sighed deeply, and this gave me back some of my self-assurance; but as soon as he was quiet again, I suddenly fancied, I don't even know why, that he was dead. I slipped quickly down to the ground. I knocked hard and dreadfully long—a whole eternity!—on T.'s wall, convinced all the time that at the distance of an outstretched arm a dead body was lying on the bunk, afraid to turn my back on it for even the shortest moment, until I felt something sticky trickling between the fingers of my clenched fist and stopped knocking. There was no answer. Could he be dead too? I was gathering my breath for a last desperate shriek, as if I wanted to shout out all the agony of my fear of death, when by my side I heard first a knocking and then the question:

"What's the matter?"

"You're alive! Thank God!"

"I don't feel well, I'm weak . . ."

"Let's give up the strike, we lost anyway when the others gave in. . . . The nuns have been shot . . ."

"No. *I* won't," he answered with unexpected force.

I did not stir from my place. But when the body on the lower bunk sighed again and shouted something, I fell asleep heavily, and for the first time in many weeks I slept with a feeling of calmness and peace.

On the evening of the eighth day the unknown prisoner did not appear as usual, but Zyskind opened the door and told me to get ready to come out.

"Where to?" I asked.

"The guard-house."

In the corridor I waited while Zyskind called out T. When he came out, I looked at his swollen face, and I saw in his stare the effort and the difficulty with which he was recognising my familiar face.

"I suppose this is the end?" he asked quietly.

I shrugged my shoulders. "I don't know. There aren't any guards."

At the guard-house, in the presence of an officer from the Third Section, we signed the text of a telegram to Professor Kot, the

Polish Ambassador then officiating in Kuibyshev, and then, still escorted by Zyskind, we set off for the small hospital which had recently been opened at the other end of the zone. We walked supporting each other, yet lightly, as if we could take off from the earth at any moment. Thick snow was falling, covering the barracks up to their lighted windows. It was quiet, empty and peaceful.

*   *   *   *   *

In the hospital our lives were saved by the silent "old Pole" from the Ukraine, Dr. Zabyelski, who, contrary to explicit instructions, gave us each two milk injections instead of the usual bread and soup. Thanks to them, we avoided instantaneous and fatal cramp of the intestines, and on the next evening, having eaten my first solid food for nine days—a plate of thin boiled barley—I went out to the latrine. In the small, hastily erected closet, with only a few planks in place of a door, I suffered the worst physical torments of my life, as the stone-hard turd, which my thirsting organism had sucked dry of all its juices during eight days of hunger, forced its way through my guts, wounding and tearing them until the blood flowed. I must have been a sorry sight, crouching over a frozen plank, my jerkin blowing in the wind, looking out at the snowstorm which blew over the plain, with eyes full of tears of pain and pride.

CHAPTER 14

THE MORTUARY

THE last stage of a prisoner's life in the camp was the mortuary, a large barrack situated between the kitchen and the maternity hut, where prisoners no longer capable of working were directed before their names were finally crossed off the list of the living.

A prisoner was transferred to the mortuary on the basis of a medical examination, which could be repeated, when he stopped being a "working man" and became a "dokhadyaga"—a word which can best be translated as "one who is dying by inches". Women prisoners who were unfit for work were either left in their barracks or sent from Yercevo to some unknown destination, as there was no separate mortuary for them. In theory, the mortuary provided an opportunity for the exhausted organism to recover its strength, but rest and idleness alone, without better nourishment, were not sufficient to revive even the youngest and healthiest prisoners. The mortuary brought release from the torture of daily work, but no relief from the agonies of daily hunger. On the contrary, hunger becomes really dangerous, and leads men to the verge of madness, particularly during long periods of idleness, when one has time to become fully conscious of it, when thoughts of it invade and fill every moment of the endless rest on the bunks. The crowd of beggars which gathered round the kitchen every evening, waiting for the dregs of soup from the cauldrons to be given out, came for the most part from the mortuary.

The originally intended function of the mortuary was probably to make sick and exhausted prisoners fit enough to go back to work, to serve as a kind of miniature health resort; in practice, however, its nature was summed up in the nickname given to it by the prisoners —a mortuary, a charnel-house. The mortuary food ration, although, as a shame-faced compensation for years of labour, it was usually fixed at the level of the second cauldron, was insufficient to stop the disintegration of body tissues; the occasional coveted spoonful of raw vegetables could not cure the usual diseases of the north—scurvy and pylagra. Only a man with a very strong constitution, exhausted by work but still free from disease, could hope to regain strength in the mortuary, to live and work for a short time until he broke down again. Regular medical inspections divided the inhabitants of the mortuary into the "weaklings" and the "incurables". The weaklings were prisoners like myself who, it was considered, still had a prospect of returning to work after a period of rest; we were given a small additional ration, the so-called "weaklings' extra", and formed into a special brigade used for occasional light work inside the zone. The second category involved a diagnosis of "incurability in camp conditions", or in practice a sentence of slow death in the mortuary; the incurables were not forced to work, but neither did they receive any additional food. They could only wait patiently for the end.

There were so few cases of recovery and return to work even among the weaklings that this division into categories was no more than a polite fiction, yet the inhabitants of the mortuary, though fully realising that despite artificial differentiations they were all doomed, always begged to be included in the first division. They were not so much eager for the additional food, as terrified by the death sentence contained in the word incurable.

The hard price of complete peace and idleness was the irrevocable loss of all remaining hope. No one, thinking of the barrack to which sooner or later all the paths of the camp led, would have dared to compare its aimless idleness with the restfulness of the hospital. It stood a little apart from the zone, snowbound, solitary, abandoned by hope and avoided by the living, with frosted windows gleaming opaquely like the eyes of a blind man, and a white rag of smoke hanging over its roof like the flag of surrender. One might have said that it was not even in the camp, but beyond the wires, already on the side of eternal freedom. . . . And yet a prisoner in the mortuary did not even have the sympathy of others to accompany him on the last stage of his life's journey. "That rubbish, that shit, they eat our bread and do nothing for it. Better for us and for them if they were put out of their misery"—that was the usual comment whenever the mortuary was mentioned in the barracks.

My feelings as I walked to the mortuary for the first time from the hospital must have differed from those of my Russian fellow-prisoners in the same situation. Five days in hospital had not cured the swelling of my whole body or healed the sores on my legs; my nerves were relaxed after the tension of the hunger-strike, my whole organism open to a fresh attack of scurvy; but the taste of victory was still fresh enough to revive my hopes of survival. The mortuary seemed to be the best solution for me, as without a temperature I had no formal right to occupy a bed in the hospital, and with the prospect of a speedy release from the camp before me I preferred to spend my remaining days there in idleness, even in the constant presence of death, than to cling to the appearance of life by going out to work. I felt as if I was entering a leper colony, protected against the disease by impenetrable armour. And now, as once before, I felt ashamed because my fate was pushing me off the paths trodden before me by thousands of swollen and scrofulous legs like mine.

I walked past the infirmary, past the new outbuilding of the technical barrack, past the maternity hut. I stopped at every few steps, laying down the bundle with all my possessions, to look back at the zone. Below me, lit up by the frosty December sun and surrounded by a high wall of drifted snow, stood my old barrack, to which I knew that I should never return. Two pregnant women walked slowly to the infirmary, clasping their dumpy stomachs with red, frost-bitten hands. Beyond the wire, as far as the eye could see, stretched the white desert plain, bounded on the horizon by the thick line of the forest. As I stopped before the door of the mortuary to get my breath back, I saw the porters' brigade leaving the barrack and walking towards the bath-house. So much time had passed since I had marched out to work with them, so many new, unknown faces had taken the place of those whose names now dimly rattled in my memory like stones in an empty box. When they were passing the mortuary one of the porters recognised me, waved his hand in greeting and gaily called out: "Hullo, friend! Dying already?"

In the mortuary I was greeted by curious glances from both the rows of two-tiered bunks. I laid my bundle on the table and started to look for Dimka. I found him in a far corner, on a lower bunk as usual (he believed that lying above other prisoners gave one a valuable sense of superiority, but his pin leg made it difficult for him to climb into the upper bunks), sleeping peacefully with his old wooden spoon in his hand. He had grown thinner since he had been classified as an incurable, but his greying beard was beautifully trimmed and pointed, and gave to his angular face an expression of mental resignation and inward peace. He woke when I touched his arm lightly. For a moment he seemed not to recognise me, painfully screwing up his eyes, hazy with sleep and so pale as to seem almost colourless, but then he raised himself on the bunk and welcomed me with a friendly smile. I am ashamed to say that I had not tried to see him from the moment when, having gathered up his things in our barrack, he shook my hand before leaving for the mortuary. Now he said almost through tears: "My son, my son, I've heard about everything. You're a brave boy!" and added, looking at my bundle: "Did they give you back the bread for those eight days?" He was indignant when I told him that after my hunger-strike the pile of untouched bread from my cell had been sent back to the bread store, on Samsonov's express orders. Dimka did not once ask me why I had moved into the mortuary; he had already guessed it all with that sixth sense which allows veteran prisoners to read everything in the faces of their companions.

Near Dimka's bunk I found M., the Polish engineer, who had visited us in hospital twice, but had avoided mentioning the hunger-strike. Thanks to his tact the whole business was passing into oblivion, giving every one of us six Poles an equal share of hope. His silence, his forbearance to ask questions and require explanations, was a sincere, convincing gesture of solidarity. M. was also a new arrival at the mortuary, for until then, despite his inclusion in the weaklings' category, he had been allowed to go on living in one of the general barracks. He was lying on an upper bunk, and I recognised him from a distance by his long legs, wrapped in rags and hanging out beyond its edge. When I shook his leg he awoke from his dreams, or possibly his prayers, and made room for me on the bunk. There I stayed, sleeping and living on three narrow planks, since my neighbour on my right, the schoolteacher from Novosybirsk who had once worked in the bathhouse, refused to give up another inch of space for me.

About midday Sadovski came back to the mortuary from the zone. They had already told me that he went out every day, morning and evening, to beg for soup by the kitchen. He always returned with an empty can, though not necessarily with an empty stomach, for he had reached that stage of hunger when he could not even wait until he had carried the soup back to the barrack, but gulped it down where he stood, rapidly and burning his lips. In his rare moments of sanity Sadovski's stories and his conversation were lively and interesting as before, but there were whole days when he seemed to notice nothing, and sat immovable on a bench at the table or by the fire, staring at one point with a fanatic stubbornness, crouching back as if ready to jump at the throat of anyone who interfered with him; from this demented reverie he was roused only at meal-times by the tinkling of mess-cans outside. A silent but nonetheless passionate rivalry had developed between him and Dimka, for both had the reputation of being the most successful beggars at the kitchen and they must frequently have got in each other's way. Dimka treated Sadovski with unconcealed dislike, occasionally, without reason, justifying it by political arguments. But Sadovski, the old bolshevik, had long ago given up the brilliant displays of dialectic reasoning which had sometimes led him to logical self-annihilation, and if he talked at all it was only to recall the past. After my arrival at the mortuary relations between them improved considerably, so much so that in the evenings the three of us, together with M., would often sit down at the table to play draughts or talk. But I never saw them talking to each other when alone, and they never went out to the kitchen with the other inhabitants of the mortuary.

The interior of the mortuary differed in its appearance from all other barracks. About a hundred and fifty of us lived in there. The first, and to some extent accurate, impression was that of a hostel for tramps and beggars. In the daytime some of the prisoners went out into the zone to look for food or to do the light work assigned to them, while the rest lay on their bunks talking in whispers, darning clothes, playing cards or writing letters. The most striking thing about the mortuary was the silence. No one commanded or enjoined it, but it was observed as strictly as if it had been enforced with regulations. We talked only in whispers, and then politely, with that typical guilty courtesy and consideration for others which is at once noticed in hospitals for the incurably sick. But for the fact that most of its inmates were no longer capable of controlling their natural functions, the mortuary could also have passed for the cleanest and tidiest barrack in the whole camp. We did not have our own orderly, but every day a different prisoner scrubbed the floor, washed down the tables and benches, wiped the windowpanes with a wet rag, lit the fire and brought in the water. Pictures cut out of newspapers and family photographs in tin frames, decorated with a faded field flower, were pinned to the walls over some bunks. The room was bright, in good repair, with spaces between the bunks at every tenth sleeping-place. Frequently, after breakfast, arguments broke out between prisoners who each wanted to do the day's cleaning, for time hung on our hands dreadfully, and seemed to be seeping slowly away from us with our lives. Only towards evening, when the prisoners from the weaklings' brigade returned with news and gossip from the zone, and the electric lights went on, the mortuary came to life for a time with quite unsuspected reserves of energy. The very sight of prisoners playing draughts round the table or gathering in groups in the spaces between bunks was encouraging and comforting. Heat filled the barrack, opening the sores on our legs, opening too our hearts and our mouths. The bulbs shone above us, handfuls of light thrown at the frosted white tiles of window-panes. Voices were raised above a whisper, laughter was heard, and even the tentative harmonies of mouth-organs circled in the air, fluttering like moths in the bright circles of light. After nightfall the mortuary was silent again, but its accumulated suffering burst out with screams and babblings more piercing and more desperate than in any other barrack. The atmosphere was a stifling compound of exhaled breath, feverish sleep, and fetid excrements.

But the peaceful illusion of normality was a mask which hid a brutal reality, seen and recognised only after a longer stay in the mortuary. Even the beggars and tramps of a prison camp had evolved a code of existence, a set of rules of behaviour which were themselves a caricature of the laws governing the lives of ordinary prisoners. For instance, in other barracks universal envy and greed were checked by the fact that everyone ate only as much he had earned by his work; mutual hatred was forgotten in common work and the consciousness of a common fate; even despair was sometimes drowned by fatigue. But in the mortuary, where time dragged unbearably slowly, all these emotions were given full rein, and in the emptiness of an aimless life without hope the barrack became charged with an atmosphere of malice and hatred which grew in intensity like a flooding river behind the dam of artificial courtesy, almost, but never quite, sweeping it completely away. Sitting on those bunks in rotting clothes, with unshaven faces and dangling, swollen legs, the prisoners watched each other with suspicion, followed each other's every movement, wanted to know everything about each other. Those who were dying could not avoid the unspoken question "When?" reflected in the eyes of their companions; those who were returning to life bragged cruelly of their health. Expiring human emotions revealed themselves here in their primordial form, distorted and deformed but horribly vivid. One evening when I came into the barrack I found the Novosybirsk schoolteacher mercilessly tormenting two incurables, both in the last stages of pylagra. Once, for a pinch of tobacco, he used to tell us about the naked women he saw in the bath-house; now he was leaning back against a vertical beam, with his hands in his pockets and a cigarette-end in the corner of his mouth, and shouting at the incurables in his squeaky voice, encouraged by laughter from the neighbouring bunks: "That's what women are—legs, thighs, breasts! It's no good even dreaming about it, brothers, you're no good for that sort of thing any more." Without even noticing it myself I was also beginning to accept and obey the cruel unwritten code of mortuary behaviour. I shall never forget the day when I was fortunate enough to be taken on to help in the kitchen for a few hours. I was forbidden to take food out from the kitchen and into the zone with me; but in the evening, when I had scrubbed all the cauldrons clean, and had eaten my fill in there, I suddenly saw, behind the frozen window-pane, Dimka's face, then Sadovski's, and two hands holding out empty mess-cans through the serving-hatch under the window-pane. One of the cooks walked up to the window and suddenly slammed the hatch-cover down over the opening; the begging hands jerked with a spasm of pain, but rapidly withdrew outside without dropping their cans. I looked at the wretches on the other side of the glass with disgust, with loathing, although not long before I myself had started to come out in the evenings to beg for dregs of soup at the kitchen. It is a mistake to suppose that only a beggar who has broken away from it can understand the misery and suffering of his former companions. On the contrary, nothing repels a man so much and rouses him to rebellion as the picture of his own human condition carried to the lowest extreme of degradation, suddenly brought before his eyes.

Nevertheless the mortuary gave prisoners who had known each other previously in the zone better opportunities for closer friendship. For over a year my relations with Dimka had been those of father and son, but it was only during our long conversations in the mortuary that I found out something about his old life. When the Revolution broke out, he was a very young priest in Verkhoyansk;

they left him alone during the first few years, but then he himself rebelled, threw off his cassock, and became a notary's clerk. About 1930 he married and went to the south of Russia, where he found work as a manual labourer. He worked hard, having in his own fashion become reconciled to communism, and forgot the past almost completely. He was the only man that I met in the whole camp who had wiped out thirty years from his memory so thoroughly that he seemed to grope with difficulty among the indistinct and vague recollections of his youth. The renunciation of his priestly calling in 1925 was the "second birth" to which he owed his youthfulness, but at the same time he had the mature wisdom of an old man which was rooted in a dim and already non-existent past. He was a strange combination of two personalities, and he himself often did not know which was the genuine one. From his youth he retained an understanding, sympathetic, instinctively religious attitude to human suffering, but whenever he became conscious of this, his fear expressed itself by a cynical scoffing at every kind of faith. The most important thing for him—and this was the echo of a young man, deformed by a premature struggle with life—was to eat and sleep as much as possible, to "take good care of yourself", as he would say. But like most atheists, he did not even suspect that his great gesture of religious rebellion was fundamentally more Christian than a thousand miraculous conversions. One evening I asked him when he had definitely stopped believing in God, and he told me that it was in 1937, when he had chopped off his foot with an axe in Yercevo forest, in order to go to the hospital and save his faith in his own will, faith in himself, faith in man. In this respect he was the very antithesis of Sadovski, who until his last conscious moment in the mortuary retained his deep contempt for the human personality and his faith in an abstract philosophical system devised by the human brain. Dimka was arrested in 1936 for the crime of "priesthood" which he himself had forgotten, and belonged to the almost extinct "old guard" of the Kargopol pioneers. His wife and his two children were arrested with him and transported to Central Asia. For five years he had heard nothing of them, and, what is stranger, did not want to know anything of them.

A completely different type was M., who had the appearance and the bearing of an aristocrat even in his prison rags. Very tall and slim, with a well-bred, narrow face and deep-set eyes which expressed sadness and pride at the same time, he moved about the barrack slowly and meditatively and did not speak to anyone there. The prisoners disliked yet respected him. He was able to remain aloof from them without offending or hurting anyone, though he did not avoid the discussion of any question which had some lasting importance. Anyone who did not know him better might have laughed at his comic aspect: incredibly long legs and arms seemed to trail behind him like those of a broken puppet, and from his eyes and nose thin streams issued and ran down his haggard face towards his mouth. Heart disease was not his only affliction; more painful were the frequent migraines connected with disturbances of the brain, when he sat over the table, supporting his head with his hands, his eyes convulsively closed, as if he was trying desperately to fall asleep. Sometimes it happened that he would suddenly stop by the bunks, lean back against a beam, close his eyes and put his hand to his forehead; then I knew that he was preparing to resist another attack. He also suffered from bad circulation, and it was pathetic to see him trying vainly to warm his limbs by the fire, crouching over it like his own shadow. But I never heard a word of complaint from his lips, and he did not allow hunger to dominate and distort his actions. He was hungry—we knew that well enough—but he ate what was given to him with dignity and calmness. His only passion, of which he could not cure himself until the end, was tobacco. Sometimes, having first looked all around, he would pick up a cigarette-end and hide it quickly in his pocket; I knew, too, that every other day he cut off half his starvation ration of bread to sell in the zone for a little tobacco. In one sense it was smoking that finished him, for he owed his prolonged detention in the camp, after the amnesty, to a denunciation by the camp official whom he had frequently visited for a cigarette and a chat. His political opinions were conservative, but he was interested deeply in only three things: God, Poland, and his wife. He had been arrested by the Russians on September 20th, 1939, three days after their entry into Poland, in one of the eastern regions where he had been working as a high official of the Ministry of Agriculture. He was sentenced first to death, then to ten years' hard labour. While he was in prison in Baranoviche he learnt that his wife had been sent into the depths of Russia, and when, in the camp, he was at last allowed to write her a monthly letter, all his attempts to contact her proved unsuccessful. His frightful headaches were, I am sure, largely caused by the effort of concentration with which, in moments of solitude and loneliness, he recalled to his memory one image to the exclusion of all others—that of his wife. At night—I slept next to him on the bunk—he found full consolation in prayer. I have never in my life heard a man pray more beautifully than M. Sitting up on the bunk, his face hidden in his hand, he pronounced the words of prayer in a whisper so moving, so pregnant with tears and pain, that he might have been prostrated at the foot of the Cross in a trance of adoration for Him whose martyred body had never broken out with a word of complaint. . . . "Who are you praying for so hard?" I once asked him when I could not sleep. "For all mankind," he answered calmly. "Even for those who are keeping us here?" He thought for a while, and then replied: "No, those are not men."

So in the evening we would sit down at one table, Dimka, Sadovski, M. and myself. Dimka enjoyed a game of draughts, and I played with him even though the monotony of the moves wearied me. Sadovski and M. cautiously discussed the latest developments at the front and watched our game. Sadovski, himself a Pole by origin (he had been born in Poland, and taken to Russia by his parents before the 1917 Revolution), hated M. for his inherent "lordliness" and his religious fervour. Dimka also mistrusted M., and yet we formed the closest and most friendly group in the whole mortuary. Sometimes, when the light came on in the barrack and we left the bunks for the table, the empty place in our corner looked like a painful gap in a row of teeth.

Just before Christmas all of us six Poles were given to read and acknowledge by signature a short verdict: "Detained in the camp by order of the Special Council of the N.K.V.D. in Moscow". This decision violently cut short our hopeful expectations of the future. I began to look at the mortuary in a different light, for it seemed that I would have to make my home there for a long time, if not for the rest of my days.

Christmas was celebrated in the camp unofficially and surreptitiously. All religious holidays and festivals have been scrupulously abolished and erased from the Soviet calendar, and replaced with historical anniversaries connected with the October Revolution and with the lives of communist heroes; at liberty in Russia Sunday was an ordinary working-day, followed by the official "day off" on Monday. Among younger prisoners, brought up in the bolshevik mentality, there were some who did not even know the Christian traditions underlying the divisions of the week and the annual festivals. But older prisoners preserved the old calendar in their hearts and memories, carrying out its injunctions humbly and in secret. During my first Christmas in Yercevo, in 1940, I was struck by the festive appearance of the barrack on Christmas Eve, and the large number of prisoners whose eyes were reddened by weeping. "All the best to you," they would say, shaking my hand, "for the next year—at liberty." That was all. But anyone who knows a Russian prison camp will understand how much this meant. In Russia the name of liberty is not taken in vain.

In 1941 we, i.e. the six Poles left in Yercevo, decided to celebrate Christmas together because the feeling of utter despair with which we greeted it was a common bond between us. The other four came to the mortuary in the evening, and before we broke the piece of bread which had been saved for this occasion, Miss Z. gave to each of us a handkerchief which she had embroidered with a Polish eagle, a fir branch, the date and a monogram. It was impossible to guess how she had got hold of the thread and the thin linen to make them, and difficult to believe that despite her heavy work at the saw-mill she had devoted at least five evenings to sewing them. Timidly and happily we handled these gifts (I have kept mine to this day), and thanks to them we were able for a moment to forget that our whole Christmas dinner was to consist of a piece of bread and a mugful of hot water. The sight of that small group of people, sitting round an empty table and crying with longing for their distant country, must have commanded the unwilling respect of the mortuary's other inhabitants, who watched us from their bunks with gravity, while Dimka and Sadovski quickly went out into the zone. Late in the evening our conversation became more animated, and to this day I can remember the story of B., who, as a former officer of reserve of the Polish Army, was arrested in his barrack in Yercevo on the day after the outbreak of the Russo-German war and detained in the central prison. B. started talking unwillingly (most prisoners are superstitiously afraid of recalling their prison hearings and the whole period between their arrest and the passing of sentence), but as he continued he talked faster and eagerly, as if this revelation of events usually shrouded in mystery among prisoners was giving him relief. When he had finished the mortuary was already plunged in sleep.

B.'S STORY*

"I could not sleep on the night of June 22nd. The bunk seemed to be harder than usual. I could not stop thinking about the changes which the outbreak of war might bring in my life. I didn't go to sleep until it was nearly morning. As soon as I had fallen asleep, I was woken by a movement unlike the normal morning push. Samsonov's deputy was standing by my bunk and told me to get dressed quickly, but he wouldn't let me put on all my clothes, saying that I would come back to the barrack straight away.

"Everyone was still asleep and the zone was peaceful. In the N.K.V.D. office Strumina was waiting for me with two armed soldiers. I was still sleepy, but I woke up with a start when I saw the indictment which she gave me to sign. I was accused of twofold treason against the Soviet Union, but despite pressure I did not sign it. Strumina told the soldiers to take me to the central prison. They did not allow me to collect the rest of my things from the barrack, but promised to let me have them in prison.

"They pushed me into a small cell, about three yards by five, with double-tiered bunks and a small window with thick iron bars covered with boards on the outside. Over the door, in a small opening in the wall, there was a bulb in a wire cage. I was all alone. I began to realise what had happened, but I still didn't know why I had been arrested. Anyway, I thought, I was a prisoner twice over.

"After an hour the door opened and five new prisoners from Yercevo came in. They were terrified. It's the war—they kept repeating—we'll all be shot. Why should they shoot us? I asked. As an example to others, they said. By morning there were already twenty-two prisoners in the cell, the remaining sixteen from other camp sections. I took a place on the bunk next to the window, it was my right as the first in the cell. Death was staring me in the face, but the instinct of self-preservation was as dominant as ever.

"We spent the day discussing various possible reasons for our arrest. I was the only Pole there. Next to me lay Selezyonka, an Ukrainian lawyer from Poland. From other camp sections came

---

* My memory of the above story has been confirmed by a letter from its narrator, who emigrated to Canada after the war. Some of the details, like the names of his companions in the prison, had to go out of necessity, erased by the passage of so many years, but the simple continuity of the narrative has been faithfully preserved.

two Soviet generals, four lawyers—one of them, Grosfeld, Professor of Law at Moscow University, claimed to have 'taught Stalin'—two journalists, four students, one high-ranking officer of the N.K.V.D., a former camp chief, and a former camp supply officer. Of the other five, one was a hairdresser from Moscow who lamented his fate more than any of us, anxious for the safety of his family at home.

"The air in the cell became more oppressive every day. You know what the summer is like here, thousands of mosquitoes flying into the cell through the small opening which served us for a window, hordes of fleas on the bunks, we all felt as if we were living through a fantastic, terrifying nightmare.

"The cross-examinations began soon after. Every night two or three of us were taken out to the N.K.V.D. office. They would come back toward morning, beaten up and dreadfully shaken. They were forced to make fictitious confessions and to sign faked 'protocols' of the hearings which had been prepared beforehand. The hairdresser, on the day after the war broke out, had been shaving a Jewish prisoner, who jokingly remarked that the labour camps would now become the recruiting ground of the Red Army. The hairdresser had answered laughing: 'Maybe, but I don't expect they'll take you—you need a crooked rifle to shoot round the corner of a house. But still, we have plenty of rifles like that here, so perhaps even you will get into the Army." For those words he was accused of betraying his country. Another prisoner, when the bread ration was lowered after the outbreak of war, had remarked: 'If they're short of bread already, what'll happen to us in a month's time?' He too was accused of treason to the Soviet Union. Then it was my turn. I was taken at night to the N.K.V.D. office, about a mile from the central prison. They took me into a room where there was no furniture except a desk and two chairs. Then a captain of the N.K.V.D. came in with a thick file of documents—it turned out to be the dossier of my first interrogation in prison. He let me sit down and offered me a cigarette, but I don't smoke anyway, and I refused it. It took him two hours to read through the documents, two hours which seemed like eternity to me. The examining judge broke the silence first, and gave me a long lecture about the war with Germany, the power of the Soviet Union, and the wisdom and infallibility of Stalin. When he had finished, he told me to read and sign an indictment and confession which had been prepared in advance. I was accused of accepting work as a State official in bourgeois-capitalist Poland" (B. had been a high-school teacher), "although I was a farmer's son, thus betraying my class, and of discussing life in the West with my fellow-prisoners, thus betraying the Soviet Union. I wouldn't sign. The judge got up and kicked me suddenly so hard that I fell off the chair. Then he told me to squat on my heels and began all over again. I still wouldn't give in, so he kicked me once more, and threatened me with a revolver. The hearing went on till seven in the morning, and during the whole time I wasn't allowed to sit on the floor or to stop squatting. In the morning the judge told the soldiers to take me to the guard-house and to see that I didn't go to sleep. I sat at the guard-house, without food and water, till ten o'clock in the evening. I was taken back before the judge, and the whole procedure of the previous night was repeated. He kicked me and hit me in the face continuously and sent me back to the cell towards morning completely exhausted.

"Then they left me alone for two weeks. All the others in the cell had finished their hearings.

"After two weeks I was again told to sign the confession. This time there were four witnesses from the camp in the judge's office, two of whom I had never set eyes on in my life. Their testimony was hopelessly incriminating, but I still wouldn't sign. The judge lost all control over himself, beat me blindly and furiously, and threatened to 'shoot me like a dog' whether I signed or not.

"Several days passed. Some of those in the cell advised me to sign the indictment, others encouraged me to hold out. At that time the trials began. The prisoners were called out of the cell at night, two at a time. Those who had been tried and sentenced did not return to our cell, but were placed in one opposite. The corridor in the prison was very narrow, so that we could shout across to them through the tiny opening for the light bulb. From their side we heard shouts announcing death sentences. After a few days there were only five of us left in the cell; one of the generals, Grosfeld, the self-styled 'tutor' of Stalin, one student, Selezyonka the lawyer and myself. One night they too were taken out, and I was left alone. But they came back towards morning, full of fresh hope. 'Our cases have been postponed,' they said, 'we've still got some life in front of us.' After a week we were woken one night by unusual movements in the corridor. The door of the condemned cell was

opened and our neighbours opposite told to come out. Those who
resisted were dragged out forcibly. I heard them sobbing and
screaming. The hairdresser shouted loudly: 'Whoever hears me
and remains alive, tell my family in Moscow that I've been shot.'
After a few minutes we heard the sounds of single shots and
screams coming from the prison courtyard. Can you imagine what
I felt like? My heart stopped beating and I could feel every vein in
my skull pounding. After another few days my four companions
were taken from the cell, and this time they did not come back. I
was alone again.

"Several weeks went by. One night I was woken up and taken
before a tribunal which was sitting in the village school at Yercevo.
Two women were the judges, the prosecutor was also a woman. I
was expecting a sentence of death, but the prosecutor got up and
announced that, in view of the agreement signed in London between
the Polish and the Soviet Governments, I would not be tried at all.
I couldn't at first understand what it was all about. On the judges'
desk lay an open calendar, and I saw that the date was August 29th.
I suspected a trap, but the court's decision was repeated to me and I
was taken back to the cell.

"Only there did I fully realise that, during my two-month stay in
prison, the political situation must have undergone some change.
In the first days of September I was told, through the opening in the
door, to get ready to move out in ten minutes' time. In the courtyard six prisoners and five soldiers of the N.K.V.D. were already
waiting. We marched off, towards an unknown destination.

"In the evening our convoy reached the Second Alexeyevka. The
penal camp there is divided into two zones. In one, the so-called
free zone, the prisoners live normally in common barracks. In the
other, called the isolation zone, and enclosed by a high fence and
barbed wire, the penal brigades are imprisoned. We, of course,
were directed to the isolation zone.

"In the morning, when we were being driven out to work, I had an
opportunity of learning more about conditions in the Alexeyevka. Despite severe frost the prisoners were almost all barefoot
and dressed in rags, and they could hardly move, they were so
exhausted. Before my eyes two prisoners fell down and died on the
spot as they were going out of the gate. In accordance with the
orders of Soroka, the camp chief, the prisoners marching out to
work did so to the strains of an accordion. On my first day three

prisoners in the brigade dropped dead at work. Within the isolation zone stronger prisoners murdered the weaker and took their food with perfect impunity.

"I worked hard, and after two weeks I managed, by promising to behave well, to obtain a transfer to the free zone. This part of the story won't interest you so much, but I'll just tell you that in the free zone I found a barrack inhabited exclusively by 123 Polish prisoners. One day we all decided to strike and we refused to go to work, demanding to be released from the camp in accordance with the terms of the amnesty. The very idea of an amnesty was something so unprecedented in the annals of Soviet labour camps that Soroka, instead of taking his usual course in such cases and sending a platoon of soldiers with a light machine-gun to the barrack to shoot every one of us down, hastily sent us off to Krouglitza. From there I, and I alone, was sent to Yercevo with a detachment at the end of September. I don't know what happened to the others but, believe me, when I saw Yercevo I felt as if I was returning home."

*   *   *   *   *

Life in the mortuary was approaching its predestined end. In January my body began to swell again, and I stayed on my bunk most of the time, eating only what Dimka brought me. I was not hungry, though, but lay for days on end without moving, with the greatest consolation that a dying man can enjoy—the comfort of memory. Most often I dreamed (for I was really half-asleep) that, late in the evening, I was walking home from the railway station of my native village in Poland. And though it was after nightfall I could see distinctly, as if in a dark light, first the sandy road which ran parallel to the railway track, then the small spinney, then the large clearing with a deserted villa in the middle, the stream, and next to it the hill where during the First World War they had buried dead artillery horses, and finally the road leading to our pond, overgrown with rushes and reeds. I climbed down to the shallow stream, jumped over a few stepping-stones and walked slowly towards the house along the bank planted with tall alder trees. The evening was cool, but dry after a whole day's drought, and a full moon hung above the old mill like a gleaming ducat, leaning gently against the point of the lightning-conductor; and from the direction of the fields I caught the crying of wild ducks and the plashing of feeding carp. As I approached the two larches which my childish imagination had fixed as the meeting-place of two ghosts who were imprisoned in the daytime under the large mill-stone, I was seized by my old fear and started to run. I opened the garden gate carefully and climbed up on to the ledge of the wall under the window; round the table I could see my father, our housekeeper, both my sisters, my brother with his wife and her daughter. I tapped on the window, and at the moment when they all got up from the table to welcome me after so many years of absence, I woke on the bunk, crying, with my hand pressed to my heart. This dream returned so exactly and with such unfailing regularity that I found fresh happiness in the expectation of it, in humbly praying for it when it began to get grey in the barrack.

Many storms troubled the peaceful course of life in the mortuary. One evening an old collective farmer from the region of Kalouga jumped down from a bunk, and frantically beating with his fist on the bottom of an empty tin, proclaimed "the end of all this suffering", with his own Second Coming—"I am Christ in the rags of a prisoner." When this was greeted with derisive laughter, he stood with his face to the bunks and his back to the fire and looked at us for a moment—imposing, tall, almost splendid with his outstretched arms and the blunted face of a madman—then rapidly turned round and jumped into the open fire. His body terribly burnt, he was taken to the hospital the same evening.

Another time Sadovski, who for several days had not spoken to anyone, placed a table in the middle of the barrack, sat down behind it as if at a desk, and shouting out a string of strange foreign names, he added to each, with frightening monotony and fury, the command: "This is a revolution! Firing squad for you! To the wall with him! To the wall!" All this lasted no longer than a quarter of an hour, but, perhaps because he had been my friend, this nightmarish cry, in which his whole life, from the past, through the present, and into the future, was contained, has lodged deepest in my memory as the last dominating impression of my stay in the mortuary.

CHAPTER 15

IN THE URALS, 1942

ON January 19th the junior officer of the Second Section, who used to walk round the timber depot, when I worked there, with a list of releases in his hand, finally remembered my existence, and told me to report the next morning at the office for a certificate of my release from the camp. It came just in time; I crawled off my bunk with difficulty and, together with M., went round to say good-bye to all my Polish friends in the camp. In everyone's life there are moments of such stupefaction that a long time passes before the organism wakes from its numbness, sleepiness and insensibility. When I looked at the small group of people with whom only six weeks ago I had agreed to strike, I understood that it is possible to suffer in solitude, but not to be happy. "Don't forget us", they said, shaking my hand, "tell them where we are, tell them to get us out."

To M. I said good-bye in the morning, on our bunk. He was due to visit the medical hut that morning, and could not see me to the guard-house on my way out. "God won't abandon us," he said, embracing me affectionately. "But in case we shouldn't meet again, I wish you all the best." He walked out of the mortuary without looking back, and his long legs seemed to be dragging two heavy stones behind them.

So only two friends saw me off at the guard-house, Dimka and Olga. I woke Sadovski in the mortuary to say good-bye, but he simply stared at me deliriously for a moment, swore vilely, and covered his head again with a stinking jerkin; Dimka, when he heard that I was being released, put on the clean shirt in which he wanted to be buried and, limping on his wooden leg, held my hand until we reached the guard-house. "My son," he repeated with trembling lips, "my son, good luck to you. We are all finished, there is only death in store for us, but you're still a boy, you deserve to be free." Olga was waiting by the guard-house to see me off; she had grown thin and withered since she had been sent to the timber depot to load wood, and now could not keep her tears back as we said good-bye. I felt dreadfully sad and unhappy. Dante did not know that there is no suffering in this world greater than to experience happiness before the unhappy, to eat in front of the hungry. I kissed them both in silence. Just as I was leaving, old Iganov ran out from the barrack (it was the first rest-day in the camp since the New Year), and, taking me aside, gave me a card to post to his family. I walked slowly beyond the zone—for the first time in two years without a guard—to the office of the Second Section, where my papers had been prepared for me. At the bend of the road I turned round for a last glimpse of the camp. Dimka was still waving his wooden stick from the distance, and Olga was wearily walking back to the women's barrack.

In the Second Section I was given a list of the places for which I could get a railway ticket and a permit for residence. There was no possibility of joining the Polish Army. The N.K.V.D. officer, now all politeness, pretended ignorance of its whereabouts; even if he had known its exact location, I could not have got there, for the route that prisoners released from the Kargopol camp were allowed to take stopped at the Urals. Haphazardly, I chose Zlatoust, near Chelyabinsk, though I never reached it. Large towns like Sverdlovsk or Chelyabinsk were "rezhimnye goroda"—literally "régime towns"—where it was possible to reside only by special permission, which needless to say would not be granted to prisoners newly-released from labour camps.

At Yercevo station I learnt that the next train for Vologda would not leave till dawn on the following day. I found a warm resting-place on the floor near the stove in the waiting-room, and I went out to look at all the places which before I had seen only through barbed wire. As I walked I constantly fingered through my clothes my rustling new papers and Iganov's postcard. I am ashamed to confess it, but I never did post that card, and it lies before me on the table as I write. As long as I was within five hundred kilometres of the camp, I became panic-stricken whenever I approached a postbox, as if paralysed by the thought that I might return to Yercevo for helping Iganov to commit this offence. Once I got beyond the Urals, I forgot about it completely in my breathless pursuit of the Polish Army. Poor, honest Iganov! For a long time he must have wondered, praying at night on his bunk, how it was that the card, put into such apparently safe hands, had never reached its destination. Today I read it as I might a document, taken from a bottle thrown up by a stormy wave on a safe shore. It is addressed to his wife in Kazakhstan, though Iganov came from the Volga country, so I suppose that after his imprisonment his family was sent into exile in Asia. The card's text, besides numerous greetings to all nearer and more distant relations whose names are preceded by the traditional "most honoured", contains only one sentence which could explain and justify Iganov's attempt to evade the scrutiny of the camp censor's office: "I am *still* alive and well." And despite his religious faith, Iganov was cautious enough, when thanking God for watching over his family, to write His name with a small letter.

That evening I saw the camp from a hill near the station; it looked so small that I could have put it in the palm of my hand. Vertical columns of smoke rose from the barracks, lights shone in the windows, and but for the silhouettes of four high crow's-nests, cutting the night with the long knives of searchlight-beams, Yercevo could have passed for a quiet, peaceful settlement of foresters or charcoal-burners, resting after a heavy day's work. Straining my ears, I could catch the sound of chains and capstans turning on the wells—from the earliest days of civilisation a sign of untroubled peace.

*   *   *   *   *

In Vologda our train ran into a siding and the guard calmly announced that for the moment the journey was over. I had not come far, and if I went on travelling at this pace, I could have little hope of reaching the nearest detachment of Polish troops before spring. But at least I had arrived at Vologda station early enough to reserve a sleeping-place on the bare earth floor of the station waiting-room. Several hundred released prisoners had been living here for a month; apart from a handful of Poles, they were mostly short-term criminal prisoners, released from the camps as volunteers for the front before their sentences were finished. In the day-time they were driven out into the town, where they spent their time looking for food, and in the evening the enormous waiting-room, by permission of the N.K.V.D., served as a dormitory for them. I hesitate before describing the four nights which I spent in Vologda, for I do not believe that literature could sink so low without losing some of its character as the artistic expression of things commonly known and experienced. Enough, then, to say that we slept next to each other, lying on our sides packed together like herrings in a barrel, and giving out an inhuman stench. In the yellowish-green light of the night bulbs, the faces of sleepers, their open mouths gaping like holes, looked like the death-masks of drowned men. Every attempt to wade through the mass of bodies at night to reach the nearest bucket usually ended in someone's death. If the foot landed on someone's chest, rising and falling with the unquiet breath of feverish sleep, a short choking moan gave warning that one should step aside, but I myself, still half-conscious after waking up suddenly, once stepped on someone's face. One of my legs was wedged between two bodies, and trying to free it I moved my whole weight on to my other leg, and felt a spongy mass splintering and crackling under my heavy boot, while blood spurted from under the sole. A moment later I was sick into the bucket, though I had not come to it for that. Every morning at least ten bodies, stripped naked by their fellow-guests in the waiting-room, were carried out and laid on the open trucks.

At dawn we had to leave the station and we went begging in the town. I found a small street in the working-class district, where every day about noon a grey-haired old woman beckoned to me, first having made certain that no one was looking, and took me into her kitchen, where she gave me a mugful of unsweetened herb tea and a slice of stale bread. We never exchanged a word beyond my "spasiba"—"thank you", and her "idi z Bogom"—"God be with you". Once, wandering aimlessly round the town, I blundered into a small square and found in a red-brick house the local office of the People's Commisariat for War, something like a recruiting centre for volunteers. A stout captain received me behind his desk, backed by an enormous wall-map of the Soviet Union, politely offered me a cigarette, and, when I asked him where the Polish Army in Russia was being formed, suggested that I would do far better to join the Red Army. Another time, I remember, I stood in a bread queue and witnessed an incident which I shall remember all my life. A wounded Soviet soldier, who had lost his right leg during the defence of Leningrad, dragged himself to the queue on crutches and asked, quietly and politely, if he might not enter the shop without having to wait, for he had only been out of hospital a few days and found it difficult to stand for any length of time on his one healthy leg. He was answered by a hostile murmur and maliciously told that he need be in no hurry, for with only one leg he would not be taken back to the front anyway. His face was full of such helpless despair that I would willingly have given him my bread, but my weak and diseased legs would not allow me to stand in the queue until I reached the door of the shop. Thus the contempt for a damaged machine which is out of circulation has permeated all strata of the Russian people and has polluted fundamentally honest hearts. Besides, the war itself was not particularly popular in Vologda in January 1942. The queues were full of complaints about the food shortages and the chaotic conscription which had left many families without a single bread-winner, and twice I even overheard the whispered question: "When are these Germans coming?" Vologda was a bottleneck on the railway, corked with consignments of damaged furniture, machinery and factory plant from Leningrad. In all larger public buildings detachments of soldiers, moved back from the front for a short rest, were bivouacking; in the evenings they haunted private flats and living quarters like a flock of hungry birds, playing sadly on mouth-organs, and always eagerly searching for vodka. I had nothing to wait for in Vologda. On the morning of the fifth day, instead of going out into the town as usual, I walked out along the railway tracks, and about midday I jumped on a train, whose destination was then quite unknown to me, which had stopped for a moment about half a mile outside Vologda station.

Inside the warm and comfortable compartment I was welcomed with surprise, though without a word of protest, by several sleepy naval officers, who were travelling on orders from Archangel to the Black Sea. For the first time since I left the camp I recognised, in their conversation, the quiet and discreet feeling of Russian patriotism. It did not appear to me to be very spontaneous, for after the inevitable "We shall win" which accompanied every fresh revelation about the new epaulettes and medals which were being issued to the officers, the speakers would go back to sleep, shading their eyes with the lowered peaks of their caps. After three hours' journey the guard found me in the compartment and put me out of the train at the tiny station of Bouy.

*   *   *   *   *

In Bouy fate smiled at me when I was near despair. I spent the night at the station, and in the morning I went out to look at the small pleasant town. In the square I saw a small church painted gold and green, and with astonishment I noticed that the sign "anti-religious museum", which I had seen hanging in front of the

Vitebsk church, was absent from its rotting wooden doors. In the dark, chilly nave three old women knelt together; at the sound of my footsteps they raised their heads, got up, and walked quickly out without looking at me or at each other. I was evidently young enough to arouse fear and suspicion.

The day was frosty and sunny, but there was no wind, and on the brittle, powdery snow my steps sounded confident, almost gay. I wandered among the small streets, I walked beyond the town into a large field, and returned to the square: everywhere the same thing— closed shutters and not a soul in sight. Near the wooden head-quarters of the fire brigade I found on a rubbish heap a large piece of black bread. I scraped it clean of mud and mould with my camp penknife and, having moistened it with snow, I ate it hungrily and greedily. The station waiting-room was still empty, but my morning walk had so refreshed me that the very sight of a lonely station-master in a red cap, tapping out mysterious signals in the silence of the frosty morning, his hand on the brass hammer of his telegraph set, brought to light from under the rubble of my damaged memory the first verse of Tuvim's well-known poem about the life of a love-sick telegraphist on a lonely, isolated Russian railway station. Things could not be so bad, I thought, if I can still remember poetry.

The stationmaster looked at me with suspicion for a few minutes. Finally he got up from his desk, came up to me and asked me if, for a plateful of soup and a pound of bread, I would unload a truckful of railway sleepers, which, for lack of labour in the town, had been standing for several days in a siding. If I had not just eaten my breakfast by the fire-brigade headquarters, I would have agreed without a moment's hesitation. But now I put a higher price on myself, and demanded, in return for my work, a seat on the next train for Sverdlovsk. The stationmaster shrugged his shoulders and returned to his work. Fifteen minutes later, after much haggling, the bargain was struck: he would give me immediately a plateful of hot soup, and if I worked till evening he agreed to put me on the express from Moscow to Sverdlovsk, which at midnight stopped at Bouy for one minute. Exactly at eleven that night I came for my pay with bleeding hands and frost-bitten legs. The stationmaster kept his word, and an hour later I was sitting huddled in the dark corridor of a railway carriage, travelling rapidly towards Sverdlovsk.

I fell asleep almost instantly, and as I thawed in the warmth of the corridor, my dreams became pleasant and peaceful. I was woken by a hand which reached out from within a dark compartment, inviting me inside. Unwillingly, rather nervous, I entered the compartment. By the light of a shaded blue bulb I could just make out the forms of six sleeping women. The woman who had asked me in woke her companions, and a few minutes later I was sitting back on a bench strewn with cushions, drinking sweetened tea from a thermos flask and eating bread with dripping on it. My hospitable fellow-travellers turned out to be workers from a Moscow steel works which was being evacuated wholesale into the Urals; their machines stood on open trucks at the rear of the train. They were indeed kind to me—they concealed me on the upper bunk of the compartment until we reached Sverdlovsk and they shared their food with me the whole way; but I shall never forget that they respected me as a human being, refusing to be put off by my filthy, lousy rags, and bearing bravely the stench of my dirty, festering body. I mentioned only once my stay in prison and in the camp, but I said no more about it when I saw the expression of fear and distrust in their eyes. But we talked much of the war, of the winter offensive which was being prepared, of the partial evacuation of heavy industry from Moscow, and the cruelties committed by the Germans in the occupied regions. It is possible that at the time I was moved by this unexpected kindness, or else my mental faculties, weakened by so many painful experiences, suddenly relaxed in the safe warmth of the compartment, but I believe that never again, not even in the Polish Army in Russia, did I meet with such a sincere and touching expression of patriotism. The women outdid each other in telling me stories of the courage and sacrifice of the people of besieged Moscow, of their own work, which often continued, with short breaks, during whole days and nights, of the readiness with which they now abandoned their homes and families in order to rush to the Urals at the call of "the Government and the Party"; the gleam of hatred and enthusiasm in their eyes was unfeigned as they assured me that they would not hesitate to give up their lives in the defence of their Fatherland against the German invader. I particularly remember one of them, a young girl in the sixth month of her pregnancy, who writhed with pain at every sharp jolt of the carriage, and as she talked laid her thin and work-soiled hands on her bulging belly, like a Dutch peasant woman from one of Van Gogh's earlier canvases. A little later I learnt of what inhuman effort the Soviet industry is capable. On the third day of my short stay in Sverdlovsk I went for a lonely walk round the town, and in a small valley I found the women of the same Moscow steel works standing on improvised wooden scaffoldings, busy at their machines with bare hands. Thick snow fell all round them, as over their heads carpenters and builders were putting the first tiles of the roof into position over hastily erected beams.

The greater part of my journey I spent on the luggage-rack, and I remember only that the train stopped at Vyatka and Perm.

*   *   *   *   *

It was January 30th when I arrived in Sverdlovsk. This is the first date which I quote not from memory, but from the evidence of a diary which I kept at the time. It was a sign of my rapid return to health that as soon as I came to Sverdlovsk I was seized with a desire to write, and with my last few kopeks I bought a little note-book and pencil at the station. The writing on its pages is now worn and hardly legible. "The town"—I wrote—"resembles a contour-map made of plasticine. The old 'Ekaterynburg' is built mostly of wood. Even in the centre of the town one can find small wooden one-storeyed houses with curious little domes and carved orna-ments—this is the architecture of the Russian mercantile middle class. Beyond, it is all brick factory-blocks with tall chimneys, and red churches. The third layer is the modern Sverdlovsk—hideous, vulgar houses, hung with portraits of Lenin and Stalin, covered with garish posters and slogans. The town has no vitality, it rolls over from side to side like a wounded animal, plagued by its human vermin. The effect of war can be seen at every step. Over two million natives, refugees and evacuees are living in the town. Nothing but queues and tired faces everywhere. In the street where the headquarters of district administration and local offices of the Government are collected there is no distribution of bread and soup, nothing to stand in the queues for. Few soldiers, but many new recruits in their old civilian clothes, with rifles slung over their shoulders. Everywhere can be seen efforts of organisation which produce no result. Life here is competitive—if you want anything, you must fight for it yourself. The evenings are more pleasant, the trams are crowded, the streets fill with people. Sverdlovsk has no blackout."

This colourless, but on the whole I believe faithful, description was the first thing that I had written for two years. What strikes me about it now is the exaggeration (that "wounded animal"!) so typical of a young writer who tries to capture an impression while it is still fresh in his mind. If today I were to attempt a description of Sverdlovsk, I should probably lay greater emphasis on human beings than on architecture. I remember workers, returning from factories in the evening, who gathered under the street megaphones to hear the latest war news. Their faces were grimy, unshaved, their eyes without a spark of life. They listened in silence, and then departed in twos and threes for their evening dose of political discussion and propaganda. Their hunched shadows merged into the grey snow-mist, like water rats which creep out at dusk from their holes in the ice. The silent crowd moved slowly through the narrow streets into the squares and dispersed, some joining the queues, others entering the brightly-lit doors of eating-houses. Only the clanging trams formed any sort of livelier contrast to the enormous five-pronged star of electric bulbs which glared from the roof of one of the Government offices. I remember a group of soldiers who knelt in the frozen road, patiently breaking up the ice with sharp little hammers to make a way for a convoy of tanks. About midday a shrill whistle from one end of the street caused all the junior officers to spring up from the pavements. After a moment a gentle cloud of perfume which floated on the air from a distance was followed by a Russian general, covered with medals and surrounded by his staff. He walked slowly, kicking his way through the kneeling soldiers with violent asides of his boot. I also remember a perfectly-equipped and armed Siberian division, in white uniforms like siren-suits and hoods of white fur with holes for the eyes and mouth. The soldiers spent several hours at Sverdlovsk station on their way from the Far East to the Leningrad front; before the eyes of the hungry crowd they ate tinned meat and biscuits made of white flour, but not one of them dropped a scrap of food into the trembling, expectant hands held out all round him. Finally, I remember a Russian soldier who was having his photograph taken for his family outside the station. He spread his right hand on his chest, like Balzac in the well-known daguerreotype, but he would not allow the photographer to press the little rubber bulb until he had pushed back the sleeve of his greatcoat to show an enormous wrist-watch. . . .

When I moved into the station waiting-room on my first day in

Sverdlovsk I joined a small handful of Poles who were living there.
They informed me that the next train for Chelyabinsk would leave
in about ten days' time, that soup was distributed every day in an
abandoned truck beyond the main line, that any solitary woman
waiting for a train could be had in a dark corner near the cloak-
room, and that no one in Sverdlovsk had ever heard of the Polish
Army in Russia. In the afternoon I went out into the town. On the
day before I had left Yercevo, a prisoner in the transit barrack
had asked me to visit the wife and children of General Kruglov, if
ever during my wanderings I happened to pass through Sverdlovsk.
Kruglov himself was a prisoner in the Ostrovnoye camp section,
and immediately after the outbreak of the Russo-German war he
had received an additional sentence, rounding off his seven remaining years to fifteen. My mission was not very pleasant, but I held on
to it as the only point of stability in my life at freedom. I found the
address—a tall, dirty apartment house, in a narrow street whose
name I have now forgotten. There an old housekeeper, glancing at
me suspiciously, led me through the courtyard to a small flat on the
ground floor. I found the general's daughter, Nadia Kruglov, a
lovely fourteen-year-old girl with dark, thoughtful eyes, sitting at
the table over a stack of notes and text-books. She received me
politely, and with a certain eagerness when she learnt that I had
come from her father's camp. The dark room was crowded with
shabby antique furniture, and the murky yellow air of evening was
seeping in through a broken window which was partly covered with
plywood. It was so cold in the flat that the girl was wearing felt
boots, mittens, and a fur coat thrown over her shoulders. I had a
thorough wash in the kitchen, my first in two months. While
waiting for Mrs. Kruglov, I sat at the table with Nadia and helped
her with her work; as we pored over maps and struggled with sums
together, we became good friends. In the evening her mother
returned, a woman still beautiful despite signs of tiredness and lack
of sleep, and the horn-rimmed glasses which hid dark, sparkling
eyes like Nadia's. She laid a pound loaf of bread on the table and
looked enquiringly at her daughter. When she learnt that I had
brought news of the general, she immediately asked me to go into
the kitchen with her.

"Did you tell Nadia about her father's new sentence?" she asked
anxiously.

"No," I answered, "I quite forgot about it. In the camp no one pays much attention to sentences, for it is impossible to imagine oneself living to the end of them."

"Oh, thank God," she cried, taking no notice of the meaning hidden in my words. "You see, her teachers and school-friends persecute Nadia so much because her father is in a camp, that she would never go to school again if she knew that his sentence had been increased."

We came back into the room just as the Kruglovs' old nurse, who had come in to eat as usual with her former mistress, was serving dinner. On a white tablecloth appeared a steaming tureen of soup and a samovar. I was strangely moved and a little intimidated by it all. The nurse cut a piece of bread from her ration and handed it to me across the table, saying that at her age one can do without bread; we sat round the table and warmed our hands on the heated metal of the samovar. Mrs. Kruglov never mentioned her husband, and cut short any of my allusions to the camp with a warning glance of her sad eyes; we talked of indifferent matters. She told me that she worked very hard as a typist, that she earned little, and that in the evenings she could hardly keep awake during the political discussions which the whole office had to attend after work. Her eighteen-year-old son, who had always wanted to be an officer, was turned down by the Army "because of his father", and was now digging trenches in Leningrad in an auxiliary brigade of volunteers. Nadia complained with tears in her eyes that they would not take her into the school "Komsomol", the Communist Youth Organisation, "because of Father," and that she was not allowed to join in sports and games after school, but added that in two years' time, "when Daddy comes back," everything would be changed. The old nurse rocked sleepily in her chair like an owl, mumbling with toothless gums her eternal, monotonous "God help us." After dinner we opened a large atlas on the table under the porcelain shade of the oil-lamp, and, laughing together, we planned long journeys abroad. The old nurse would not join us, saying "Don't worry about me— I was born in Russia, and in Russia I want to die." I was so happy there that suddenly I thought how much I would give to be able to spend just one night under a family roof—even on the floor in the tiny kitchen. Mrs. Kruglov, however, did not invite me, and looked at her watch repeatedly. During my two years in prison and camp I had almost completely lost any feeling of sensitivity or politeness, but now, in this atmosphere of genteel poverty, I felt so timid that it was only with difficulty that I managed to ask for the favour of one night's lodging.

"Did anyone see you come in?" Mrs. Kruglov asked nervously.

"Yes, the caretaker showed me the way here."

She suddenly seemed to lose control of herself and began to sob. "I can't, for God's sake, I really can't. My husband in prison, my children treated like outcasts . . . they hardly allow us to breathe. . . . Do you know what it feels like to be dragged out at night by the N.K.V.D. . . . to beg for work as if it were charity? Don't bring any more suffering to this house! Please go, please go at once, and never come back here!"

It was past midnight when I made my way to the station through the deserted streets.

My diary here describes, in touchingly naïve and sentimental language, a romantic episode which, looking back on it seven years later, hardly appears to be romantic at all. On my fifth day in Sverdlovsk I met Fatima Soboleva, a young Georgian woman who was dozing on a bench like the rest of us, waiting for a train to Magnitogorsk. I felt attracted to her not only because she was exceptionally pretty—a round face with a dark complexion, skin covered with a soft down, long jet-black hair which in the daytime she wound round her head in plaits and at night combed out round her shoulders, her ivory-white teeth gleaming in the dark— but also because I noticed that she often took from a small basket portions of cheese, cold meat, and butter for her bread. Fatima was an official of the Communist Party's City Executive Committee at Magnitogorsk, and her Party card opened the doors of the shops which remained closed to us. She was stranded in Sverdlovsk for several days on her way home from Omsk, where she had travelled to visit her wounded husband, also a Georgian, an officer of the artillery, who at the time of the outbreak of war had been stationed in Lithuania. She spoke of him often, chattering unconcernedly about his wound: "He's no good to me any more, they've amputated both his legs. Of course it's a pity, but I can't be expected to sleep with an invalid for the rest of my life."

I became very fond of her, and once or twice we even went together into the dark corner by the cloak-room. Fatima tried to persuade me to give up all thought of going off to the war, and to come with her to Magnitogorsk. "What nonsense you talk!" she would say in a complaining voice, "life is too short for that sort of thing. They're not dragging you off to the Red Army, why push yourself in? You're well educated, I'm a Party member, I can fix you a good job at home."

She would not believe a word of what I told her about the labour camps. "Nonsense, nonsense," she would shake her head decisively. "There is nothing like that in the Soviet Union. Anyone can get scurvy up in the north, and their clothes torn at work. If you come with me your legs will heal, I'll see that you get clothing coupons, and everything will be all right." But in the evenings, when we would walk aimlessly about in the snow, she would interrupt my prison reminiscences with a nervous tug at my arm. "Didn't they teach you in the camp," she would whisper, looking carefully behind her, "to keep your mouth shut in the street. Anyone might be passing by in the dark. You could be picked up here and now." Indeed I could not distinguish anyone in the shadowy, murmuring, and horribly anonymous crowd which flowed through the streets. We would stop in front of the bright windows of eating-houses to read the list of dishes, headed by the eternal cabbage soup.

"Why don't you ever take me in on your Party ticket for a meal? Ashamed of my rags?" I asked her once.

"No, it's not that," she answered, "but someone might recognise me and write to the committee at home."

"And in Magnitogorsk, won't they recognise you there?"

"That's different. At home it's always easier. They might not allow you to go in, but as long as I had asked permission first they'd never punish me."

Five days later Fatima left for Magnitogorsk. From the window of her compartment she shouted loudly at me: "Don't forget, Leninskaya Street!"

The next morning my group of Poles met, and welcomed with almost religious awe, the first Polish officer that we had seen in Russia, who was travelling from his detachment to collect his family from Archangel. He told us that the nearest office of the Polish Army was in Chelyabinsk, and the latest division of the Army was being formed in Kazakhstan.

*   *   *   *   *

In Chelyabinsk our small company,* led by the energetic

* In Chelyabinsk I met three of my friends from the camp, M., T. and B., who had been released soon after me. Despite our enquiries, we never discovered what had happened to L. and Miss Z.

Lieutenant C., found the smart "Ural" hotel near a tractor factory, and in the hotel the chief of the Polish Army office, a tall captain in battle-dress with a swagger-stick. He received us without any particular sign of enthusiasm, scarcely listened to our chaotic stories, and opened a window, even though February is not usually accounted to be one of the warmest months in the Urals. He gave us ten roubles each and assured us that, if the Russian authorities did not object, he would put us through an improvised medical examination (luckily there was a doctor among us), and that he would try to arrange for a separate railway carriage and travel documents which would get us to Kazakhstan. As we said good-bye, the captain gave Lieutenant C. several small crosses with the legend "Pledge for Victory" in English and some copies of the litany to the Miraculous Virgin of Ostrobrama printed on vellum paper. "Please give these out to your men," he said, pushing us out through the door, "they must have forgotten about God in those camps." Secure in the thought that we were at last "men", human beings, even though we had indeed forgotten about God in the camps, we made our way towards the station, where, we had been told immediately after our arrival, it was possible to steal food from the stores.

My diary breaks off at this point—evidently I was too busy and excited at the prospect of joining the Army—and instead of careful notes and observations it contains only a detailed itinerary of our route: Chelyabinsk-Orsk-Orenburg-Aktubinsk-Aralsk-Kyzyl-Orda-Arys-Chymkent-Dzambul-Lugovoye. In the first days of February we left Chelyabinsk in a goods truck which had been provided with two tiers of wooden bunks, two buckets, a sack of flour and one of barley, and two holes in the floor for our most immediate needs. On March 9th we were already in Lugovoye. I remember almost nothing of this journey, for we seldom left the truck, which at every large station was coupled to a different train, for fear that we should not be able to find it again. We spent that month on our bunks, sleeping and eating, sometimes finding a distraction in hunting for lice in the folds of our clothes. But in Orsk, where our truck had to wait several hours, I remember seeing a magnificent sunset over the snowy steppe—a sky changing from dark blue to rusty red, and brown camels carrying solitary travellers on their rocking humps across the steppe to the station.

On March 12th, in Lugovoye, I was accepted for the tenth

regiment of light artillery. The first person that I met in Lugovoye, as I walked through the rain to my tent carrying a new battle-dress, underwear, a pair of boots and a billy-can, was the thin Captain K., whom I used to drag from his bunk to the bucket in the Vitebsk prison when he could no longer walk there himself. I knocked into him by accident, sliding down a muddy slope on my wet boots, and when I saw who it was I opened my arms wide with astonishment so that my whole bundle fell into the mud. He looked at me fiercely, dusted his beautifully-cut breeches, and threatened me with "disciplinary action" the moment I was in uniform. I knew then that I was really in the Army, that I was at last among my compatriots, who after all that they had gone through during the past two years were rapidly returning to normal.

The tenth division, containing almost entirely those most recently released from the camps and therefore the weakest and most undernourished prisoners, was the first to be evacuated to Persia from Russia. On March 26th my regiment was transported on a goods train through Dzambul, Arys, Tashkent, Dzizak, Samarkand, Bukhara, Tchardzhau and Ashkhabad, to Krasnovodsk on the Caspian Sea; on March 30th we embarked on two ships, the *Agamali Ogly* and the *Turkmenistan*. The night of April 2nd, 1942, I spent on the beach at Pahlevi, beyond the frontiers of that country where, as I wrote in my diary at the time, "it is possible to cease to believe in man, and in the purpose of the struggle to improve his lot on earth."

THE FALL OF PARIS

"It is hard to imagine how far a man's nature
may be distorted!"
          —DOSTOEVSKY—*The House of the Dead.*

1

IN Vitebsk prison I learnt that Paris had fallen from a small dark
prisoner who was pushed into our cell on a June day in 1940.

The summer was at its height. Every day we would gaze, in
silence and with painful stubbornness, at the square of blue sky,
pale, almost white from the heat, which was framed by our small
window. Shadows of invisible birds flitted across it and disappeared
with a cry in the silence of the afternoon which was as thick and
sticky as honey. Almost immediately after our arrival at Vitebsk,
in the first days of June, we learnt to look at the sky without a
word, a sky which every day was clearer, every day hotter. Most of
the prisoners in the cell were soldiers, scattered refugees from the
Polish Army, the first to be defeated by Germany in the war. When
it was cooler, they would sit up on the palliasses after lunch, and
spend the afternoons spitting on their heavy army boots and
polishing them, rubbing for hours on their sleeves the metal
buttons and little silver eagles which they had hidden in their packs,
and carefully winding cloth puttees round their legs. Their faces
were covered with a hard bristle, which grew over dirty wrinkled
skin, their shaved heads were like shapeless lumps of stone, their
necks covered with carbuncles and boils, their lips cracked and
swollen, their eyes and legs red, the first from weariness, the others
from burns. Heavy leaden tears sprang to their eyes whenever the
sound of horses' hooves metallically treading on the cobbled streets
reached the cell from some distant horizon of silence.

The new prisoner laid his bundle on the bucket, looked round
with distrust and alighted timidly on a palliasse by the door. He
was like a bird who flies into a cage with much flapping of wings,
with eyes veiled by a white cataract, and a half-open sharply-

hooked beak, and grips the wooden perch with determination. There was silence in the cell. We had all spent enough time in Soviet prisons to know that out of ten newly-arrived prisoners five at least were informers who had been sent in from another cell to see what they could pick up. The quiet, whispered conversations stopped even in remote corners of the cell where the new arrival's hearing could not have penetrated. The prisoners' stooping figures became tense, their hands clasped their bent knees, their fascinated gaze hung on the small face twisted with a grimace of fear. It was clear that in order to break the wall of suspicion which surrounded him on all sides the unknown man would have to speak first.

He did not, it is true, look like an informer. In his ungainly figure with elongated hands and crooked legs, his face with two abnormally large ears sprouting from it like wings and black eyes looking anxiously around, I sensed rather a great tragedy, one of many which the war then revealed in the lives of those who in slavery had seen the best guarantee of freedom for themselves. He raised his head from his bundle abruptly, and in a voice movingly quiet whispered: "Paris has fallen. . . ."

One of those sitting by him blew up this flickering whisper into a sharp flaming shout: "Paris has fallen!"

The tense figures relaxed, and sighs could be heard from almost all bunks. We lay down comfortably with our faces turned towards the window and our hands folded behind our heads. We had nothing to wait for any longer. Paris had fallen. Paris, Paris. . . . It is unbelievable that even the simplest people there, people who had never set eyes on France, felt the fall of Paris as the death of their last hope, a defeat more irrevocable even than the surrender of Warsaw. The night of slavery, which hung over Europe like a dark cloud, covered too the small scrap of sky quartered by prison bars.

2

I became closely acquainted with the new arrival during the next few weeks, for his news had in some ways drawn us together. In the evenings he told me the story of his life, so banal in its matter that it could serve as an example for text-books of the late war. He was born in Grodno, the son of a rich Jewish merchant. After finishing his high school in Poland, he left for Paris in 1935 to continue his studies. There he became a communist, he even attempted to slip into Spain at the time of the Civil War, but the Party ordered him to stay where he was and organise a Party cell of foreign students at the Paris School of Architecture. He continued to study architecture, and in June 1939 received his degree. A month later, just before the outbreak of war, he returned to Poland.

It would be a vain pursuit to attempt an analysis of his communism. In moments of clarity he made himself understood, and I gathered that his faith was a compound of Marx and Le Corbusier, in which the economic contradictions of capitalism are solved by the planning of an urbanistic Utopia. This sounds naïve, even comic, but his Jewish idealism, recognising a heavenly kingdom only in this world, needed some basis of rationalist construction, and found it in huge dream garden cities, inhabited by the Paris proletariat and the scum of Polish ghettoes.

When the Soviet Army marched into Grodno, in September 1939, he was appointed building adviser to the Town Council, and filled that post until May 1940, when he was imprisoned for refusing to agree to a voluntary exile in the depths of Russia. The fall of Paris was a personal defeat for him: it was not only the final seal of conquest over the whole Continent, but also the capture of the city in which his Utopia was conceived, by a state allied to the fatherland of his Utopia.

He soon became popular in the cell, for in the evenings he talked vividly and convincingly of life in pre-war Paris. But besides the tragedy of a betrayed idealist he was undergoing another drama, perhaps even more difficult to bear and more painful: an inward conflict of loyalties. In his heart he thought of himself as a Pole. But when, on the evening after his arrival in the cell, the block sergeant asked him formally what his nationality was, he replied quietly, looking down at the ground: "Jewish."

3

In June 1945 I almost bumped into him in Rome, as I was walking at midday out of the editorial offices of the army paper on which I was then working.

"I'd heard that you were working here," he said shyly, "and I came from Florence to see you. . . ."

"But you, how did you get to Italy?"

"Oh, that's a longish story," he answered with a smile, "let's go and have coffee somewhere."

At that time of day it is difficult to sit for any length of time in the hot cafés and taverns of Rome, so we decided to talk in my hotel. Rome was then slowly returning to life. Horses' hooves made a hollow sound on the scorching paving-stones, and a sad, ragged crowd trickled over the bridges and stopped half-way across, looking down at the dirty waves of the Tiber. In the distance, over it all, the Castello Angelo rose like a winged rock.

He could not wait and started talking in the street. He had been taken from the cell in Vitebsk a month after me, and sent to the Pechora camp with a ten-year sentence. He was first put to heavy work in the forest, and then to floating wood down the river. When the Russo-German war broke out he was near the end. The amnesty for Poles passed him by because at his first prison roll-call he had answered "Jewish" when asked to give his nationality. The Russians put their own interpretation on the Polish-Russian agreement; they considered Polish citizens to be only those of Polish racial origin, retaining in the camps all Ukrainians, White Russians and Jews from east of the Curzon Line, who had before the war been Polish citizens, and towards the end of 1941 even Jews from Central and Western, i.e. German-occupied, Poland. It could almost be said that the Russians treated the Jews as their own property, and it must be admitted that they had some reason for this attitude—in Hitler's continental empire, between the years 1941 and 1943, the fate of the Jews was indeed tragically connected with the existence of Russia.

He was saved from dying of exhaustion by the fact that in January 1942 the camp authorities remembered his high technical qualifications, and made him a foreman in the building brigade. Transferred to the technical barrack, he returned to health comparatively quickly. In January 1944 he was suddenly released before time, and immediately conscripted into the Red Army. Almost without any military training, he found himself, in the spring of that year, in the army marching on Hungary. He was wounded in battle near Budapest. Straight from the hospital he was transferred to the Polish units then being formed by the communist Committee of National Liberation in Moscow, and with them he reached Warsaw. He obtained his discharge from the army at the first opportunity, and illegally fled to Italy. The Jewish organisation, Joint, gave him a room in their house in Florence, where he was waiting for a visa to South America.

In the requisitioned hotel on the corner of Tritone and Corso Umberto I ordered a bottle of iced wine and took him up to my room on the third floor. It was hot and stuffy, through the drawn blinds flattened rays of light broke into the room, and we could hear the shouting of drunken soldiers and the squeals of street girls in other rooms. A lazy crowd moved along the streets. The heat was approaching its daily zenith. We sat down together on the bed. I looked vacantly at the patterns on the wallpaper, not knowing where to begin. For I felt instinctively that he had not told me everything.

"In the whole story," he began carefully, "there is one thing that I have not mentioned, and which I would still like to tell you. I haven't talked about it with anybody because, to tell you the truth, there has been nobody to talk to. When I got back to Poland I found no one alive; my whole family, all near and distant relatives, were dead. But through so many sleepless nights I have longed to meet someone who could understand me, who had also known a Soviet prison camp. . . . I'm not asking you for anything. I have changed my name since the war, and in a few months' time, a year at most, I shall start a new life in America. But before that happens, I would like you to listen, and when you have heard me out, to say just one word, say only: 'I understand'. . . ."

I refilled our glasses. "You can speak freely. After all, we were in the same prison cell, and after this war that is almost like having been to school together. . . ."

"It wasn't so easy, then, to maintain myself in the position of foreman with the building brigade. In Russia, as you know, you have to pay for everything. In February 1942, barely a month after I had left general work for the technical barrack, I was summoned at night to the Third Section. It was a period when the Russians were retaliating for their defeats at the front even in the camps. I had four Germans in my brigade, two completely russified, from the Volga settlements, and two communists who had fled to Russia in 1935. They worked well, and I had nothing against them except possibly the fact that they avoided any discussion of politics like the plague. Well, the Third Section told me to sign a deposition, testifying that I had heard them talking in German of the speedy

coming of Hitler. My God, surely one of the greatest nightmares of
the whole Soviet system is that mania for liquidating their victims
with all legal formalities. . . . It isn't enough to put a bullet through
someone's head, no, he must himself politely ask for it at the trial.
Not enough to involve someone in a grim fiction, but they must
have witnesses to prove it. The N.K.V.D. did not conceal from me
that I would be sent back to the forest if I refused. . . . I had to
choose between my own death and that of those four. . . ."

He poured himself out some more wine and with a trembling
hand lifted the glass to his lips. From under my lowered eyelids I
saw his perspiring, frightened face.

"I chose. I had had enough of the forest, and of that terrible
daily struggle with death—I wanted to live. I testified. Two days
later they were shot beyond the zone."

We were both silent. He placed his empty glass on the table and
curled up on the bed, as if expecting a blow. On the other side of
the wall a woman's shrill soprano crowed a phrase of an Italian
song and stopped suddenly, cut short by a curse. It had become a
little cooler, but I could almost hear the heated car tyres tearing
themselves away from the sticky asphalt with a slight crackle.

"If I told that story to any of the people among whom I
am now living, they would either not believe me or, if they
believed, would refuse to shake my hand. But you must know to
what they drove us, how low they brought us there. Say only that
you understand. . . ."

I felt the blood rushing to my head. Images and memories
crowded before my eyes. At that time, three years after I had left
Russia, when I was forcing the camp from my mind in order to
preserve faith in human dignity, these images were blurred and indistinct, though now when I have finally obtained some peace, I look
at them with detachment and they are clear but quite remote. I
might have been able to pronounce the word that was asked of me,
on the day after my release from the camp. I might have done . . .
In 1945 I already had three years of freedom behind me, three years
of military wandering and battles, of normal feelings, love, friendship and sympathy. . . . The days of our life are not like the days
of our death, and the laws of our life are not the laws of our death.
I had come back among people, with human standards and conceptions, and was I now to escape from them, abandon them,
voluntarily betray them? The choice was the same: then it had

been his life or the lives of the four Germans, now it was his peace or mine. No, I could not say it.

"Well?" he asked quietly.

I got up from the bed and without looking him in the eyes walked over to the window. With my back to the room I heard him going out and gently closing the door. I pushed the blind up. On the Piazza Colonna a cool breath of afternoon air had straightened the passers-by, as it would a field of corn bowed to the ground by drought. Drunk American and English soldiers walked along the pavements, pushing the Italians aside, picking up girls, looking for shade under the striped awnings of shops. Under the pillars of the corner house the black market was in full swing. The Roman "lazzaroni", small ragged war-children, dived in and out between the legs of enormous negroes in American uniforms. The war had ended a month ago. Rome was free, Brussels was free, Oslo was free, Paris was free. Paris, Paris, Paris. . . .

I watched him as he walked out of the hotel, tripped across the road like a bird with a broken wing, and disappeared in the crowd without looking back.

June 1949–*June* 1950.

THE END

I. POSTSCRIPT TO THE MOSCOW TRIALS

THE circumstances of Gorki's death have never been cleared up. During the Moscow Trials of 1936-7 the State Prosecutor mentioned in an aside the fact that besides Kirov, Kuibyshev and Gorki had also fallen victims to the "Trotsky-Zinoviev conspiracy", though he did not go into details about the method in which the great writer was murdered. Only during the last Moscow trials of 1938 three Kremlin doctors, Levin, Pletnyev and Kasakov, confessed that at the command of Yagoda (who was allegedly acting at the instigation of Bukharin and Rykov) they murdered, among others, Gorki. Brigadier Fitzroy Maclean, in his book, *Eastern Approaches*, reports their admission that "Maxim Gorki had deliberately been sat by them in a draught and had caught pneumonia." Both Levin and Kasakov received death sentences. Isaac Deutscher, in his book on Stalin, mentions, however, a book published in 1940 by Stalin's private secretary, Poskrebyshev, in which Gorki's death is described as natural.

While writing the chapter entitled "A Game of Chess", I was struck by the resemblance between the conviction of Dr. Levin for the assassination of Gorki and the nickname "Gorkist" which was given to Dr. Loevenstein in the camp because he had neglected Gorki during his last illness. The similarity of the names made me suspect either that, after so many years, I had unintentionally changed Levin into Loevenstein, or that Levin, though sentenced to death, had been sent to the camp with a new name. Excited by the probable discovery that not all the verdicts of the Moscow Trials were carried out, I wrote to Brigadier Maclean, who was an eye-witness of Levin's trial, giving him a description of Loevenstein ("a man of about fifty-five, short, stoutish, with a small belly, a pleasant and intelligent face with slightly protruding eyes, gold spectacles and locks of greying hair"). Brigadier Maclean replied: "As far as I can remember, your description of your fellow-prisoner generally corresponds to my recollection of Dr. Levin. In fact it looks very much as if it might have been the same man."

Further confirmation of what would be a most interesting

discovery is provided by a letter from Kazimierz Chmielowski, a former Soviet prisoner now living in Italy, which contains the following description of a meeting in prison:

"I wish to describe an occurrence which I witnessed in the Lukyanovka prison in Kiev. I was in the 'special penal block', in cell 18 on the second floor. In March or April 1941, as we were on our way to exercise, we stopped for a moment in the corridor. One of the prisoners, a Jew who had once been a chief of the N.K.V.D. in Odessa (his Christian name was Boris, his surname I cannot remember), taking advantage of our guard's momentary absence, looked into one of the cells through the judas, and his face changed as if he had seen something incredible inside. He whispered something to another prisoner, Colonel Nicolai Borodin, who also looked into the cell; the effect on him of what he saw was the same. As we moved off again, I lifted the judas curiously, and caught a brief glimpse of a half-naked man (like a terribly emaciated Gandhi) sitting on the floor by a low table with a typewriter and some papers on it. The behaviour of the other two prisoners after they had looked into the solitary skeleton's cell and after our return to our common cell No. 18, decided me, after a few days, to ask Colonel Borodin, whom I knew slightly better than the other (I had spent sixteen months in cell 18 by then), why Boris had been so frightened by what he had seen. Borodin was confused by my question and did not answer. But later on the same day Boris came up to me and asked me whether I had seen the prisoner in the solitary cell, and whether I had told anyone about it. I answered that I had seen the prisoner, and that I had told no one. Boris then told me that if I should mention it to anybody, the N.K.V.D. would promptly liquidate me, him and Colonel Borodin, for the solitary prisoner was a personal friend of Tukhachevsky, a former general and lecturer at the Army Academy in Moscow, who had been sentenced to death with Tukhachevsky; after the trial, the Press had printed official confirmations that the sentence had been carried out. It turned out that Boris had known him personally and that he (Boris) had been a witness in the Tukhachevsky trial; Colonel Borodin had also known the general. I promised to say nothing, and from that time Boris and Borodin watched me closely, but at the same time doing me various favours.

"Several days after the outbreak of the Russo-German war the prison was evacuated. The occupants of our cell were moved to the ground floor. After a month the prisoners still remaining, about 2,000 Russians, Poles, Lithuanians, Czechs, Germans and Jews, were led out into the large courtyard between the main block and the 'special' block. There the officers began to check the numbers and compare them with their documents. After three days of muddled counting, checking and rechecking, we were surrounded by an escort and marched off. After three weeks' march we reached the railway station at Preluka, about 200 miles from Kiev, where we were loaded on to a goods train. A few weeks later what was left of the 2,000 was unloaded at Tomsk in Siberia. During the journey, in August, I met the general from the solitary cell, whose name unfortunately I have forgotten. I talked to him several times, and listened to his conversations with other prisoners. He was a living encyclopedia, and I could not understand how, after all that he had suffered, this walking skeleton could quote from memory whole chapters of General Sikorski's book about the year 1920. I remember the general's answers to three of my questions:

"1. Who will win the war?—Russia. Particularly now, when it is certain that England and America will help her. Russia was waiting until the capitalist world should exhaust itself in the war with Germany, but the Germans, by their action, have frustrated these plans.

"2. Will there be a Poland after this war?—Yes, but it will be a communist Poland.

"3. Why did the Russians, when they occupied Eastern Poland, send the population into exile, imprison innocent people, separate families, and so on?—Most of those N.K.V.D. men should be in prison themselves. If the Germans did not employ even more cruel methods, they could gain a great number of allies for themselves.

"When asked why he had not been shot after his death sentence, despite the official announcements in the press, he answered that he was necessary to the Government, and that several times in Kiev he had been summoned from his cell to talk to high Soviet dignitaries. He added that his present circumstances and the events of the last few years had not altered his convictions, that he had remained a communist, and that soon the whole world would be communist."

II. TWO EXCHANGES OF LETTERS

1

Alexei Stakhanov, originator of the Soviet Stakhanov Movement, published the following letter in *Tribune* of July 23rd, 1948:

"A few days ago I attended a lecture on international affairs. Among other things, the lecturer referred to slanderous articles appearing in some British newspapers and magazines, in which it is asserted that we have 'forced labour' in our country. I decided to make a closer study of the writings in question and found out that particularly active in this respect are two traitors to our country—a certain Dallin and a Nikolayevsky. It seems that they have published a disgusting book piled high with all sorts of monstrous fabrications about the Soviet Union. And what seems particularly strange is that their 'treatise' has been much commented on in the Labour Press, which has gone out of its way to advertise the slanderous book.

"You can hardly imagine what indignation and disgust such vile and utterly false tales about our country arouse in a man like myself, who has devoted and is devoting all his efforts to serve his country.

"You love your people and your country. I am a patriot of my Socialist motherland. And I, like every Soviet citizen, have every reason to be proud of my country, in which the workers and peasants have for the first time in history become the real masters.

"My life does not differ much from that of thousands of other Soviet workers. If I have become known as the initiator of a widespread movement for higher productivity, it is only because all the conditions and opportunities are provided in our country for free, creative work. That is why I feel that I cannot pass over in silence the lies spread by the Dallins and similar renegades.

"Thirteen years ago I, Alexei Stakhanov, a common Donetz miner, pondered over how to make work in the colliery more efficient and thus help my country sooner to carry out the second Five-Year Plan. Millions of other workers in the Soviet Union, who created and carried out the Five-Year Plans, had the same idea and we were fired by the same ambition. I devised methods of work which made it possible to save not only minutes, but even seconds. I said to myself: 'You must try hard, Alexei, because there's no one to spur you on—you, too, are your country's master.' My output kept increasing, and on August 31st, 1935, I established a record: I produced fourteen times as much coal as I was supposed to produce. In those days that was a big event. Today thousands of miners in the Soviet Union are producing much more than I produced thirteen years ago.

"The Soviet people have done me the great honour to call the movement for higher efficiency the 'Stakhanov' movement. Now I ask you, can people be coerced to work so highly efficiently as millions of 'Stakhanovites' do in the Soviet Union? I am sure you will agree that this is impossible. Only Soviet workers can achieve such results, because they are profoundly aware of what their work means, of its usefulness for their country.

"We Soviet workers know that the fruits of our labour belong entirely to the people, that they are not appropriated by a handful of exploiters. By the way, thousands of our foreign friends, among them people from Britain, who have visited the Soviet Union and have seen our work, can confirm this.

"In the Soviet Union, honest and efficient labour enjoys great honour and esteem. You must know that advanced workers in our country receive the title Hero of Socialist Labour, the newspapers write about them, and songs are made about them. I ask you, honestly, could forced labour, work under coercion, be so exalted?

"Every Soviet worker is interested in higher efficiency. By producing more he incessantly improves his own well-being and raises his standard of living. He is not spurred on by anyone. He is himself eager to work better and produce more.

"There is one more thing I should like to draw your attention to: I think that the slanderers who are trying to revive the old tales about forced labour in the U.S.S.R., and to create the impression that it is by such labour that our new Five-Year Plan is being accomplished, may do their peoples, including yours, a poor service. They are deceiving you, attempting to picture the Soviet Union as a weak country. Before the Second World War, as you know, the same slanderers shouted from all the house-tops that the U.S.S.R. would collapse at the first impact of enemy armies. But it turned out the other way round. The Soviet Union not only drove the Fascist invaders from its own territory, but liberated many countries of Europe from the Fascist yoke. As a matter of fact, it helped your country, too, enabling her to muster her forces and deliver the finishing blows to the enemy who had already been defeated by us. Why, then, do your newspapers offer all sorts of adventurers the opportunity again to picture the Soviet Union as a poorly knit State, where everything, allegedly, is based on forced labour? Who, save the enemies of your people and ours, can gain from this?

"My friends, miners whom I often meet (although I am now doing responsible work in the Ministry), and I, deeply resent the lies printed in your Press about the Soviet Union, particularly the revival of the old slander about forced labour in our country."

The author of this book replied as follows in *Tribune* of August 6th, 1948:

"May I point out that Mr. Alexei Stakhanov's 'protest', published in your issue of July 23rd, would surely cause great indignation and stupor among the many millions of forced-labour slaves in Russia, were they able to read it?

"It is quite obvious that, in Alexei Stakhanov's opinion, Dallin and Nikolayevsky are 'traitors' and 'renegades'. I didn't expect anything else. But perhaps, after having written a 'protest' to a Socialist weekly, Mr. Stakhanov would like to know what a Socialist, who has been a forced-labour slave in Russia for one and a half years, has to say on the question?

"While reading Mr. Stakhanov's letter, I recalled an old saying of Communists imprisoned in Soviet forced-labour camps. 'If Stalin knew what is happening here'—they used to say—'he would put into prison all these N.K.V.D. scoundrels instead of us.' It is always this same fairy tale: the good Tsar, who knows nothing about the sufferings of his devoted people, but will one day appear as the Supreme Judge and the Personification of Mercy to punish the sinners and bless the meek.

"In the same way, Mr. Stakhanov seems not to know about Soviet forced-labour camps, and from his high-placed and responsible post in the Ministry in Moscow he condemns all this story as a typical 'old slander'. To explain this mystery, we must remember that Mr. Stakhanov is probably employed in the Ministry of Industries, and thus has to do only with workers who work, more or less, of their own free will. But the recruiting of the forced-labour slaves in Russia is not the job of the Ministry of Industries (nor is it the job of the Ministry of Labour, which ceased to exist in Russia some time ago). It is the task of the N.K.V.D. hunters and N.K.V.D. prisons. The H.Q. of the Labour Camps, working under the direction and control of the N.K.V.D., is the real recruiting organisation of forced labour in the U.S.S.R.; the N.K.V.D.'s well-planned enslavement programme helps to carry out the Russian Five-Year Plans.

"I spent eighteen months, between 1940-42, in the Kargopol forced-labour camp near Archangel, on the White Sea. The camp, as all such camps, was called *Ispravitelnyi Trudovoi Lager*, which means 'Corrective Labour Camp'. The people to be 'corrected' were, except for a few notorious criminals, decent and good citizens, sentenced to five, eight or ten years' imprisonment as 'Trots-kyites', 'nationalists', 'kulaks', or 'spies'. Most of them knew quite well that their imprisonment was a mere pretext to force them into hard and unpaid labour under the most primitive conditions.

"The camp was established in 1937 in the heart of the Archangel forest as a part of a timber industry plan. The first prisoners had to build their barracks and clear the camp area, working in temperatures of 30–40° below zero. Their daily ration was two portions of soup and one pound of black bread. The few survivors of those times told me in 1940 that among the 'pioneers' there were a fairly large number of fully qualified forest engineers, who in their past life had not even heard about politics and 'counter-revolutionary deviations'.

" 'I ask you, honestly,' writes Mr. Stakhanov, 'could forced labour, work under coercion, be so exalted?' An honest question deserves an equally honest answer. I, personally, working as un-loader at the food base in the Kargopol forced-labour camp, worked at about 150—170 per cent of the average (which was twenty-five tons of flour per man daily), and my name was even put on the 'red board' as a 'recordist of Kargopol Stakhanov Movement'. Could work be so efficient under coercion? would ask Mr. Stakhanov. Yes, when one, being hungry, is promised an additional half-pound of bread per day, one can work very efficiently indeed. All I wanted, then, was to survive.

"The Stakhanovites of forced-labour camps in Soviet Russia do not receive 'the titles of Heroes of Socialist Labour'; the newspapers never mention them, and songs are not 'made about them'. But they compose songs about themselves. I remember one of them. It begins with an ironic invocation to join the Soviet Stakhanov Movement, and ends sadly with a refrain that 'You won't be even taken to the hospital, because all the hospitals are full'. This is almost true. In the Kargopol camp there was a small hospital with several beds, and a much larger barracks for completely emaciated workers, which was a kind of ossuary before going to the burial ground."

2

The following letter, from A. Trainin, D.Sc., Honoured Worker of Science, Corresponding Member of the Academy of Sciences of the U.S.S.R., Vice-President of the International Association of Democratic Lawyers, appeared in the *Manchester Guardian* of August 29th, 1949:

"SIR,—

"There has of late been some very sharp criticism in the House of Commons and the British press on the system of corrective labour in the U.S.S.R. On July 23rd your paper also published material alleging that the Corrective-Labour Code contains legal provisions for a definite system of recruiting labour, organisation and utilisation of compulsory labour. I should like, with your permission, to briefly acquaint your readers as to how I, a Soviet citizen and lawyer, regard this criticism.

"First of all, in the interests of truth let me note the following: The Corrective-Labour Code regulates the régime and conditions of people convicted for crime and therefore has not and cannot have anything in common with the labour conditions of any other people.

Then there is this yet that has to be noted. Owing to ignorance of the facts—I should be sorry to draw worse conclusions—the British critics have totally ignored the regulations of the Criminal Code of the R.S.F.S.R., organically bound with the Corrective-Labour Code. If these critics had but taken the least trouble and acquainted themselves with the fundamentals of the Criminal Code they would have easily avoided the profound and harmful confusion in their understanding of the three main types of punishment as applied in the U.S.S.R.—(1) corrective labour, (2) imprisonment and (3) corrective-labour camps.

"As is clearly and directly indicated in the law, corrective labour in the Soviet Union is one of the mildest punishments for a criminal offence. This labour ranges over a term of from one day to one year and does not include imprisonment (Art. 30 of the Criminal Code of the R.S.F.S.R.); apart from the name 'corrective labour' there is nothing in the régime that has anything in common with imprisonment or confinement in a corrective-labour camp. Finally persons who have even been sentenced to a term of imprisonment by no means always serve the sentence in the corrective labour camps. On the contrary, as directly prescribed by the law, 'imprisonment for a term of up to three years is served in general places of confinement. Sentences of from three to more years are served in the corrective-labour camps' (Art. 28 of the Criminal Code of the R.S.F.S.R.). This shows that only persons serving sentences of more than three years for grave offences are maintained in camps.

"In West Europe and America the dominating system of punishment is still imprisonment—solitary confinement, general, mixed imprisonment, and so forth. An attempt was even made to create a special science of 'prisonology'.

"Soviet law has decidedly discarded this prison cult. In the U.S.S.R. the entire penitentiary system revolves on labour. Labour is a necessary element in the camp corrective system. Naturally, a term in the corrective-labour camp means deprivation of freedom. But this loss of freedom is not the kind practised in West Europe and the U.S.A. There the prison is a place of seclusion, a place for complete isolation from the outside world, and very often from other prisoners. Offenders confined in corrective-labour camps in the U.S.S.R. are engaged in useful labour, and are free to mingle with one another, free to move about the territory of the camp. In the corrective-labour camps work is compulsory only in so far as the re-education and correction of the offender is compulsory. Labour of the convicted person is regimented. Here are some regulations from the Corrective-Labour Code:

" 'The labour of prisoners must be so organised as to promote the preservation and improvement of their qualifications and the acquirement of one by those who have none' (Art. 70). 'Work is allotted with due regard for the health of prisoners as established by the doctor' (Art. 73). 'Labour conditions of prisoners are regulated by the general rules of the Labour Code of the R.S.F.S.R. concerning the work day, rest, women's labour, labour of minors, and labour protection. Exceptions to the rule are established by the People's Commissariat of Justice in agreement with the All Union Central Council of Trade Unions' (Art. 74).

"Confinement in a corrective-labour camp is, of course, a punishment and very severe one at that, but not as tormenting as confinement in a prison cell as is practised in the West European countries, where people are 'buried alive'. Confinement in a corrective-labour camp as a means of punishment is necessarily connected with the application of a compulsory, obligatory régime for the prisoners. But does punishment in any part of the world exist without elements of compulsion? Or maybe British prisons are built up on the principle of rest homes and flogging of prisoners is a hygienic measure? Or maybe compulsory sterilisation of 25,000 people in the U.S.A. by January 1st, 1947, as against the 1,116 of Nazi Germany in the course of three years (1933–1936), is an example of humanity?

"If this be the case then why the noise, why the organised excitement around the corrective-labour camps? The following fact shows that we must be extremely wary in supplying the answer to the question.

"The Corrective-Labour Code in the U.S.S.R. was issued in 1933. In 1936—that is, three years later—it was translated into English. Thirteen to sixteen years have since passed and naturally every impartial observer will want to know: Why have the British authorities and the British organs of the press maintained silence on the question of the Corrective-Labour Code for sixteen years and now suddenly become so keenly interested in it? What has changed? The one thing that has changed, and this must be plainly stated, is the international situation, which of late has really become very aggravated and which, unfortunately, certain influential circles are striving with all possible haste to aggravate still further. The fact that the present time has been chosen for the fierce attacks against one of the codes of laws passed in the U.S.S.R. is causing grave anxiety among all loyal friends of the peace, regardless of what nation or class they belong to, anxiety in the sense—is not this campaign on the question of the Corrective-Labour Code an ideological development of the North Atlantic and other similar pacts, and is it not an attempt to work up an aggressive spirit against the U.S.S.R. under the guise of concern for the welfare of people who have been subjected to a régime of corrective labour? Does not this mask of fighters for humanism hide the organisers of crimes against mankind, the instigators of a new war?

"Genuine humanism prompts the movement for peace and democracy; and in these times of tension there can be no more humane task than the struggle against all attempts to sow discord among the States and to undermine the cause of peace, equally dear to both the Soviet peoples and the people of Britain."

The author replied, in the *Manchester Guardian* of September 3rd, 1949:

"SIR,—

"Will you allow me to give a slightly more detailed answer to Dr. Trainin, whose letter on 'Russian "Forced Labour"' appeared in your issue of August 29th?

"I am not myself an Honoured Worker of Science, but I think that my qualifications to speak on this subject are better than those of Dr. Trainin—as, between the years 1940 and 1942, I was a very unhonoured worker in the forced-labour camp at Kargopol, near Archangel. I am, therefore, not prepared to discuss scientifically with Dr. Trainin the legal aspects of the Soviet Penal Code, which none of the Soviet prisoners knows, treats seriously, or cares about, since ninety per cent of them are sentenced to forced-labour imprisonment without any trial.

" 'The Corrective-Labour Code,' writes Dr. Trainin, 'regulates the conditions of people convicted for crime and therefore has not, and cannot have, anything in common with the labour conditions of any other people.' What are these crimes of which they are convicted? My own personal experience was as follows: I was arrested by the N.K.V.D. in the territory of Eastern Poland (then ceded to Russia by Germany) while trying to cross the Lithuanian frontier in 1940. I agree that the illegal crossing of a frontier is an offence, and I remember that, before the war, my fellow-students were sentenced to twenty-four hours' imprisonment for accidentally going over the border from Poland into Czechoslovakia while climbing in the Tatra mountains. But my 'sledovatel', the judge who was conducting the preliminary investigations, was of a different opinion.

"He accused me first of being a German spy on the ground that the first part of my name, when transcribed into Russian (Gerling), made me a supposed relative of a well-known German Field Marshal. It took us one whole week of nightly hearings to dispose of this argument, and at last the sledovatel agreed that in any case Gerling is not the same thing as Göring. His second accusation against me was that 'I tried to cross the frontier in order to join the Polish Army in France and fight against Soviet Russia.' I do not pretend to have played the hero during these hearings, but at that one moment I asked the sledovatel to substitute the word 'Germany' for 'Soviet Russia'. A blow full in the face, accompanied by the encouraging sentence, 'It means the same thing,' made up my mind for me, and I signed the accusation form which had been drawn up by the judge. I had no trial, no counsel, and no opportunity to defend myself before the verdict was given. After the preliminary hearings in Grodno prison, which lasted for three whole months, I had to wait four months more in Vitebsk prison for my sentence. At last I was summoned to the N.K.V.D. office in Vitebsk prison, to be told that I had been sentenced, in my absence, to five years in a forced-labour camp.

"Let us even suppose that my case was not typical, since I was a Polish citizen searching for an opportunity of fighting against Germany during the war and—what is more important—at the time of the Ribbentrop-Molotov friendship pact. But in the Kargopol camp I met many people who had been sentenced, also without trial—by Osoboye Sovestchanye (the Special Court) of the N.K.V.D.—to terms of eight or ten years, on the sole ground that they were kulaks, priests, Germans, Poles, or Marxist-deviationists. I think Dr. Trainin has made his voice heard in the West a little too late; there can now be no doubt among honest people of the West that behind the smoke-screen of a penal code the Soviet forced-labour camps are no more than a means of recruiting cheap slave-labour in Russia.

"Dr. Trainin further writes that the Soviet system differs from that of Western Europe or the United States, where 'the prison is a place of seclusion, a place for complete isolation from the outside world, and very often from other prisoners,' and where prisoners are 'buried alive', and that 'Soviet law has decidedly discarded this prison cult' of solitary confinement, basing it instead entirely on labour. In reality, the substitution of forced labour for solitary confinement has given rise to an entirely new and distinct prison cult in Soviet Russia. A prisoner in a forced-labour camp works twelve hours a day in a temperature of thirty to forty degrees centigrade below zero, receives two plates of watery soup and a little over a pound of bread daily (an amount not sufficient even for a prisoner in a 'place of seclusion'), and has a day off once a month, or even once in two months, according to how the industrial plan on which the camp is engaged is being fulfilled.

"Under these conditions, of what use is it to him to be 'engaged in useful labour', or to be 'free to mingle with one another, free to move about the territory of the camp'? After three years of this work, prisoners are sent to the special barrack for workers who are too weak to be any longer useful as labourers; this barrack was known in the camp as 'the mortuary', and there the prisoners are allowed the privilege of dying in peace without being called out to work any more. It is in Russian camps that the better-educated prisoners think of themselves as being 'buried alive', repeating the well-known phrase from Dostoevsky's *House of the Dead*. Dr. Trainin quotes the Corrective-Labour Code, which rules that 'the labour of prisoners must be so organised as to promote the preservation and improvement of their qualifications'. After having read it now (for, of course, I never saw it in Soviet Russia), I may ask whether, as a literary critic, I should not have been employed in the camp library. But I remember that the position of librarian was reserved for common criminals, who were judged to be more trustworthy in handing out the Soviet propaganda of which the library consisted than political prisoners; and so I had to work as a common labourer.

"During my seven months' imprisonment in the prisons of Grodno, Vitebsk, and Leningrad I often longed to be sent at last to a labour camp to change the dullness of my life in the cell and to regain, while working, my physical fitness. That was nothing but a delusion. After my arrival at the Kargopol camp I soon discovered that all the forced-labour workers were dreaming of a return to prison, where they could live quietly in their cells, and not be tortured by hunger, emaciation, and frost. Is it not ironic that even in respect of the 'prison cult' Russian people are looking up to and dreaming of the Western standard of life, which Dr. Trainin so contemptuously condemns?"